The Origins of the American Detective Story

The Origins of
the American
Detective Story

LeRoy Lad Panek

McFarland & Company, Inc., Publishers
Jefferson, North Carolina, and London

Library of Congress Cataloguing-in-Publication Data

Panek, LeRoy.
    The origins of the American detective story / LeRoy Lad Panek.
        p.   cm.
    Includes bibliographical references and index.

    ISBN-13: 978-0-7864-2776-5
    softcover : 50# alkaline paper ∞

    1. Detective and mystery stories, American—History and
criticism.   2. American fiction—19th century—History and
criticism.   3. American fiction—20th century—History and
criticism.   4. Crime in literature.   5. Detectives in literature.
I. Title.
PS374.D4P33   2006
813'.087209—dc22   2006024368

British Library cataloguing data are available

On the cover: Edgar Allan Poe *(left)* and Allan Pinkerton *(Library of Congress)*

Manufactured in the United States of America

*McFarland & Company, Inc., Publishers
  Box 611, Jefferson, North Carolina 28640
  www.mcfarlandpub.com*

For Jesse James

Contents

Preface

The outlines are clear enough: from the turn of the 20th century when critics and historians first began to take the detective story seriously, the major developments have gotten their share of serious and sometimes even scholarly attention. Thus the outlines of the journey from Poe to Gaboriau, then to Collins and Dickens, then to Conan Doyle, then to Christie and Company, then to Hammett and Chandler, and finally to McBain and Wambaugh are pretty familiar. But there are plenty of dark spaces in between all of the big names, and too often the impulse is to simply pass them off as negligible and to assume that nothing really new or important happened in the interstices between all of the famous writers and eargely read and reread books. Thus, while he has cast some light on one of the most neglected periods of detective fiction—the period at the turn of the twentieth century—Hugh Greene has attached the label "rivals" to his collections of rediscovered turn of the twentieth century stories and by doing so has suggested that they defined themselves and are forever to be defined principally by their relationship to the Sherlock Holmes stories. At the same time, however, Greene has admitted that turn of the century detective fiction seemed to be a pretty much an undiscovered country because it's literally difficult to get hold of—there's no discrete bibliography for the period's detective fiction, much of it was published in magazines and even newspapers, and a lot of the books validate Raymond Chandler's comment about the genre in "The Simple Art of Murder:"

> The average detective story is probably no worse than the average novel, but you never see the average novel. It doesn't get published. The average—or only slightly above average—detective story does. Not only is it published, it is sold in small numbers to rental libraries, and it is read. There are even a few optimists who buy it at the full retail price of two dollars, because it looks so fresh and new and there is a picture of a corpse on the cover.

A lot has changed since Greene turned our attention toward the "rivals of Sherlock Holmes." For one thing, given the burgeoning resources of the Internet, much more of the fiction is readily available to

1

readers on and off-line. And this new access to that material begins to make it appear that in many significant ways there were turn of the century writers who did more than just copy Sherlock Holmes. In many significant ways some turn of the century writers were more aware of what was going on in their world than the creator of Sherlock Holmes ever touched on in print. And what that meant was that there were writers, especially in America, who were aware of the fact that the turn of the twentieth century wasn't just witnessing a rediscovery of Poe's detective stories; writers were also in the midst of what could be considered the first golden age of what we now generically call criminology. Reading turn of the century American detective fiction makes it clear that it was not only the burst of enthusiasm for Sherlock Holmes that American detective story writers experienced in that era, but they also witnessed a host of other things that influenced, even generated their fiction: the rise and fall of police as an institution, the parallel rise and fall of private detectives as a force in society, the publication of learned (and not so learned) treatises that explained why criminals were criminals, the birth of the crusading newspaper reporter and the intrusion of muck raking into political and corporate affairs, the beginning of what we now call forensic science, and the changes in rules of evidence and judicial procedures made necessary by science. And each of these had an impact on the detective story, especially the detective story as it came to be written at the turn of the twentieth century in America.

That's what the following pages look into—the formative years of American detective fiction and the seismic changes in society that helped to change the detective story from the sensation-laden fiction that dominated the middle of the 19th century into the modern detective story that appeared after World War I. Part of that change had to do with the impact of Sherlock Holmes in the U.S. But part of it also had to do with the rediscovery of Poe and the development of the detective story as separate genre. A lot of the story, too, had to do with the search for who was going to be the hero, a search that that ultimately was going to have to extend until after World War I and the creation of the hard-boiled detective. But that, of course, is another story.

As in all that I do, the mistakes in what follows are my own and the debts I owe are unpayable. Poor as they are, my thanks go to Lisa Russell of Hoover Library for her indefatigability in finding many of the quaint and curious volumes upon which this study was based. They go, as well, to the lovely Christine for her patience and hawk eyes, the least of her attributes; to Dr. D., Prince of Lorain, Ohio, for reading snippets of what follows; to Mike, Mary Ann, and the other Irregulars for lending their collective ears; and, as always, to my colleagues and students for understanding that it's really the benign and not the other kind of neglect that they've experienced.

Westminster, Maryland
June 2006

1

The First Fifty Years

It's strange that the detective story, something originally and fundamentally American, couldn't figure out how to be American for a long time—couldn't settle on who was going to be the hero, or what that hero's attributes were going to be, or what attitudes to reflect and espouse toward crime, criminals, law, and justice. Along with these ultimately societal conundrums, in the 19th century the detective story in America also had to learn how to cope with what can only be described as the one two punch of Wilkie Collins' *Moonstone* and then Arthur Conan Doyle's Sherlock Holmes stories. That's not to say that during the early years, during the second half of the 19th century, there weren't plenty of indigenous detectives and detective stories in the United States. This is something that an awful lot of commentators and historians tend to overlook or forget. There were lots of detective stories in print between Poe and Arthur Conan Doyle besides Gaboriau and the sensation novelists: there were fictional detectives like Cap Collier, Nick Carter, and the Sleuths (both Young and Old); there were made up boy detectives, ventriloquist detectives, and even boot black detectives; and there were detectives doing battle with proliferating mysteries and miseries in New York, Chicago, San Francisco, Denver, Cincinnati, Baltimore, and Boston. Family story papers like *Leslie's Illustrated Weekly*, *The Flag of our Union*, and *The Fireside Companion* published weekly servings of crime and crime fiction before the dime novel houses of Beadle and Smith and Street took over the business of purveying popular fiction in the United States. Indeed, what purported to be the true-life adventures of the 19th century's most celebrated and marketed real detective, Allan Pinkerton, were there for purchase from 1874 with *The Expressman and the Detective* through 1884 with *A Double Life and the Detectives*. But all of these stories about detectives, imaginary and real, were on or over the edge of being sub-literary, aimed by their publishers at adolescents and the newly literate readers produced by the post Civil War movement toward universal education in the U.S. These man hunters plied their trade in the pages of inexpensive publications—family story papers and then dime novels—that Anthony Comstock, the country's most outspoken defender of propriety, decried as being virulently immoral, as being (to use the title of Comstock's published diatribe) Traps for the Young. And besides that, on the basis of class prejudice and perceived literary quality, no self-respecting middle class adult would openly admit to reading them. Just imagine a grown man (or worse yet a woman) reading, to say nothing of enjoying, a yarn about Nick Carter and the bicycle thieves. To 19th century America, this seemed inconceivable, although, in truth, it was very much conceivable; turn of the 20th century detective writers, when they wish to separate fact from fiction, allude to dime novels as often as they cite Poe and almost as often as they mention Sherlock Holmes. Melville Davisson Post, for example, in his introduction to *The Strange Schemes of Randolph Mason* (1897) saw dime novels as a flood of fiction that came between Poe and Conan Doyle:

> Thus it happens that the toiler has tramped and retramped the field of crime. Poe and the French writers constructed masterpieces in the early day. Later came the flood of " Detective Stories " until the stomach of the reader failed. Yesterday, Mr. Conan Doyle created Sherlock Holmes, and the public pricked up its ears and listened with interest [3].

Arthur B. Maurice comes right out into the open with all of this in his 1902 essay "The Detective in Fiction." Thus his explanation of the detective story's history begins with a reminiscence of the furtive adolescent pleasures of reading dime novels before, more soberly, he turns to Poe, Gaboriau, and Conan Doyle. When he turns that corner from boyhood escape to serious literary history, Maurice says that

> The different types of detectives in fiction may be classified according to the social scale. Old Rafferty, Chink, Sleuth, Butts, and all of that ilk may be designated as the *canaille*, the *proletarians*; Poe's Dupin, Gaboriau's Lecoq and Pere Tirauclair, and Dr. Doyle's Sherlock Holmes are the *patricians* [*Bookman*, 15, May, 1902 234].

As a waypoint in the history of detective fiction, on the social status map, it is worth noting that here Maurice (and many other early literary commentators in the U.S.) refers to the author of the Sherlock Holmes stories as Dr. Conan Doyle, and not Arthur Conan Doyle. And for American readers, if that title gave the author a certain cachet, one can only imagine what happened once the Dr. Arthur Conan Doyle became Sir Arthur Conan Doyle.

POE AND THE DETECTIVE STORY

While from the 1870s through the turn of the century "dime novel" detectives lay thick on the American landscape, the first American detective, indeed the first ever fictional detective, wasn't American at all—even though he was dreamed up in Philadelphia. The name, Auguste Dupin— C. for Chevalier Auguste Dupin no less—says it all. He's French. C. Auguste Dupin appears in three of Poe's tales: "The Murders in the Rue Morgue," "The Mystery of Marie Roget," and "The Purloined Letter." They all appeared in middle class periodicals in the early 1840s (*Graham's Magazine, Snowden's Lady's Companion*, and *The Gift for 1845* respectively). This meant that they did not have the kind of exposure available to the family story paper or dime novel detectives: *Graham's Magazine*, for example, had a subscribers' list of 3,500 names when Poe became editor versus the average circulation of 200,000 to 300,000 of the most popular family story papers. On top of that, they appeared half a century before mass circulation, middle class magazines like *Collier's, McClure's, Redbook*, etc. took off in the United States and Britain.

There is something a bit odd about the fact that Poe made the first fictional detective a Frenchman and not an American. Poe, to be sure, drew a modicum of his inspiration for creating his fictional detective from reading the memoirs of the first actual modern detective, the Frenchman Eugene Francois Vidocq. Poe, however, actually borrowed very little from Vidocq. In his memoirs the French sleuth recounts exploits in which he depends mostly on fake whiskers or with hanging around with crooks and accumulating knowledge of the underworld in order to get his man. Rather than emulating this particular Frenchman, Poe's Frenchman holds Vidocq up to ridicule: specifically he classifies him as a bungler. Rather than from this incidental French source, much, if not most, of Poe's inspiration for creating Dupin and writing his detective tales to begin with came from his own larger than life view of himself. But he was moved to write about the genius, not just as genius but as genius detective—as crime solver—by incidents and people in his own backyard. Some of Poe's impulse to write about police and detectives came from reading about crimes like the murder of Mary Cecelia Rogers in the New York newspapers, not in quaint and curious volumes. Some of it came from living and writing in Philadelphia during the prominent public debate about creating a police force for the City of Brotherly Love and the contested provisions of the will of philanthropist Steven Girard (one of the richest, if not the richest man in America at the time) intended to fund said police force. Some of it came from Poe's friendship with journalist George Lippard who wandered Philadelphia's streets and came to write a mysteries and miseries book about the city. There are plenty of native roots to the detective story.

Why, then, did Poe put all of the French furniture in the Dupin stories? Surely he didn't need to leave the States to create a background for the moody romantic genius—after all, Poe made LeGrand in "The Gold Bug" pretty much a southern fried Dupin and in "Thou Art the Man" he made up a crime story that took place in backwoods, small town America. In the settings of the three Dupin stories the city is no more like Paris than it is like Philadelphia or Baltimore or New York or Boston or Richmond. It just has a few funny names for places and people. Poe hardly needed a foreign setting in which to practice technical virtuosity and innovation in the short story form—as his other short fiction amply demonstrates. And he didn't have to go abroad to find crime; he just had to read the newspapers. But, first of all, Poe just plain liked the French and things French. Then, too, the Dupin stories got stuck in France because Poe wanted to focus on rationalism in them and he associated rationalism in its purest and most absolute form with France and French philosophers—just as the Italian setting of "The Cask of Amontillado," for example, was to add background and gothic credibility difficult to exactly achieve with any other place. Perhaps he set the stories in France because there he could add the luster of hereditary social class to the capabilities of his detective genius: to show, in other words, that the Chevalier Dupin differed from the proletarian prefect of police and bungler Vidocq not simply in degree but also in Degree. Maybe, too, in the case of "The Purloined Letter," before the days of the stolen papers spy novel of the next century, Poe found that the political intrigues of the French court possessed more polish and allure than ward healers in Philly, New York, Boston, or Baltimore bargaining for votes. It is also possible that Poe thought that the principal red herring in "The Murders in the Rue Morgue," the Babel of European voices allegedly issuing from the crime scene, would fit a cosmopolitan setting like Paris more naturally than one in urban America. And it's possible, too, that he placed the stories in France because the setting only thinly disguised the fact that dupin' is a contraction for duping (especially in Poe's Southern speech), the principal narrative technique of "Murders in the Rue Morgue."

While Poe certainly wrote the stories that became the origin and model for detective fiction, it's not clear that he ever thought of what he was doing as creating a new genre (he probably didn't), and he absolutely never thought he was inaugurating a genre having anything to do with crime. Certainly there was a lot of fiction about crime around long before Poe, but in it the detective, fulfilling God's justice, was not very important, and it centered on the criminal's repentance for immoral acts. In short, it was Newgate literature, confessions of criminals for their heinous acts, and, by extension, examples to society of the wages of sin. Sentiment and morality were the entire bias of the crime fiction in the 19th century family story papers and in the dime novels that Anthony Comstock, ironically, wanted to keep out of the hands of impressionable boys. Unlike what passed for crime fiction at the time, Poe's Dupin stories both center on the detective as a character and have nothing to do with morality and have nothing to do with crime, justice, or law. They also have little to do with women—or live ones on stage at least—and, therefore with sentiment. The first Dupin tale, "The Murders in the Rue Morgue," for instance, is not about crime at all but about the accidental depredations caused by an escaped wild animal, and in the last one, "The Purloined Letter," the crime really isn't that important—it's a crime, at any rate, that is either above or beyond the law. None of Poe's detective stories ends with the villain committing suicide or just spontaneously curling up and dying of guilt and shame—endings appropriate to the crime friction of the mid-19th century—and certainly Poe doesn't show anyone taken to court or hauled off to jail. Indeed, readers never meet the criminal in "Marie Roget" and Minister D. appears only at the end of "The Purloined Letter." While "The Purloined Letter" shows Dupin adept at knowing what others think (seen earlier in his demonstration on the association of ideas and his assertion that for him men have "windows in their bosoms" in "The Murders in the Rue Morgue") and the story focuses on psychology, here it is the psychology of perception and, more importantly, that of the game player. It's not the psychology of the criminal or the victim or the avenger or (as in most 19th century crime fiction) the psychology of those who suffer from crime. And as for the law, none of Poe's Dupin stories has anything to do with points of law. For Poe it's not about law or crime or criminals; it's all about playing games. He makes this clear in the build-up to the action in "The Murders in the Rue Morgue" when the narrator compares the athlete with the analyst and talks about the superiority of checkers over whist and in the middle of the narrative when Dupin decides to go to the crime scene for amusement. Poe makes the element of game playing clear again in the beginning of "The Mystery of Marie Roget" where the same narrator drops the term "calculus of possibilities," a phrase Poe borrowed from Hoyle's advice to card players that they ought to depend on the odds they calculate from counting the cards played. And "The Purloined Letter" focuses on a battle of intellects—with a bit of dress up play tossed in at the end. When the detective story got to the 20th century, it was going to be about games too—indeed, Golden Age detective fiction in Britain and America would become perhaps more emphatically engrossed in games than Poe was. But that was hardly the mood of the mid-19th century. Between 1840 and 1890, focus on the sentiment associated with crime and those touched by crime as well as a small but growing interest in the mundane, pre-modern procedures of the police and the detective took the American detective story off the path marked by Poe—for the time being at least.

SENSATION NOVELS

All of this adds up to give us some of the reasons why detective fiction didn't catch on and catch up with Poe until half a century or so after he wrote the Dupin stories: Poe wrote detective stories and not crime fiction, but from the time of Poe's pieces in the 1840s until the turn of the 20th century, popular writers' concerns in Britain and America were not principally focused on the brilliant detective or on crime *per se* or even the cleverly told tale but upon the sentiment unleashed by crime and the travail of those caught up in its toils. For most of the time this meant that writers looked to Wilkie Collins and to the rage for sensation novels that *The Woman in White* (U.S. 1860) and then *The Moonstone* (U.S. 1868) inspired.

Sensation novels are about the contrast of innocence with guilt, of purity with sin. They focus on the emotional trauma and turmoil experienced by their central characters (who are typically helpless women bereft, somehow, of familial support) and they expect readers to derive pleasure from sharing their emotional upheavals. Significantly, in the two most important American sensation novels centered on crime (to be discussed below), the narrators are not the principal detectives but the medium through which readers can witness the suffering endured by the women in the novels. Typically the sensation novel plot depends on secrets as well as upon wicked and disguised schemes often involving the transfer of wealth and power through marriage or inheritance. Some of the best of them, a la Poe, do end with surprises, but the surprise is occasioned by circumstance rather than being a direct result of the detective's brilliance. While there was a good bit of sensation fiction published in the United States during the 19th century (including more than a handful of pieces by Louisa May Alcott), the two most currently well known American sensation novels—in fact the only two well known American sensation novels—that fall into the category of crime fiction are *The Dead Letter* (1866) by Metta Fuller Victor and Anna Katharine Green's *The Leavenworth Case* (1878). Being that they are sensation novels, they both center on self-less, tragic female heroes and palpitating male admirers who witness and describe the tribulations and heroism of the women, but who are also mostly clueless about discovering the causes or cures for their suffering. In both cases the writers use crimes as the means to illustrate that suffering proves womanly virtue. Indeed, at the end of *The Dead Letter* Victor essentially beatifies the long-suffering Eleanor. Relevant to the evolution of crime fiction, both *The Dead Letter* and *The Leavenworth Case*: 1) revolve around murders, 2) have lawyers—or a lawyer and a law reader—as narrators and amateur investigators, 3) have professional police detectives who solve the crimes, and 4) eventually introduce clues and evidence that bear some relationship to the solution of the crimes. In spite of all of this, they're not detective stories, not by a long shot. They're sensation novels.

First, take the way in which *The Dead Letter* and *The Leavenworth Case* treat their detectives. Mr. Burton (in *The Dead Letter*) and Mr. Gryce (in *The Leavenworth Case*) are both official agents of the New York City Police Department. For today's readers, though, it seems at least somewhat odd that Detectives Burton and Gryce are so much masters of their own movement and time, rarely visit a police station of any sort, seem to operate out of their homes, and work on cases outside of New York City. They, in fact, act more like the private detectives, to which readers are accustomed, than cops. It's worth remembering here, however, that both authors had to deal with a recently established profession. The New York City Police Department added its detectives in 1857—only nine years before the publication of *The Dead Letter.* It's also important to understand that neither the regular police nor the detective police at that time had established an unsullied and savory reputation in New York—or anyplace else in the U.S. for that matter. Thus when Redfield first meets Mr. Burton, the detective in *The Dead Letter*, he observes that "He was intelligent, even educated, a gentleman in language and manner—a quite different person, in fact, from what I had expected in a member of the detective-police" (46). Twelve years later, Green introduces her detective with another comment on the less than heroic popular stereotype of detectives: "And here let me say that Mr. Gryce, the detective, was not the thin, wiry individual of piercing eye you are expecting to see" (5). As one sign of the novelty of the police and detectives in the middle class world of mid-19th century America, before Victor introduces her detective in *The Dead Letter*, she feels it necessary to justify Redfield's and the Argyll family's appeal to the police for help in discovering the identity of Moreland's murderer in the first place: "The public welfare demanded, as well as the interest of private individuals, that the guilty should be ferreted out, if possible" (46). Thus, before either writer can deal with the particulars of her character as a detective, she feels the need to justify the utility and propriety of detectives in general. On top of this, throughout *The Leavenworth Case* one of Green's preoccupations is in defining the social caste of her police detective compared to the status of the principal characters in the novel and in delineating its attendant difficulties:

> I can enter a house, bow to the mistress of it, let her be as elegant as she will, so long as I have a writ of arrest in my hand, or some such professional matter upon my mind; but when it comes to visiting in kid gloves, raising a glass of champagne in response to a toast—and such like, I am absolutely good for nothing ... But it is much the same with the whole of us. When we want a gentleman to work for us, we have to go outside of our profession [107].

But what kind of police "work" is Gryce talking about here? Exactly how do these two detectives detect? First of all, they mostly follow people, or track them down, or even eavesdrop on them. The first thing Mr. Gryce does in the Leavenworth house is to surreptitiously listen in on Mary and Eleanore's conversation, and one of the first things Mr. Burton does in *The Dead Letter* is to show Redfield one of the suspects whom he (or his agents) had tracked to a gambling den. In both cases these acts are at least vaguely disturbing and repugnant to the narrators. Be that as it may, both novels turn (or don't turn) on the detective and his agents finding missing persons who may or may not have light to shed on the murder. In addition to this most mundane detective skill, both Victor and Green characterize their detectives by their ability to interpret evidence. Victor, in fact, includes a paean on something she believes to be police science, handwriting analysis, or to use the elevated Latinate term, chirography:

> I do not know his name, and I have never met him. All the acquaintance I have with him, I have through the medium of chirography. It is sufficient for me; I cannot mistake.... By the way, Richard, you are not aware of my accomplishment in the art of reading men and women from a specimen of their handwriting. It is one of my greatest aids in the profession to which I have devoted myself. The results I obtain sometimes astonish my friends. But, I assure you, there is nothing marvelous in them. Patient study and unwearied observation, with naturally quick perceptions, are the only witchcraft I use [141–142].

This is the same person Victor's narrator praises for having "the subtle perceptions of the detective, a magnetism which amounted to the marvelous" (Victor 183). Along with perception, both Victor and Green include the discovery, classification, and analysis of evidence in their narratives. Indeed, one can suppose that this is one of the spin-offs of having lawyers as narrators—another one of these being Green's diatribe against circumstantial evidence, soon to become a commonplace lament in a whole lot of crime fiction in both the U.S. and Britain. In *The Leavenworth Case*, as well, Green has her storyteller include floor plans, facsimile documents, and lists for the reader to see and peruse. And in *The Dead Letter* Mr. Burton finds lots of items of evidence after breaking the code in the letter the narrator found in the Dead Letter Office.

As much as Burton and Gryce are similar, they also represent two different 19th century models of the detective character. Victor's detective is Dupin bowdlerized—the romantic, even Byronic hero as detective. First of all, with Victor's detective it's more than just the accurate use of the senses that makes him the super sleuth:

> ... there is about me a power not possessed by all—call it instinct, magnetism, clarvoyancy, or remarkable nervous and mental perception. Whatever it is, it enables me, often, to feel the presence of criminals, as well as of very good persons, poets, artists, or marked temperaments of any kind [201].

Not only does he have these powers, but so does his daughter, who bears the nevermore name from "The Raven," Lenore. Victor's Lenore is a clairvoyant who, in spite of its physically taxing nature, has used her second sight to help Burton with his cases in the past and who, once put into a trance, tells the detective the whereabouts of a key witness in *The Dead Letter*. Along with these preternatural skills, Victor gives her detective more than a tincture of tragedy—the background of how persecution for his skill and honesty has led him to become a detective and Burton's forever unsolved murder by one of his enemies at the close of the novel. If, then, Burton comes from Poe's moody detective genius, tamed and domesticated, Green's avuncular Mr. Gryce issues from Inspector Bucket in Dickens' *Bleak House* (U.S. 1853). Gryce is the same kind of open, self-deprecating, humorous, efficient, and determinedly middle class professional man as Dickens' detective.

The problem with both Burton and Gryce is that neither Victor nor Green created a plot in which the malefactor is discovered and brought to justice solely by means of the detective's exertions. In *The Dead Letter* the case is unraveled by the accident of discovering a letter from the assassin in the Dead Letter Office, and in *The Leavenworth Case* the truth comes out only after Mr. Gryce publicly accuses an innocent woman. In the historical context, recall, if you will, that Sergeant Cuff in *The Moonstone* does not solve the crime or recover the jewel either. Something more than detectives detecting, then, is going on in *The Dead Letter* and *The Leavenworth Case*—and in all sensation novels. That something has a lot to do with the views of and attitudes toward criminals and justice that lie under these kinds of books. Crime and justice in the sensation novel depend on faith in a universe that is eventually and inevitably just and governed by providence: this goes back to the sure knowledge that "murder will out" that serves as the basis for what happens in century upon century of western literature from Chaucer's "Prioress' Tale" to *Macbeth* and *Hamlet*. More contemporaneously, it's the set of assumptions on can quite literally find enunciated in 19th century American court rooms. Most famously it's there in Daniel Webster's speech at the trial of John F. Knapp in 1830. There Webster, for the prosecution, sets forth, with ringing biblical phraseology, the role that God plays in the detection and prosecution of crime:

> Ah! Gentlemen, that was a dreadful mistake. Such a secret can be safe nowhere. The whole creation of God has neither nook nor corner where the guilty can bestow it, and say it is safe. Not to speak of that eye which pierces through all disguises, and beholds every thing as in the splendor of noon, such secrets of guilt are never safe from detection, even by men. True it is, generally speaking, that "murder will out." True it is, that Providence hath so ordained, and doth so govern things, that those who break the great law of Heaven by shedding man's blood seldom succeed in avoiding discovery. Especially, in a case exciting so much attention as this, discovery must come, and will come, sooner or later. A thousand eyes turn at once to explore every man, every thing, every circumstance, connected with the time and place; a thousand ears catch every whisper; a thousand excited minds intensely dwell on the scene, shedding all their light, and ready to kindle the slightest circumstance into a blaze of discovery. Meantime the guilty soul cannot keep its own secret. It is false to itself; or rather it feels an irresistible impulse of conscience to be true to itself. It labors under its guilty possession, and knows not what to do with it. The human heart was not made for the residence of such an inhabitant. It finds itself preyed on by a torment, which it dares not acknowledge to God or man. A vulture is devouring it, and it can ask no sympathy or assistance, either from heaven or earth. The secret which the murderer possesses soon comes to possess him; and, like the evil spirits of which we read, it overcomes him, and leads him whithersoever it will. He feels it beating at his heart, rising to his throat, and demanding disclosure. He thinks the whole world sees it in his face, reads it in his eyes, and almost hears its workings in the very silence of his thoughts. It has become his master. It betrays his discretion, it breaks down his courage, it conquers his prudence. When suspicions from without begin to embarrass him, and the net of circumstance to entangle him, the fatal secret struggles with still greater violence to burst forth. It must be confessed, it will be confessed; there is no refuge from confession but suicide, and suicide is confession. [http://www.fullbooks.com-/The-Great-Speeches-and-Orations-of-Daniel8.html].

This is precisely the kind of inevitable justice that one finds set forth in Victor and Green's world. It's there on the character level. Thus this passage from *The Dead Letter*:

> While we stood there, among the others, waiting, I chanced to observe his paleness and restlessness; he tore his black gloves in putting them on; I saw his fingers trembling…. The next moment the coffin appeared; I took my place by its side, and we moved away toward the depot, passing over the very

spot where the corpse was found. James was a step in advance of me, and as we came to the place, some strong inward recoil made him pause, then step aside and walk around the ill-starred spot [Victor 39].

This guy gets the heebie jeebies when approaching the scene of the crime, and things get worse, a lot worse, as he listens to the recital of the facts in the case near the close of the action:

> I seemed to see the story reflected in his countenance, instead of hearing it. Flushes of heat passed over it, succeeded by an ashy paleness, which deepened into a sickly blue hue, curious to behold, dark passions swept like shadows over it; and gradually, as the speaker neared the climax of the story, I felt like one who gazes into an open window of the bottomless pit [197–8].

Here's Dupin's "windows in men's bosoms," but it's not their thoughts but their souls that the observer sees. From the reader's perspective, though, it hardly takes a genius to tell who's guilty. Here Victor's characterization is based upon the idea that criminal acts are so contrary to human nature, so sinful that their perpetrators cannot disguise or suppress their consciences. Guilt, sooner or later, becomes palpable and obvious.

While not as wholly and maybe even naively committed to it as was Victor, Green in *The Leavenworth Case* shows an alternate use of this traditional, literary view of crime and criminals. Thus while she refuses to reveal what she knows about the background of the crime, Eleanore Leavenworth proposes that the victim's corpse will demonstrate her innocence.

> You have said that if I declared my innocence you would believe me....
> See here," and laying her cheek against the pallid brow of her dead benefactor, she kissed the clay-cold lips softly, wildly, agonizingly, then, leaping to her feet, cried, in a subdued but thrilling tone: "Could I do that if I were guilty? Would not the breath freeze on my lips, the blood congeal in my veins, and my heart faint at this contact? Son of a father loved and reverenced. Can you believe me to be a woman stained with crime when I can do this?" and kneeling again, she cast her arms over and about that inanimate form [92].

Rather than being a purely literary practice, late 19th and early 20th century crime fiction suggests that in France at least confronting a suspect with the victim's corpse was not an uncommon police technique.

With its faith that justice is the business of providence and that guilt unambiguously marks the criminal, the sensation novel didn't look like it's going to develop into the detective story of the 20th century. There are other reasons as well that circumscribed the focus on detection in the sensation novel, but the main one is the law. One of the truisms associated with the history of detection in and out of fiction is that it requires the presence of the rule of law. The law is, of course, the law—or is it? It is perhaps worth knowing that when Poe wrote the first detective story, systematic thinking about Anglo American law was pretty much in its infancy. The codification of English law in Blackstone's *Commentaries* (1762) was not that old and as Carl Leonard points out in "Towards a Legal History of American Criminal Theory: Culture and Doctrine from Blackstone to the Model Penal Code" 19th century thinking about law on both sides of the Atlantic was undergoing a change from what Leonard calls "private moral justice" to Blackstone's newer conception of the law as having to do with the social contract and "public wrong and prevention." The shift, then, was from a view of the law as the codification, upholder, and defender of divine law and justice to one in which the law was a mechanism of the social contact and a defender of the individual against the state. In America, however, the transition away from the law as a moral/spiritual entity was complicated by the pull of Puritanism on the law. Thus the idea that

> Crime only happened through the loss of God's grace, and God might withdraw that grace at any time. The condemned, consequently, did not become an outsider, an unintelligible enemy of the community, but a kind of tragic figure with whom all could identify [Leonard 47].

Part of what we see in Victor and Green's novels, then, is the rough transition from a world in which crime allows and demonstrates the enactment of God's justice to a world in which the focus shifts from away from the criminal's moral turpitude and makes crime the public business of the community.

If the development of this kind of law is one prerequisite, one should also add the idea of scrupulous attention to objectivity and impartiality—the impartial application of the rule of law is necessary for the development of real or imaginary detection. And that's just what one does not find in *The Dead Letter* or *The Leavenworth Case*. It is apparent in both novels that class makes a very big difference. The most egregious example of this is that at the end of *The Dead Letter*, the detective, a sworn (one assumes) officer of the New York Police Department, gives the head of the injured household the option of whether or not to report the solution to the crime and whether or not to effect the arrest of the murderer; since Mr. Argyll wishes to avoid family scandal, Mr. Burton lets the murderer go free at the end of the book. While not as graphic in its effect, the social class of the Leavenworth family clearly makes a difference in the way in which they are treated by those investigating the crime. While status serves to stifle the detection in these sensation novels, in them gender provides an even greater impediment to discovering the truth. Just as *The Moon-*

stone turns on the fact that Rachael won't tell people what she knows, so do *The Dead Letter* and *The Leavenworth Case*. Indeed Green builds her novel around the Leavenworth cousins, Mary and Eleanore, and their adamant refusal to tell what they know about the background of the crime. Then, too, she focuses on the men tiptoeing around the cousins, at once frustrated by their aloofness, by their defiance of the demands of law and justice, but awed and respectful of their privileged status as upper middle class women. Partly this comes, in both novels, from women's greater investment in social propriety than men's, but partly it comes from these women writers' views of the special character of womanhood. Accepting that their gender confers a special status on women with respect to the law, however, cannot advance the cause either of the law or the development of the detective story. Indeed, one of the subtler ways in which one can mark the progress of the detective story as it emerges in the 20th century is to hold it up next to the progress of the movement for women's equality.

THE OTHER WOMAN

The year after the publication of *The Leavenworth Case*, Donnelley, Gassette & Loyd of Chicago published *Shadowed by Three*. The title page announced that it was written by Lawrence L. Lynch and that said Lynch was an "Ex-Detective." The cover of the 1883 edition which shows three shadows on a stone wall and a fleeing female form announces that the book is "Original American Fiction." Original it may have been, but there was no such author as ex-detective Lynch: the book was really written by Emma Murdoch Van Deventer. Between her debut in 1879 and World War I Emma Murdoch Van Deventer wrote almost two dozen detective stories, and while now virtually unknown, in some ways she was at least as original as Green or Victor.

Clearly Van Deventer deals with a different milieu than that one finds in Green and Victor. First of all, the action doesn't all take place in New York—*Shadowed by Three* and most of her other fiction takes place in or around Chicago; indeed, *Against Odds: A Detective Story* (1894) uses the 1893 Chicago World's Fair for its backdrop. It's not just that she sets the stories out of New York, Van Deventer also decidedly includes a far wider social and urban spectrum in the incidental details of her narratives. Thus, for example, in *Shadowed by Three* one of her characters stops by the newspaper office simply to watch minor criminals ply their scrofulous trades:

Crossing Dearborn street with the sublimest disregard for drays and news-boys, he paused before the "Tribune" building and scanned the structure with considerable interest. Finally he entered at the great door, through which anxious-looking people were constantly hurrying, and, leaning his back against the wall, lost himself for a moment, in watching and pondering the evolutions of the famous "advertisement" system. Shabby-looking men, who had advertised for a "lady correspondent," a "refined housekeeper," or a pretty "amanuensis," and who turned away from the box with a big pocket of letters, and a coarse joke, at the expense of the unknown writers; sharp-looking men who wrote "ads." For "partners" and "business chances" and handed them to the clerk with the required change... [3].

In the same novel Van Deventer takes readers not just into rich folk's houses, but also into modest rooming houses and into the haunts of 1870s vaudeville performers. And then there are her characters. In the criminal department, unlike her predecessors, Van Deventer gives her readers habit-ual, professional criminals—gamblers, forgers, counterfeiters, etc. Out-side of those from the criminal class, Van Deventer's villains differ graphically from those of run of the mill sensation novelists. While books like *Shadowed by Three* possess the same heritage as *The Dead Letter* and *The Leavenworth Case*, they focus more prominently on the action of the detectives and Van Deventer's villains come from altogether different sources than Green's or Victor's. They're hardened to evil; in other words, they don't turn to jelly or gibber and shake when their crimes are men-tioned. In *Shadowed by Three*, for instance, while one of the villains resembles Collins' Count Fosco, the other is a woman who has murdered men on two continents, expresses neither guilt nor contrition, and lives in disguise undetected and unsuspected until the very end of the novel. As revolutionary as she is in this, Van Deventer's female victim in *Shadowed by Three* is even more groundbreaking. Lenore Armyn superficially fits the outlines of the sensation novel female hero-victim. A lot of the action of the novel revolves around her inheritance—the one of which she is unaware but also the one that one of the villains passionately wishes to possess. And it's not just that persecution that she has to endure, she's also forced into a marriage with a rotter against her wishes. It all seems right out of the sensation novel pattern book. But Lenore Armyn is no sensa-tion novel suffering woman. Van Deventer draws her as an independent woman. From girlhood she has been an active foe of injustice. Indeed, when she arrives in Chicago, much to the amazement and chagrin of her companions, she interferes with a man she observes beating a woman in the street:

The woman was down on her knees beside a little pile of wood, and a mallet and wedge lay beside the man. Before we could think, Lenore had run at the man screaming in the *awfullest* way! "Stop, you beast, you devil; stop, I tell you." But the man roared out another oath and struck the woman so hard that she fell over upon the wood. In an instant Lenore had seized that great mallet and struck the man an awful blow upon the head [150].

When wronged herself, Lenore becomes determined and she acts to defend and protect herself. And on her own, in a strange city, she manages to elude and then escape from the villain who wishes her dead as well as from three clever, experienced detectives. And in the end her triumph may be providential, but she has given providence some pretty effective assistance.

The detectives in Van Deventer's first novel give providence a hand, too. But unlike the detectives in Victor and Green, they're not city detectives. The Chicago Police Department had had detectives of sorts for eighteen years before Van Deventer published *Shadowed by Three*, but one can't tell it from reading the novel. There are some references to patrolmen in the book, but none to Chicago police detectives. Van Deventer's detectives are private agents. Francis Ferrars, one of Van Deventer's gumshoes, is a Scotland Yard detective detailed by his chief to work on a private case that brings him to America—where he stays and becomes a private detective in Van Deventer's later books. The other two of the three ace detectives in *Shadowed by Three* are Neil Bathurst and Rob Jocelyn.

> They had been sworn friends and allies. As well as brother detectives, these two; friends since the very day that had brought Neil Bathurst, then a mere lad, into favorable notice among the operatives of a certain Eastern agency. One of its officers had picked him up, as it were, a runaway gamin, and had found him so quick-witted, agile, and altogether useful, that he had been retained in the service, and, at the age of fourteen, found himself fully launched as a boy detective [*Shadowed* 21–22].

While *Shadowed by Three* takes place exclusively in and around Chicago, one of the things about these detectives is that they are peripatetic—they have had cases all over the place, with the Americans chasing crooks in Europe as well as round about most of the States and the Englishman coming to America to find the lost heiress. As the title indicates, mostly these detectives follow people. While there's 1) a bit of physiognomy thrown in ("The mind, the tongue, soon learn to dissemble, to guard a secret well, but the human face is a window" 70), and 2) some mention of record keeping ("Bathurst had found that his habit of jotting down everything that came into his mind or under his observation, concerning a suspected party, or those connected with the parties or cases coming under his eyes, had often stood him in good stead" 104), Van

Deventer's detectives rely on "detective instinct" and especially on disguise—indeed, to convince readers of their expertise Van Devnter even includes episodes in which the detectives fool one another, Bathurst being especially expert at disguising himself as a woman and sneaking up on his colleagues.

In spite of her innovations, Van Deventer's Lawrence Lynch books had little impact on the development of the late 19th century detective story. In spite of her far more liberal and liberated views on crime, criminals, and on women, her take on catching criminals may have been accurate, but it centered on shadowing versus problem solving, and at the core she was committed to a lot of the techniques and principles of the sensation novel. And it didn't help, either, that she was published in Chicago and received little or no notice in the Eastern press. In a variety of ways it was the Eastern press that was going to remake the American detective story at the turn of the century. And that started—in a very small way—with Julian Hawthorne.

THE WORLD'S GREATEST DETECTIVE

But for what can only be called the fatal lure of sensation, Nathaniel Hawthorne's son, Julian, had a chance, albeit a small one, of continuing some of the detective story conventions invented by Poe and even adapting them to the real world of New York city as opposed to Poe's Paris. In *The Great Bank Robbery* (1887), in fact, he even makes an allusion to Poe before the first real interest in the history of the detective story began at the turn of the century; sadly, however, it's to the "calculus of probabilities" business rather than to the character of the detective or the way in which Poe's plots unfold. The other advantage that Hawthorne had, the one that he worked at developing, was his acquaintance with Thomas Byrnes, the most celebrated detective in America after Allan Pinkerton's death in 1884. Byrnes began his career with the New York Police Department walking a beat in 1863 and by the turn of the century ended up running the whole show—first as Inspector, then as Chief, and finally as Superintendent. He became the head of the department's first official detective division and kept the city relatively crime free through unashamedly brutal and blatantly extra constitutional means—Byrnes, for instance, is credited with coining the term "third degree" for the use of physical force and intimidation in interrogations and for establishing an arbitrary "Deadline" around New York's financial district that known felons were forbidden, upon pain of arrest, to cross. When the Jack the Ripper murders flummoxed London's Metropolitan Police, Byrnes boasted that if any such crimes occurred in his city he could solve them in thirty six hours; and in the one parallel case of a prostitute being murdered and mutilated in New York, Byrnes made good his boast by arresting a man who was convicted of the crime (but who history suggests was probably not guilty). On top of all of this, perhaps in spite of it, Byrnes also made real contributions to "scientific" police work, especially with the publication of his *Professional Criminals of America* (1886), a photographic "rogues' gallery" of arrested felons that offered a solution to one of the most pressing problems of 19th century criminology—how to identify people.

Hawthorne became (following, perhaps, Allan Pinkerton's efforts at literary self-promotion) the *de facto* publicist for the policeman who came to be styled the world's greatest detective: on Nov 29, 1890 the *New York Times* carried this ad for a feature to appear in the *Sunday Herald* of the next day:

> INSPECTOR BYRNES
>
> Giving the inside views and methods of the
> world's greatest Thief Taker, written by his
> literary "Pard," Julian Hawthorne.

The newspaper pieces were only the latest manifestation of a partnership that began in 1887 with the publication of the first of Hawthorne's series of books subtitled "From the Diary of Inspector Byrnes," *The Great Bank Robbery* (1887), which was followed by *An American Penman* (1887), *A Tragic Mystery* (1887), *Section 558* (1888), and *Another's Crime* (1888).

Just as Victor and Green went to some pains in their novels to present the police detective as a legitimate, heroic individual to counter the less than savory contemporary reputation of the profession, in his Inspector Byrnes books—written almost a decade after *The Leavenworth Case*—Hawthorne still felt that he had to make the same point about the social class of detectives and the respectability of the police. In *The Great Bank Robbery*, therefore, he describes Byrnes as looking like a "businessman" and repeats the business allusion in this passage from *A Tragic Mystery*:

> In this apartment ... sat ... a well-dressed and powerfully built man of something less than forty years of age. His face was pleasant and his expression combined in a singular manner the qualities of frankness and impenetrability. He commonly wore an air of seeming abstraction, which, however, disguised a rare faculty of close and accurate observation. Quiet in manner and affable in speech, he might, so far as appearances went, have discharged any of the hundred functions of prosperous business life. In fact, however, he filled one of the most important and responsible offices in the gift of the city—that of chief of the detective force [26].

Indeed, in *Section 558* Hawthorne both makes Byrnes eminently respectable and also makes him an exemplar of the American Way: "He has the air of good society, and yet there is something about him that distinguishes him from the ordinary 'society man.' We feel that he must have raised himself in some way above the common level..." (5).

Unlike earlier writers, however, Hawthorne's interest in police work went beyond simply establishing the police detective as a legitimate hero. He was one of the first, if not the first, writer in America to manifest an interest in the police and what they do. Significantly he framed *The Great Bank Robbery* with a discussion between the Journalist and the Novelist, both of whom are familiar, or become familiar, with Inspector Byrnes and feel free to pop into his headquarters on Mulberry Street. Thus in that novel, when discussing criminals, one of the disputants says "The next time you go down town, stop in at Mulberry Street, and ask Byrnes to let you have a look at his collection of portraits" (9). This sounds very much like Dickens' habit of dropping in on Inspector Field and his fellow detectives, to smoke cigars and listen to cop tales that would later turn up in his magazine *Household Words*. More detailed than this allusion to the Rogues' Gallery, in *A Tragic Mystery* Hawthorne presents readers with a page and a half describing the gruesome exhibits (including the black hoods worn by hanged murderers) of the police museum. On the personnel side, in the same novel, he describes the New York Police Department's routine response to a crime—going from the reports of the patrolman on the scene, to the roundsman, to the detectives, to Inspector Byrnes, and finally to the shadowers. Significantly, too, Hawthorne is one of the first, if not the first, to connect the work of the police with descriptions of the real city with its tenements, pawn shops, and scrofulous dives as well as mansions and gentlemen's clubs.

One problem that confronted Hawthorne in writing about police work in the 1880s (the same problem that confronted Pinkerton or his ghost-writer a decade earlier) was that before the advent of police science and technology at the turn of the 20th century, police work was not very complicated—or interesting. Hawthorne pays some small attention in *The Great Bank Robbery* and *A Tragic Mystery* to the techniques Byrnes used to skirt the law in order to solve his cases—like rearresting suspects or moving them from precinct to precinct to avoid courts' rulings on suspects' rights. Nevertheless, much of what Hawthorne describes the police doing in all of the books is either rounding up the "usual suspects" (known because of Byrnes' data collection) or having an undercover agent follow people—in contemporary parlance, "shadow" them (a chapter in *A Tragic Mystery*, in fact, is entitled "Shadows"). This connects with the fact that in the slow evolution of modern police science and technique, even before the New York Police Department had an official detective division, there was a group of plain clothesmen called "shadows."

In that Hawthorne's Inspector Byrnes books purport to be realistic portraits of actual, day to day police work, their principal failure is the lack of even a whisper about the epidemic corruption in the New York Police Department that would lead to the Lexow Commission blowup less than a decade after their enthusiastic chronicling of Inspector Byrnes. More subtly off the mark, the books portray police work as the achievement of one, larger-than-life individual. Thus, while in every book the solution to the crime is the work of many men—both shadows and subsidiary detectives, Hawthorne never even gives them names. Indeed, in *A Tragic Mystery*, virtually all of the real investigation is done by the anonymous detective called only the "Shambling Man." This exclusive focus on Byrnes' brilliance and the implied necessity of visionary leadership and obedient, nameless workers—parallel, Hawthorne would have us believe, to that of a "successful businessman" or captain of industry—is not a wholly successful way to create a popular hero. It, however, is the same idea that led police reformers and writers of police fiction in the first half of the 20th century to adopt the metaphors of generalship and armies as the key to successful urban policing.

If Hawthorne had little that he could describe about actual police work and little that his position as Byrnes' advocate and "literary pard" would permit him to say about the real world of the police, there were always criminals, and his interest in Byrnes and in police work led him to manifest an awareness of crime and criminals absent in other 19th century works of American crime fiction. Real crimes were what got Hawthorne into the crime fiction business to begin with. Thus, the October 1878 robbery of the Manhattan Savings Institution (with its $3 million take the largest bank robbery to that date) formed the basis of his first Byrnes book, *The Great Bank Robbery*. Not only does Hawthorne treat actual crime, but he also brings in a wider variety of crime than usual in crime friction—thus there is extortion in *Section 558*, robbery, murder, and espionage *in A Tragic Mystery*, and forgery in *An American Penman*. In the books, too, he recognizes the public's periodically heightened sensitivity to particularly heinous crimes: thus Hawthorne mentions the assassination of President Garfield in *Section 558* and alludes to anarchists in *A Tragic Mystery*. On both levels, his awareness of real crime is something new in American crime fiction.

Along with a more forthright presentation of crime than had been the practice in incipient American crime fiction, Hawthorne also presents a portrait of criminals as a separate social class—something that had been done in British crime fiction from at least the time of Bulwer-Lytton but was absent in America. It begins with the discussion in *The Great Bank Robbery* where Hawthorne inserts a six page debate between the Novelist and the Journalist that ends up describing professional criminals as a separate social class. This takes off from, and is inspired by, talking about Byrnes' Rogues' Gallery (and, by extension, his *Professional Criminal of America*). Early in the discussion the Novelist notes that one cannot distinguish a criminal by means of his appearance: thus when viewing the Rogues' Gallery

> You will think ... that you have seldom seen an equal number of intelligent, respectable, self-satisfied persons. Nothing diabolic, nothing brutal, no signs of corroding anxiety or secret agony [9].

And yet they're all known felons. Given the influence of physiognomy and phrenology on American thought in the 19th century and the fact that when Hawthorne wrote this, Caesare Lombroso in Italy was off measuring heads and charting physical characteristics, he seems remarkably modern in this assertion that one cannot judge a person simply by his appearance. At the end of the set piece on professional criminals in the novel, Hawthorne concludes the argument with an assertion of relatively simplistic social cause and effect:

> My argument, as you call it, was simply undertaken to explain how it is that professional criminals have smooth faces.... I will only add that the true burden of sin consists in feeling it to be such. In our Puritan forefathers, the conscience was abnormally developed, and to sleep in church or to smile on Sunday was a deadly sin. Among Sandwich Islanders, on the other hand, it is a point of piety to eat your grandmother when she has reached a certain age. Now, thanks to my peculiar education, it will go against my conscience to steal your watch or cut your throat; but if I passed all my life among professional criminals, and still more if I were the descendant of such, I should consider it quite in the ordinary day's work to perform either of those services for you, and I should sleep not a jot worse for it. In other words, what to you or me is crime, to the genuine criminal is business, and his mood after committing it is not remorse, but satisfaction [16–17].

In the discussion in *The Great Bank Robbery*—one that, in its assertion that criminals live a more carefree life than the law abiding, has more than a hint of the premise of John Gay's *Beggar's Opera*—Hawthorne ignores the most important factors that determine class—economic status, education, etc. In his creation of criminal characters in the novels, however, these do play a significant role. Consistently in the books he presents two sets of people who commit criminal acts. There are the lower class criminals like the gang that knocked over the Manhattan Savings Institution in *The Great Bank Robbery* or the low-class thugs who robbed and wrecked the wine shop and then murdered its proprietor in *A Tragic Mystery*, based on the December 29, 1881 murder of Louis Hanier. And then there are the upper class folks, those people whom Hawthorne presents as more or less tragic figures like Mrs. Nelson (*The Great Bank Robbery*) or Kitty Clive (*Section 558*) or Mme. Desmond (*A Tragic Mystery*) motivated by hidden and mysterious passions.

Here was that fatal lure of sensation making itself felt. *The Dead Letter* and *The Leavenworth Case* both depend upon women with secrets. In both cases it's a character point and a plot device. Just as in *The Woman in White* or *The Moonstone,* readers are supposed to suffer for perverse circumstances that affect them and admire the silent suffering of Victor's and Green's female characters. Watching innocent women suffer, as perverse as that seems, was not the only emotional entertainment of the sensation novel. There came to be a set of sensation novels about the horrors and suffering that come about when women go bad. The most prominent examples of the when women go bad school of sensation fiction are Mrs. Henry Wood's wildly popular *East Lynne, or the Earl's Daughter* (1851) and Mary Elizabeth Braddon's widely read *Lady Audley's Secret* (1862). They both feature female characters who, ruled by passion, cause social havoc and ruin lives—their own as well as others'. Hawthorne's Inspector Byrnes books, more than being about crime and detection—the sort of thing one ought to expect coming "from the diary" of a high ranking police official— are about women and passion. This is particularly the case in *The Great Bank Robbery*. There Hawthorne gives decidedly short shrift to the details of solving the crime and catching the criminals in order to devote attention to his made-up story of Mrs. Nelson—as opposed to the real story of the bank heist. In Mrs. (not her real name) Nelson Hawthorne presents the awesome (and awful) effects of a woman's unbridled passions. At first her desire for social prominence exhausts the family's means, especially after her husband suffers business reverses. Not to be denied, she becomes involved with the underworld at first as a means of obtaining money and then as an adjunct to her increasing addiction to excitement. Indeed, Hawthorne uses an episode of her facing down an untamed horse as the fulcrum for the Novelist's interest in looking into the details of the bank robbery in the first place. But Mrs. Nelson is not the only sensation novel woman in the Byrnes books. There is Vera, the subject of this passage in *An American Penman*:

> But you are a woman, and I once loved you. A year ago, when I found you in danger and distress, I would have saved you, if you would have come with me. But even then you loved your shameful life too well to accept my offer [272].

Section 558 ends with the revelation that Kitty Clive has been writing threatening extortion letters fueled by her passionate (but mistaken) belief that Maxwell Golding, the financier, had wronged the philanthropic General Weymouth. In *A Tragic Mystery* there is much ado about Mme. Desmond's secret—that her family background didn't match her husband's expectations. And *Another's Crime*, too, features a sister suffering for and covering up for her brother. In truth, Hawthorne's Inspector Byrnes books have multiple plots, one about crime and detection and one about emotional travail of the distaff members of the smart set. And the sensation takes over, strangling whatever small chance the detective material might have had.

THE FIRST FIFTY YEARS REPRISE

It took half a century, from 1841 to 1891, to get from Poe's "The Murders in the Rue Morgue" and the invention of the detective story to Arthur Conan Doyle's "Scandal in Bohemia" and the real beginning of the detective story as a separate, popular literary genre. During that fifty year hiatus writers in Europe began to look at Poe, to look at crime, and to look at the newly invented institutions of the police and the detective police for material upon which to base new and (they hoped) profitable fiction. Almost at the same time that Poe wrote his detective tales, in Britain Charles Dickens grew more and more interested in police and detectives as characters, and in narrative technique very similar to Poe's as a new means of creating character and articulating plot in his *Barnaby Rudge* (1841), *Martin Chuzzlewit* (1844), *Bleak House* (1853) and, perhaps, in the unfinished *Mystery of Edwin Drood*. His friend Wilkie Collins not only gave the world its most influential sensation novel, *The Woman in White* (1860), but he also gave readers a chance to be the detective while reading *The Moonstone* (1868). At almost the same time, across the Channel Emile Gaboriau invented what would become the French version of the detective story, the *roman policier*, with his *L'Affaire Lerouge* (1865), *Monsieur Lecoq* (1869), and other narratives about heroic Parisian police. And in America adolescents could read about the daring do of dime novel detectives, and their elders could savor the passions evoked by crime and the sensation novel. Nowhere was there the kind of fiction that came to be called detective fiction. But the conditions that would make the detective story possible, even inevitable, were slowly emerging in the fifty years between Poe and Conan Doyle.

In America a number of those conditions came about after the Civil

War. The war, of course, speeded up the technology of violence, best illustrated, perhaps, by the introduction of the point and click firearm made possible by the invention of the self-contained cartridge. It also accustomed tens of thousands of men to the use of violence, and after the war there was an undeniable and dramatic increase in violent crime in America's cities—violence that would soon extend to two assassinated Presidents. The war also fueled the immense increase in individual wealth that would usher in what Mark Twain would later label "the Gilded Age." What all of this amounts to is that by the 1880s crime and violence had become new, significant problems in America—crime and violence that the newly created law enforcement community (public and private) was ill-designed and ill-equipped to handle. What it means, too, is that crime was not only more common and violent, but also that newly amassed and conspicuously consumed wealth led to new types of crime, the kind of crime reflected in the gentleman burglar stories in Britain and the U.S. and in the many stories about stolen jewels appearing at the turn of the century. Affluence, for better or for worse, also led to making detection a private enterprise for sale to the wealthy. Just as social conditions in the last quarter of the 19th century changed radically, so did the law. Always a point of controversy in a country that nurtured individualists like Thoreau with his attachment to natural law, the law in the courts and the statutes underwent a metamorphosis during the last half of the 19th century. The weight of evidence offered in trails slowly shifted from people to things, from the witness' word to the mute evidence science and scientists could adduce from the minutiae of the material world. Along side this evolution in the law, the concept of the nature of the criminal changed as the century progressed from Galt and phrenology to Freud and psychiatry. As dissimilar as were these views of human nature, both banished the concept of sin from the explanation of human behavior. Crime, detection, and punishment, then, became less directly the province of the priest and more that of the police and the courts.

Books and readers changed as well. Shortly after the Civil War, state by state, universal education spread across the country and the reading public widened and deepened. In Britain where a parallel phenomenon appeared, a new class of fiction emerged for the new readers—*Treasure Island, The Prisoner of Zenda, The White Company, King Solomon's Mines, Dr. Jekyll and Mr. Hyde.* In America the family story paper and the dime novel tried to do the same thing, presenting fledgling readers with a variety of new heroes—cowboys, soldiers, physicians, adventurers, detectives, and the upwardly mobile Horatio Alger kids. But, as we have seen, most were stigmatized as being juvenile, puerile, and not respectable—they had too much *dolce* and not enough *utile*. Maybe something that preached duty but more prominently about clear and close reasoning seasoned with a dash of danger and a pinch of excitement would fill the bill. Maybe something that would begin with

> In the year 1878 I took my degree of Doctor of Medicine of the University of London, and proceeded to Netley to go through the course prescribed for surgeons in the army.

2

Enter the Great Detective

It would be difficult to imagine what shape crime fiction would have taken in America (or anywhere else for that matter) without Sherlock Holmes. Such speculation about that road not taken, however, is hardly necessary: nobody doubts that the modern detective story and maybe even the detective story itself began in earnest when Conan Doyle switched from writing short novels to writing short stories with "A Scandal in Bohemia" in 1891. Sherlock Holmes, consulting detective, changed forever the hero and the atmosphere (if not the narrative framework) of the detective story everywhere. To his credit, Conan Doyle was never hesitant about attributing a significant portion of his success to traits and techniques he borrowed from Poe: it was one of the first things he talked about to reporters when he arrived in America in 1894. Nevertheless, his success ultimately depended as much upon the originality and humaneness of the Sherlock Holmes stories as it did upon using bits borrowed from Poe. And in no small measure that success also depended on Conan Doyle simply being at the right place at the right time. In his case the fortunate convergences were: 1. the appearance of new media (newspaper syndication and mass circulation magazines); 2. the availability of a significantly larger adult readership resulting from universal education in Britain and the U.S.; 3. the emergence of real detectives and detective police in Britain and the U.S.; 4. the invention or discovery of revolutionary scientific and analytical tools that could be applied to the solution of crime; and 5. the emergence of new attitudes toward crime and criminals. They all joined together to make the last decade of the 19th century the right time. The right place for Conan Doyle turned out to be not Great Britain but America. At the turn of the 20th century what would become known to some as the "sacred writings" gained greater popularity, and perhaps even wider influence in the U.S. than they achieved in Great Britain. There was also unarguably more money to be made in the U.S. than in Britain, and that was something that it did not take Dr. Conan Doyle long to figure out.

READ ALL ABOUT IT

Bookish people tend to think first about books — that fiction and fictional characters become popular because people have met them between the covers of books. This, however, was not the way in which readers, especially American readers, originally became acquainted with the adventures of Sherlock Holmes. In Britain, of course, magazine publication was the engine that moved Holmes from the obscurity of *Beeton's Christmas Annual* and sensation novels patterned on Gaboriau into the limelight of the short stories — Conan Doyle's association with *The Strand* magazine is a familiar story. It was perhaps no coincidence, then, that a magazine first brought Sherlock Holmes officially to America — in 1890 *Lippincott's Magazine* was the first publisher of *The Sign of the Four* on both sides of the Atlantic. But while magazine publication certainly played a role in bringing Holmes to American readers, newspapers played an even more important one. They were the first place that American readers were exposed to the short stories that made the Great Detective great. And here, too, their popularity depended on a new development in publishing. In the last decade of the 19th century, American publisher S. S. McClure invented (or at least exploited) the idea of newspaper syndication, of purchasing stories and selling them at a discounted price to a number of newspapers. McClure bought the rights to the stories that eventually would form Conan Doyle's first collection of Holmes pieces, *The Adventures of Sherlock Holmes*. And he then sold the rights to reprint those eleven stories (from "Scandal in Bohemia" through "Copper Beeches") to a variety of American newspapers where they ran from July 1891 through June 1892. A variety of American newspapers? The papers printing some or all of this first run of Sherlock Holmes in America included: *The Baltimore Sun, The Boston Daily Traveler, The Boston Sunday Globe, The Boston Herald, The Buffalo Sunday News, The Buffalo Courier, The Cincinnati Commercial Gazette, The* [Louisville] *Courier-Journal, The Detroit Sunday News, The* [Pennsylvania] *Grit, The Indianapolis News,* the [Chicago] *Inter-Ocean, The Minneapolis Journal, The New York Sun, The New York World, The Philadelphia Inquirer, The Pittsburgh Press, The Pittsburgh Commercial Gazette, The Providence Sunday Journal, The Toledo Blade, The St. Louis Post-Dispatch, The Saint Louis Sunday Star, The San Francisco Examiner, The Seattle Post-Intelligencer, The [New Orleans] Times-Picayune,* and *The Washington Post.* The list is a roll call of some of the country's greatest newspapers as well as a gazetteer of American cities, large and small. What it means is that from 1891 through 1892 newspapers pretty much blanketed the country with Sherlock Holmes stories (and some of the cities left out of the

1891–2 Holmes rush [i.e. Atlanta, Omaha] carried Holmes stories later in the decade). And they did so at a price (typically papers cost two cents a copy) that almost everyone could afford. Syndication, then, enabled a larger number as well as a greater variety of people in the United States to read the Sherlock Holmes stories than any other medium available before the cinema. And the movies, too, brought Holmes to the American public during its earliest years.

Holmes and the Slicks

The year after what surely amounts to a protracted newspaper blitz of Sherlock Holmes stories, *Harper's Weekly* ran the second batch of them, those pieces that would become *The Memoirs of Sherlock Holmes*. So in 1893 the Holmes stories moved a step up the social ladder to a middle class literary medium with the publication of "The Cardboard Box," "The Crooked Men," "The Gloria Scott," "The Greek Interpreter," "The Musgrave Ritual," "The Lost Naval Treaty," "The Reigate Squires," "The Resident Patient," "Silver Blaze," "The Stockbroker's Clerk," and "The Yellow Face" in *Harper's*. Not entirely out of the race, in 1893 S. S. McClure acquired rights to the last, most important story *in The Memoirs*, "The Final Problem," and published it in his new *McClure's Magazine* after it ran in newspapers in five cities. Other pieces from *The Memoirs of Sherlock Holmes* appeared in newspapers, too, but there were only one or two of them—*Harper's* efforts at syndication were no match for S.S. McClure's.

Fully a decade after Holmes' introduction to American readers in newspapers and magazines, a third Sherlock Holmes wave hit American streets. It started with an advertising campaign that saw devices like a medallion featuring one of the stick figures from "The Dancing Men" followed by

I am good for 10 cents.
Tear me out and give me to a newsdealer
Sherlock Holmes will tell you all about me in the Christmas Collier's. Its regular price is 25 cents, but by handing the above circle to a newsdealer you can get the holiday number for 15 cents [*Washington Post* December 7, 1903].

Running from 1903 to 1905 *Collier's Weekly* published thirteen of the Holmes stories that would eventually become *The Return of Sherlock Holmes*. Unlike *Harper's* or *McClure's*, when *Collier's* ran the Holmes stories, they put the hero on the cover—in color renditions by Frederic Dorr Steele whose concept of the Great Detective became almost as famous as that of Sidney Paget's whose illustrations were published in *The Strand*. It is most assuredly a sign both of the popularity of Sherlock Holmes in the United States as well as of the economic power of American publishing that at the turn of the century Conan Doyle sold first publication rights of his latest detective stories to *Collier's Weekly* and that they appeared in America before they appeared in Britain in *The Strand Magazine*.

DR. CONAN DOYLE ON TOUR

American newspapers almost inevitably called him Dr. Conan Doyle. And when Arthur Conan Doyle came to the U.S. in 1894 to lecture (and perhaps even to look for a suitable climate for his consumptive wife), he got the red carpet treatment. Newspapers announced his arrival, his comings and goings and, as the highlight of his arrival in any town, gave advance notice and then rave reviews of his lectures. When Conan Doyle took to the lecture circuit, Sherlock Holmes had supposedly been dashed to pieces in Switzerland and Conan Doyle thought that he was going to tour the States talking about contemporary literature with maybe a plug or two for *The White Company* and his other literary endeavors. Thus the piece from *The Washington Post* before Conan Doyle's talk (October 3, 1894) promises the literati and cognoscenti of the nation's capital a long, long evening:

> He will lecture on "Facts About Fiction," including the tendency of fiction in England, Hanly's country pictures, Stevenson's influence, "A Master of Phrases," "A Great Book," Olive Schreiner, Barrie and Scotland, the short tale, Rudyard Kipling, and recent humor.
> He will analyze the novels of George Meredith, describe the author as the novelist's novelist, tell the permanent influence on his work on literature, review his earlier writings, discuss style and its uses, Meredith's humor, his phrase making, his types of women, and his renovating force in letters.

The news stories after Conan Doyle's talk, however, make it sound like all his listeners wanted to hear about was about Sherlock Holmes and that the good doctor acquiesced and told the story of how he came to invent the world's most well-known detective. Audiences and reporters alike also wanted to know why on earth he wanted to kill off their favorite character.

SHERLOCK ON STAGE

It is not hyperbole, then, to say that before the First World War quite literally millions of Americans had been exposed to Sherlock Holmes in newspapers and in the burgeoning slick magazine market (*McClure's*, for instance, had an estimated circulation of 300,000). But some American audiences of the time came to know the Great Detective in other ways, too. The most prominent of these was from the stage. There were detective stories on the American stage before Sherlock Holmes made his appearance. Most notably, Charles Rohlfs, Anna Katharine Green's husband, appeared in a stage version of *The Leavenworth Case* in 1891. But the big news of the decade was going to be William Gillette's play about the great detective. Even before the famous actor and inventor of stage effects opened his new play about Sherlock Holmes, however, New York theatrical impresario George Lederer produced "The Man in the Moon" with music by the well-known composer Reginald DeKoven (who wrote "Oh Promise Me") and libretto by Louis Harrison and Stanislaus Stange. Part ballet, part operetta, part "women in lingerie" (*Washington Post* April 30, 1899), "The Man in the Moon" featured both Sherlock Holmes and Arthur Conan Doyle as characters, with Conan Doyle for a reason that is difficult to fathom, affecting a Dutch accent. Before going on tour, "The Man in the Moon" ran 182 performances in New York. Not bad. But the real blockbuster was going to be Gillette's play.

In 1899 William Gillette, coming off of his success in *Secret Service*, cobbled together a play based on *A Study in Scarlet*, "A Scandal in Bohemia," and "The Final Problem," went to England and got Conan Doyle's okay, and opened his play, *Sherlock Holmes,* at the Star Theater in Buffalo, New York (a provincial city where, nevertheless, two local newspapers had run the Holmes stories earlier in the decade and, perhaps not by coincidence, the home of Anna Katharine Green and her actor husband) on October 23. In 1900 he took the play to New York for an eight-month run, toured the U.S., and finally opened in England in the fall of 1901. All told, Gillette played Holmes on stage for thirty three years. In 1916 he minimally altered his play and appeared on both stage and screen as the embodiment of Sherlock Holmes. While scarcely the real thing, Gillette's performances returned the spotlight to Holmes toward the end of those years between "The Final Problem" (December 1893) and *The Hound of the Baskervilles* (1901) when Conan Doyle refused to write about his detective and it prepared the reception for the third Sherlock Holmes novel and for *Collier's* run of the stories from *The Return of Sherlock Holmes* in 1903. Aware of Gillette's success, Conan Doyle himself apparently started, but did not finish, a play based on *The Hound of the Baskervilles*—three of four acts exist in a typescript prepared in London in 1902. Also inspired, no doubt, by the popularity of Gillette's play, in 1901 Charles P. Rice opened a mediocre theatrical adaptation of *The Sign of the Four,* but this wasn't the most important reverberation of Sherlock Holmes on the stage. While by the mid-1890s occasional plays like R.H. Stephens' *The White Rat* had been performed about detectives who were very much like Sherlock Holmes, Gillette's success playing the great detective gave rise to what amounted to a rage for plays about detectives. Thus in a stroll past D.C.'s theaters on November 25, 1900, the Theatrical Notes and Gossip section of *The Washington Post* finds detectives everywhere:

> At the National was the celebrated Sherlock Holmes and his associate detectives preparing to put the nippers on a gang of crooks. At the Lafayette was another detective of the Sherlock Holmes type who chased the diamond gang through five acts and fourteen scenes of "The Great Ruby." At the Columbia even Denman Thompson had to play detective to catch his erring boy, while, for further realism, up to date policemen were introduced. At the Grand a lady detective was on view, her specialty being divorce cases. Down the theatrical line at the Lyceum and the Bijou, stage detectives made their appearance in each of the burlesques.

HOLMES HUMOR

Even before Gillette became the embodiment of Sherlock Holmes for American theater goers, American humorists began to discover that Conan Doyle's stories provided them with plenty upon which to base burlesques, parodies, and assorted other kinds of gags—as well as upon which comic writers like Gelette Burgess, Octavius Roy Cohen and others could base their more-or-less straight detective stories. Indeed, at the turn of the century Holmes take offs were almost everywhere in American newspapers and these ranged from three column inch tongue in cheek anecdotes to full blown parodies and burlesques.

Among the earliest of the American comic admirers of Sherlock Holmes was John Kendrick Bangs. His *The Pursuit of the House-Boat* (1897) is a light and frothy narrative in which the recently deceased Sherlock Holmes joins Socrates, Walter Raleigh and the shades of other immortals in pursuit of their pleasure craft (also containing their wives) which has been hi-jacked by Captain Kidd. Bangs also wrote a newspaper serial, *Shylock Holmes: His Posthumous Adventures* that appeared in newspaper syndication in 1903 (Penzler, *Encyclopedia* 19). Interested in crime from the time he invented the keystone kops antics of the incompetent police in "The Stolen White Elephant" (1882), his use of fingerprints in *Pudd'nhead Wilson* (1894), and Tom's forensic foolery in *Tom Sawyer, Detective* (1896), Mark Twain focused his gaze directly on Sherlock Holmes in *The Double Barreled Detective Story* (1902). There the much celebrated detective, Sherlock Holmes, arrives at a mining camp and by means of abstruse measurements and tortuous logic attempts to rescue Fetlock, his nephew, from an accusation for a murder he actually committed. The same year Twain came out in the open with Holmes' name, Bret Harte published "The Stolen Cigar Case" in *Pearson's Magazine* in which an abjectly sycophantic Watson—"With the freedom of an old friend I at once threw myself in my old familiar attitude at his feet, and gently caressed his boot"—asks Hemlock Jones for help only to witness the creation of an elaborate artifice of reasoning and then its collapse when it comes in contact with mundane reality. Almost a decade later, in 1911, O. Henry began a short series of stories about Shamrock Jolnes who is first an official New York police detective and then a consulting detective. In both cases, over elaborate and ultra sophisticated thinking proves to be his downfall. Among the many other burlesques and pastiches published in America at the same time the Holmes juggernaut had gathered steam, in "The Succored Beauty" (*Smart Set* October 1905) William B. Kahn seems to have noticed how many of the early Holmes pieces deal with marital difficulties and has his Spotson complain that he's broke because Orlock Combs has helped his wife procure evidence for divorce. James J. Montague, on the other hand, in "Dr. Watson Gets Peevish" (*Chicago Sunday Examiner* August 30, 1908), has Holmes taking a break from crime with the sure knowledge that he has set the detective story machine going and that it has energy sufficient to run without him. Overall American humorists before World War I tend to ridicule (gently or otherwise—mostly otherwise) 1. Holmes' deduction demonstrations ("you have been in Afghanistan"), 2. his endless store of esoteric and abstruse knowledge, 3. the blind hero-worship explicit in the Watson-Holmes relationship, and 4. the marked contrast between sophisticated, complex, and self-righteous logic and downright common sense.

DROPPING HOLMES' NAME

At the same time that the Sherlock Holmes stories provided fodder for the canon of American humor—to say nothing of comic writers in Canada (like Stephen Leacock) and Britain (like A. A. Milne)—a lot of writers took to writing straight detective stories because of Conan Doyle's success and popularity. Indeed, early on the new crop of detective story writers in the U.S. began to identify themselves with the popularity of the detective story by including allusions to Conan Doyle's stories in their own fiction. Rodriguez Ottolengui, for example, gives readers a Holmesean deduction demonstration along with an admonition about fact versus fiction in *The Final Proof, or The Value of Evidence* (1898):

> "It seems to me that if you can tell that, you are becoming as clever as the famous Sherlock Holmes."
> "Oh, no, indeed! You and I can hardly expect to be a shrewd as the detectives of romance. As to my guessing that you have had no coffee, that is not very troublesome. I notice three drops of milk on your coat, and one on your shoe, from which I deduce, first, that you have had no coffee, for a man who has his coffee in the morning is not apt to drink a glass of milk besides...."
> "Correct in every detail. Sherlock Holmes could have done no better" [2].

Melvin L. Severy's detective in Th*e Darrow Enigma* (1904) trots over to the public library to find the clue he needs to solve the crime:

> I began to read detective stories, with all the avidity of a Western Union Telegraph messenger, and, of course, read those by Conan Doyle. The assertion of 'Sherlock Holmes' that there is no novelty in crime; that crimes, like history, repeat themselves; and that criminals read and copy each other's methods, deeply impressed me, and I at once said to myself: 'If our assassin was not original, whom did he copy?' "It was while reading 'The Sign of the Four,' which I had procured at the Public Library, that I made the first discovery. The crime therein narrated had been committed in such a singular manner that it at once attracted my attention. The victim had apparently been murdered without anyone having either entered or left the room. In this respect it was like the problem we are trying to solve. I was fully aware that the chance of my learning anything in this way was very slight, In the first place; I reasoned that it was not especially likely your father's murderer had read 'The Sign of the Four,' and, in the second place, even if he had, what assurance had I that he had read this particular copy of it? Notwithstanding this, however, I felt impelled to give my synthetical theory a fair experimental trial. I was informed by the Library attendants that the book had been much read, and given the list of some twenty names of persons who had borrowed the book during the time I had specified [www.gutenberg.org].

It's not the little blowpipe guy with his poisoned darts from *The Sign of the Four* who attracts attention in Charles Carey's *The Van Suyden Sapphires* (1905), but Holmes' mastery of minutiae. "Did not Conan Doyle's sagacious hero once deduce the entire structure of a complicated case from the half-smoked butt of a 'Trichinopoly'? (150). Holmes' name was common knowledge even when it was shortened, as in Nelson R. Gilbert's *The Affair at Pine Court* (1907):

> "You aren't much of a S.H."
> "S.H.?"
> "Sherlock Holmes. Apply his methods..." [111].

And it is equally apparent that some of the new writers copied, sometimes playfully sometimes not, Conan Doyle's narrative techniques. In

Hugh C. Weir's Madelyn Mack stories (1914), for example, the detective frequently stretches the stories out between enigmatic statements about clues that the Watson character, Nora Noraker, can't comprehend and then later has Madelyn the detective resolve them, a practice that gets her labeled as "Miss Sherlock Holmes" (181). It is entirely evident that even before the turn of the century the name Sherlock Holmes had become synonymous with detective in fiction. Not a lot of examination is necessary either to find that new detective writers in America as in Britain copied some of Conan Doyle's narrative techniques because they believed that readers expected to find them in their detective stories. That Burton Stevenson dedicates *The Mystery of the Boule Cabinet* (1912) to a "Fellow Sherlockean" long before the founding of the Baker Street Irregulars demonstrates not simply that Conan Doyle's detective stories had dedicated readers, but also that some of those readers were aficionados, enthusiasts, fans.

GABORIAU AND POE

In addition to developing the audience and the nascent imaginary play world of detective fiction that would become a defining feature of Golden Age detective stories, the publication of the Sherlock Holmes stories in America gave rise to new interest in the true but brief history of the detective story. Thus, along with allusions to Holmes, turn of the century detective fiction also tips its collective hat to Poe and, less often, to Emile Gaboriau. Burton Stevenson in *The Holladay Case* (1903) has a Frenchman (who else) sing the praises of Gaboriau:.

> "I have read it, oh, ver' many times, as well as all the others—though this, of course, is the masterpiece."
> He held it so that I could see the title. It was "Monsieur Lecoq."
> "I have read it in English," I said.
> "And did you not like it—yes? I am ver' fond of stories of detection" [135].

After Sherlock Holmes and far more often than Gaboriau, it's Poe who is summoned up in turn of the century detective stories. Samuel Gardenhire filled his LeDroit Conners stories collected in *The Long Arm* (1906), with references to Poe: Conners not only has a bust of Poe in his studio but paintings of Dupin as well. Just as Madelyn Mack is Miss Sherlock Holmes, the hero of Edith Buckley's *The Snare of Circumstance* (1910) calls a young woman whom he's trying to butter up "M'lle Dupin" (95). More often, though, when writers summon up Poe, it's in reference to his term borrowed from Hoyle, "the calculus of probabilities." Thus this passage from Severy's *The Darrow Enigma*:

> I told him that I could scarcely account for it on the ground of mere coinci-
> dence, and I called his attention to that part of "The Mystery of Marie Roget,"
> where Poe figures out the mathematical likelihood of a certain combination of
> peculiarities of clothing being found to obtain in the case of two young
> women who were unknown to each other [www.gutenberg.org].

Poe, in spite of his role as the inventor of the form, never even gets close Holmes in the recognition given to literary influences in turn of the century detective fiction. The few critics who wrote about literary history aside, when writers mentioned Poe it was usually in reference to intellectual things (the calculus of probabilities) or narrative technique; it was never about the character of the detective. Sherlock Holmes owned character.

DIME DETECTIVES

To define the detective story by opposition, turn of the century writers occasionally look to the dime novel. Mostly writers dismiss Nick Carter, Old Sleuth, and other denizens of the dime world as adolescent reading material. In *The Crime of the Century* (1903), therefore, Ottolengui's smart detective (there's a not so smart one, too) differentiates real detective work from fantasy by referring to shadowing suspects and wearing disguises: "But I do not admire this masquerading. It is too theatrical. It savors too much of the dime novel detective" (115), and Frank Packard, when describing the dangers his rogue hero encounters notes that "They were exactly what they purported to be, dime-novelish, of the deepest hue of yellow, melodramatic in the extreme..." (*The Adventures of Jimmy Dale* 286). If allusions to Sherlock Holmes and Dupin served to create a sense of fellowship among readers of detective stories, the allusions to dime novels in turn of the century detective fiction reassure those same readers that theirs was a respectable avocation. Whether it's factual, or whether it's a case of the reviewer doth protest too much, this attitude comes across pretty clearly in the review of Gillette's detective drama in *The Washington Post*:

> It requires a keen understanding and sharp wits to appreciate all the fine
> points of "Sherlock Holmes." In a popular-priced house, acted by an inferior
> company, this play would be almost unintelligible to the ordinary Bowery
> type of audience. Why? Simply because such an audience would never dis-
> cover the intellectual side of Sherlock Holmes... "Sherlock Homes" is essen-
> tially high class entertainment. It is not cheap melodrama in showy wrapper...
> November 25, 1900].

This is the same kind of attitude that later in the century would give rise to lists of famous people who read detective stories as well as the popularity of using the idea of the puzzle to explain and justify the form.

THE DETECTIVE STORY FORMS

With the publication of Conan Doyle's stories in the 1890s, writers in the U.S. began to see that he did something special and different, and that that particular something special and different was part of a movement begun by Poe. Poe didn't call them detective stories, his label for the Dupin stories was "tales of ratiocination." And before the days of professional critics and modern marketing by publishers, sensation novels didn't have a particular name: sensation novels about crime were just novels. While in France, Gaboriau's works picked up the term *roman policier*, nobody applied that translated label to novels in English until the 1960s and Joseph Wambaugh's police novels. Nobody called any of the early works detective stories. But the Sherlock Holmes stories were detective stories—and then so were everyone else's. Twain, for example, always alert to marketing, didn't call them *Tom Sawyer, Detective* (1896) or *Double Barreled Detective Story* (1902) for nothing. And with the popularity of the Sherlock Holmes stories at the turn of the century, critics began to see detective stories as a separate category of fiction and to begin a search to uncover its history. Thus Arthur B. Maurice, who had written early pieces on the Sherlock Holmes stories for the *Bookman* ("Some Inconsistencies of Sherlock Holmes" and "More Sherlock Holmes Theories" both 1902), traces the ancestry of the detective back to Poe in his "The Detective in Fiction" (*Bookman* 1902). The publishers of *The Reader's Guide to Periodical Literature* granted official sanction to the form in 1905 by giving the detective story its own heading beginning in that year's reference volume. In 1907 *The Washington Post* reflected popular interest in the literary history of the form by devoting thirty-five column inches to a piece entitled "Tale of Zadig Proves Voltaire Father of the Detective Story" (August 25, 1907). A bit later (in February 1910) *Harper's Weekly* carried a piece entitled "The Detective Story's Origin" that traces the form from Voltaire, to *The Arabian Nights*, to Apocryphal Old Testament stories, and finally to Herodotus' tale of Rhampsinitus' treasure house. *The Nation* also published an early history with "Detectives in Fiction" in 1912. Aware of the emerging interest in and market for detective fiction, publishers began to issue anthologies with the terms "mystery" and "detective" as bait for readers. There was the G.P. Putnam's collection of ten titles by Green, Ottolungui, Melville Davisson Post, and Richard Dallas, *Stories of Mystery and Crime*. The

Review of Reviews used Julian Hawthorne as editor of a six volume set, *Library of the World's Best Mystery and Detective Stories*, published in 1908, and in the next year he served as editor of their of the ten volume *Lock and Key Library; Classic Mystery and Detective Stories,* a collection that had volumes dedicated to Old Time English, Modern English, American, and Real Life mystery and detective fiction. Neither of these collections, it should be noted, really delivered the detective goods but depended heavily on the "mystery" side to fill up the pages. The American volume of the *Lock and Key Library*, for example, has stories by Poe and Melville Davisson Post, but also has pieces by Washington Irving, Charles Brockden Brown, Ambrose Bierce, and the editor's daddy's "The Minister's Black Veil."

Reflecting on the fact that a lot of people apparently were talking about detective stories, Melvin Severy in the Forward to *The Mystery of June 13th* (1905), warns readers that

> Lest a misapprehension spread still further, it is perhaps but fair to state here that I am not a student of detective literature: that I know little of the methods usually employed in such stories, and have not felt it necessary to follow that little.

Those "methods usually employed" had penetrated U.S. readership so deeply that in 1913, for the Home Correspondence School, librarian turned detective writer Carolyn Wells wrote *The Technique of the Mystery Story*, a how-to guide for aspiring detective story writers. Prefatory to the practical advice, Wells gives her readers a heavy dose of Holmes (including sections on The Detectives of Poe, Conan Doyle, and Gaboriau; The Real Sherlock Holmes; Sherlock Holmes' Method; Holmes' Method Evaluated; etc) and begins in earnest with a chapter discussing "The Rightful Place of the Mystery Story in Fiction" followed by chapters featuring literary archeology and history. None of this would have happened without the Sherlock Holmes stories.

TURN OF THE CENTURY FICTION

But what does all of this mean—besides providing some interesting glimpses into the history of one of the great ages of American publishing? How did the introduction of Sherlock Holmes change popular fiction and, more to the point, how did the introduction of the Holmes stories change American crime fiction? The opening part of that question is dynamite fishing: the introduction of Sherlock Holmes created the modern detective story. Period. But when one adds the term "American" things get considerably more difficult. First of all, detective fiction in the U.S. before World War I is a largely unexplored field. Lots of people have believed Howard Haycraft's pronouncement that "It cannot be pretended that the American detective story revealed anything like the quantity of its English counterparts in the years up to the first world conflagration" (*Murder for Pleasure* 101–102). Hugh Greene, in his preface to *The American Rivals of Sherlock Holmes* (1976), comes closer to the truth when he recognizes that a lot more went on in the detective fiction department in the U.S. than Haycraft recognized, but that it's damnably hard to find in Britain—and not that easy in the U.S. Truth to be told, from the mid-1890s onward a good bit of detective fiction, both short and long, was published in the U.S. And, if everything above holds true—that the publication of the Holmes stories created modern detective fiction—the issue at hand is whether and how the detective stories written in response to Holmes differed in the United States from the way in which turn of the century writers in Britain responded to the public's demand for stories like those written by Arthur Conan Doyle. On one level, that such a difference exists can be seen is by comparing the illustrations Paget did for *The Strand* in London with those Steel did for *Collier's* in New York—or better yet, the illustrations from serialization in U.S. papers that can be found in Leslie Klinger's *The Annotated Sherlock Holmes*. If not as graphically, then just as significantly, the difference can be seen when looking at the themes and characters of turn of the century detective fiction in the U.S. They are not always what one might expect them to be. Or maybe, considering the state of the nation, they are what one would expect them to be.

How Much Crime?

One of the major differences between the Sherlock Holmes stories—or at least the first series—and those of writers working in their wake can be found in their respective subject matter. Twice in the stories that would go on to form part of *The Adventures of Sherlock Holmes* (in "The Blue Carbuncle" and again in "Copper Beeches") Holmes and Watson note that many of their adventures have had little to do with crime. Here's "The Blue Carbuncle" passage:

> "No, no. No crime," said Sherlock Holmes. Laughing. "Only one of those whimsical little incidents which will happen when you have four million human beings all jostling each in the space of a few square miles. Amid the action and reaction of so dense a swarm of humanity, every possible combination of events may be expected to take place, and many a little problem will

be presented which may be striking and bizarre without being criminal. We have already had experience of such."

"So much so," I remarked, "that of the last six cases which I have added to my notes, three have been entirely free of any legal crime" [Klinger I, 198].

Indeed, in the first run of stories Holmes' solutions often have to do more with relationships than with the law: thus the King of Bohemia's love life, an impersonated suitor ("A Case of Identity"), a missing husband ("The Man with the Twisted Lip"), reunited lovers ("The Noble Bachelor"), and separated lovers ("Copper Beeches") all have to do with dysfunctional courtship or marriage. Almost half of the first collection of stories has to do with the matter of the sensation novel, an inclination made most apparent by the repeated theme of the stolen inheritance — a theme also touched on in *The Sign of the Four*. Not much reflection reveals that the theme of wronged women looms large in *A Study in Scarlet*. This is one of the areas in which writers after Conan Doyle differed. While sensation novel themes would remain standard in detective fiction for a long, long time, almost immediately writers, particularly American writers, moved from focusing on crimes against relationships and made their detectives go after other kinds of criminals and other kinds of crime. Some turn of that fiction focuses on robbery, especially jewel robbery, but long before S.S. Van Dine's rules made it mandatory, a lot of American detective fiction was about murder.

DIVINE LAW RULES

No hurt, as the saying goes, no foul; in Sherlock Holmes' domestic cases that means no crime, no punishment — except maybe the thrashing Holmes threatens to mete out at the end of "A Case of Identity." When serious crime does occur in the tales, most frequently punishment doesn't come from Holmes or Gregson or Lestrade or the assizes. Most often it's a case of traditional (divine, as it were) retributive justice. This goes back as far as *A Study in Scarlet* with the fate of Jefferson Hope:

We had all been warned to appear before the magistrates upon the Thursday; but when the Thursday came there was no occasion for our testimony. A higher Judge had taken the matter in hand. And Jefferson Hope had been summoned before a tribunal where strict justice would be meted out to him [Baring Gold I, 230].

Things take off from there: diabetes kills John Turner in "The Boscombe Valley Mystery," a furious Atlantic gale drowns the murderers in "The Five Orange Pips," the spotted snake kills Grimsby Roylott in "The

Speckled Band," and the family mastiff tears open fatty Runcastle's throat in "Copper Beeches." Villains all, in a very real sense that "higher Judge" in the form of nature takes care of them. Holmes and Watson only serve as observers. It's just in domestic and lesser crimes—like those in "The Blue Carbuncle" and "The Red Headed League"—that the detective and his friend are actually in on what happens at the end. Furthermore, while Conan Doyle does mention the tenuousness of circumstantial evidence several times in the stories, law and the courts are conspicuously absent in the Holmes stories and this exclusion of the civil machinery of justice makes a difference. It's something that turn of the century writers in America jumped right on. They focused on the law not only as a source of narrative devices (the faulty coroner's hearing, for instance) but also as subject matter—to discuss the changing nature of law-related issues such as the legitimacy of expert testimony and rules of evidence, as well as the fundamental nature of the law itself.

What about the Cops?

If the Sherlock Holmes stories do not reflect much complex or contemporary thinking about the law and its nature, they have even less to say about the police. Transparently, Conan Doyle follows literary convention with his policemen. They're boobs. Lestrade and the rest of them are arrogant, ignorant, and socially backward. Inevitably, based on Conan Doyle's experience as a general practitioner vis a vis medical consultants, the police come to Holmes hat in hand because they're stumped by unusual symptoms and need expert advice. If this had very little to do with actual policing in Britain at the time, it had less than nothing to do with policing in the United States at the turn of the 20th century. Then, for the first time, the cops were very much in the news. The Lexow Commission of 1894 (the same year Conan Doyle did his first American tour) brought to light that the police of New York were as corrupt as many of the city's criminals. And other American cities differed in degree but not kind when it came to police corruption. On top of that there was violence and writers accepted, even almost relished things like the third degree that were, sadly, uniquely American. All of this made American writers treat the police in particular ways. It led to Melville Davisson Post's series of articles on police work and foreign police forces that ran in the *Saturday Evening Post* in 1916 ("The Man Hunters: American Influences," Mar 18 1916 ; "The Man Hunters: German Detective Methods," Mar 11 1916; "The Man Hunters: Scotland Yard," Jan 22 1916; "The Man Hunters: The Detective Department of Paris, Jan 29 1916; and "The Man Hunters: The Dragnet," Feb 19 1916). It made some writers like Alfred H. Lewis in his *Confessions of a Detective* (1906) use corruption as a major theme, and it made many others give up on the police as a source of heroes and heroism. The problem, however, was that private detectives didn't have much of a reputation for honesty either. That, too, the fiction of the period reflects—as did state legislatures when at the turn of the century they passed laws requiring the licensing of private detectives.

LOMBROSO WHO?

Just as the workings and nature of the law have little bearing on the Holmes stories, neither does Conan Doyle pay much serious attention to the background, the formation of the character, or the psychology of the criminal. Of course Conan Doyle, like all of his contemporaries, divides his criminals into lower class, professional felons (like those in "The Red Headed League" and "The Blue Carbuncle") and more frightening upper class folk who take to crime on the more or less expert level. Excepting his later creations Professor Moriarty and Colonel Moran, Conan Doyle connects passion of one sort or another with his upper crust criminals. In some cases, circumstances unleash the passions of otherwise honorable men like Jefferson Hope in *A Study in Scarlet* or John Turner in "The Boscombe Valley Mystery." That's when it's all about love; and these characters die fortunate, natural, albeit untimely, deaths. When the passion that drives the character is greed—as in "Copper Beeches" and "The Speckled Band"—the villains are killed by their own devices, just as is Professor Moriarty. But that's the business of a world that runs on the principle of retributive justice and demonstrates that evil is self-destructive. With all of his characters who commit criminal acts, however, Conan Doyle avoids really explaining why people do wicked things. Instead, he implies a simple, blanket solution to explain most of his villains' actions: they have been tainted by foreigners and foreign places and that's why they're bad. Thus in *A Study in Scarlet* and "The Five Orange Pips" it's America; in *The Sign of the Four* and "The Speckled Band" it's India; and in "The Boscombe Valley Mystery" it's Australia. Here, to be sure, Conan Doyle was completely out of step with what was going on around him: during the time he was writing the Sherlock Holmes stories there was more serious thought being given to human behavior, particularly aberrant human behavior, than ever before. In Italy there was Lombroso, in Vienna there was Freud, in Britain there were Francis Galton and Havelock Ellis (who published *The*

Criminal in 1889). Notably, S.S. McClure, one of Conan Doyle's American publishers, hired Harvard's German import, Hugo Munsterberg, to write about criminology for his magazine. While they have no impact on the world of Sherlock Holmes, the fledgling disciplines of psychology and sociology became common adjuncts to the detective story in America at the turn of the century.

DOMESTIC MALICE ONLY

Looking backward, there's something else missing in the Sherlock Holmes tales besides any significant concern for the nature of the criminal. In "The Reigate Squires" Watson talks about the subject matter of his sketches and emphasizes his sense of decorum:

> The whole question of the Netherland-Sumatra Company and of the colossal schemes of Baron Maupertuis is too recent in the minds of the public, and too intimately concerned with politics and finance, to be fitting subjects for this series of sketches [557].

Turn of the century British detective fiction observes this same condition—politics and finance are not fit subjects for the genre. They're maybe fit for the fledgling spy novel as written by Oppenheim and LeQueux, but not the detective story. The very opposite is the case with American fiction at the beginning of the 20th century. In this regard, it is more than worth noticing that S. S. McClure also financed and published the works of Ida Tarbel, Lincoln Steffens, and the other muck-rakers whose mission was to discover and expose the illegal, immoral, and even unsanitary practices of robber barons and their paid lackeys. This same group was also interested in police work—both the old fashioned, third-degree kind, and the new kind being developed in Europe, in England even. A number of the founding band of muck-rakers also wrote detective fiction. Then, too finance and politics are never very far from the surface of other American writers' work whose day jobs did not involve the exposure of public and corporate perfidy. So one finds that social comment looms rather large in turn of the century detective fiction in the U.S.

SCIENCE AND THE DETECTIVE

Running Watson over to meet Holmes in *A Study in Scarlet*, young Stamford tells the future chronicler that "Holmes is a little too scientific for my tastes" (149). And indeed, when Conan Doyle first introduced his sleuth he decorated him with some of the furniture of progressive science of the late 19th century. Coupled with the previous comment, Stamford mentions Holmes hypothetically fiddling with "the latest vegetable alkaloids" (a class of organic chemicals including nicotine, caffeine, and strychnine) and the first thing we hear from Holmes is "I've found it! I've found it!... I have found a reagent that is precipitated by haemoglobin, and by nothing else" (150). While the vegetable alkaloid business may have been a bit of old hat, Holmes' purported discovery of a means of classifying blood stains is pretty much state of the art. Holmes announces that his new discovery will replace "the old guaiacum test." As late as 1911, however, the British Pharmaceutical Codex listed the guaiacum test (invented by Izaac Van Deen in 1862) as one in which "a simple tincture of guaiacum [the wood of a West Indian evergreen tree] is employed with ozonic ether as a test for blood"(ibiblio.org/herbmed/eclectic/bpc1911). Among its other drawbacks, the guaiacum test couldn't distinguish between human and animal blood—something that had to wait until Paul Uhlenhuth in 1900 invented the test that Conan Doyle forecast more than a decade earlier, the precipitin test that could distinguish human from animal blood. All in all, when readers first meet Holmes, they see him as what we would now call a forensic scientist. But that didn't last long.

Conan Doyle may have been attentive to accuracy and to giving Holmes credentials as a scientist in his first adventure in *A Study in Scarlet*, but after that he let things slip. Granted, Conan Doyle does very occasionally mention the detective's chem. lab in the Baker Street rooms: thus "A formidable array of bottles and test tubes, with the pungent cleanly smell of hydrochloric acid, told me that he had spent his day in chemical work which was so dear to him" ("A Case of Identity" 92). In the first novel Watson comments that Holmes has a "profound" knowledge of chemistry, but in "The Five Orange Pips" his knowledge of chemistry has become "eccentric," and Klinger's note on that passage comments that "Perhaps closer observation had led Watson to amend his earlier characterization" (151) and change "profound" to "eccentric." "Copper Beeches" contains another throw-away line about Holmes needing "to postpone my analysis of acetones" (362) in the middle of the narrative. Indeed, as the stories proceed, the comments about Holmes and chemistry become more and more problematic, illustrated best, perhaps, with Holmes' itinerary during the missing years in "The Empty House": "Returning to France, I spent some months in a research into the coal-tar derivatives, which I conducted in a laboratory at Montpellier" (794). Coal-tar derivatives, during Conan Doyle's day, were the place that chemists looked for new dyes and a discovery that could benefit humanity mostly in the realm of providing us with more colorful clothes. If Conan Doyle became less and less interested in providing for Holmes a detailed and accurate involvement with organic and biochemistry, he was, if anything, just as cavalier about biology. As a physician Conan Doyle knew about diabetes and brought it into "The Boscombe Valley Mystery," but it was not until years after World War I that he actually used medical diagnoses as significant elements in his stories "The Creeping Man" and "The Blanched Soldier." One proof of Doyle's general indifference to using the details of bio-medical science in his detective stories is in the identity of the snake ("it is a swamp adder!… The deadliest snake in India") in "The Speckled Band." Klinger includes a section of two and a half pages of speculation (I. 259–261) about what kind of snake it really was—there being no such thing as a swamp adder. Indeed the final proof of Conan Doyle's general indifference to what became the scientific detective story is that Holmes doesn't use science to solve any of his cases until well after World War I. During Conan Doyle's life time the germ theory of disease was put forth by Pasteur, Martinus Beijerinck identified the first virus, Karl Landsteiner discovered blood types, Henri Becquerel discovered radioactivity to cite only a few of the fruits of science at the turn of the century. By accident or by design, writing during a period of great scientific ferment and discovery, Conan Doyle never saw the possible connections between the detective story and science. His contemporaries did both in Britain and in America. Even before Arthur B. Reeve made the science/ technology story his own, writers in America saw the scientist as the detective and linked scientific discovery with the uncovering of whodunit.

ONE MAN'S ECCENTRICITY

Going back to Poe, the detective character was not a real regular guy. Of course, Dupin's eccentricities incline him to misanthropy and he's just not very cuddly: he lives in a shuttered mansion, only comes out at night, and is at best aloof and at worst an arrogant prig. Conan Doyle turned aberration into eccentricity and idiosyncrasy. Holmes' eccentricities may be odd —it is not quite normal to pock the initials VR on one's walls with bullet holes—but they are somehow charming. In part this comes from context: the Baker Street setting, from Conan Doyle's familiarity with the physician-patient relationship, and even, perhaps, from the fact that the English value and nurture eccentricity and eccentrics as no other nation does. Eccentricity, then, is one of the things that turn of the century writers in Britain picked up on—creating idiosyncratic detectives. Thus there is Chesterton's priest detective, Max Carrados the blind detective, the grumpy Old Man in the Corner, and Lady Molly of Scotland Yard. While writers on the other side of the Atlantic had a few of their own atypical detectives (Madelyn Mack and the Thinking Machine spring immediately to mind) there is a tendency in a lot of turn of the century American fiction toward featuring the hard-working, earnest, socially normal detective hero. Scientific Sprague, Ebenezer Gryce, and Luther Trant are a few of the almost well-known normal detective heroes—and although he may not be, Samuel Hopkins Adams called his detective character Average Jones. Between Sherlock Holmes and the First World War more than a few American writers created detective heroes who were both detectives and engaged in the business of a detective agency: thus Kauffman's Frances Baird, Hugh C. Weir's Madelyn Mack, Robert Chambers' Keen Tracer of Lost Persons, Pidgin's Quincy Adams Sawyer, Anna Katharine Green's Violet Strange, and others. And earnest crime solvers are thick on the ground of turn of the century American crime fiction. They have causes ranging from campaigning for psychology, the new answer to society's ills, to the manifold practical uses of technology. Part of this arises from the strain of seriousness that runs deep in Puritan culture. Part of it, too, comes the fact that a staple of the American dime novel was the unusual detective—from the boot black detective, to railroad detective, tramp detective, and even, in a Smith and Street title, a dog detective. In terms of oddities, American detective fiction, then, had been there and done that. For any number of other reasons—not the least of which was the contemporary ill repute of both public and private detectives—at the turn of the century the American detective story needed a solid and respectable hero.

THE FOUNDER OF THE FEAST

In summary, then, the Sherlock Holmes stories represented both an attractive model for others to follow and validation of the importance of being at the right place at the right time. On the model front, one of the most attractive things about the Holmes stories is that they possess features that are easy to reproduce. That they almost immediately spawned what amounts to a parody industry serves as more than sufficient demonstration of the imitable nature of Conan Doyle's fiction. One of the reasons for this lies in the fact that a number of elements in the Sherlock Holmes stories are themselves reproductions. Great literature is great when copying comes to be labeled as literary convention or archetype. And there are plenty of those in Conan Doyle's stories. Take the deduction demonstration, for instance—that set piece that occurs at the start of most of the stories. Here Holmes extrapolates the unseen from a bit of the seen—revealing a chain of events or inclination of character by looking at a watch, a hat, a callused index finger, a raised eyebrow. It's something that Holmes does, inevitably, telling Watson things the poor doctor hasn't noticed. This was one of the first elements of Conan Doyle's storytelling that humorists jumped on with a vengeance and one that straight writers, as can be seen above, used to showcase their detectives' perspicacity. And, of course, it comes from Poe. If the deduction demonstration came from Poe, so did a number of other things—the obtuse and admiring narrator, the bumbling police detectives, the misinterpreted clue, the inspiration to write short stories, the plot outline of the first Holmes short story—the list, as many have noted, could go on and on. But it's not just from Poe that Conan Doyle borrowed in his creation of the world's most well known detective. He took the prejudice in favor of sentimental subject matter, especially of women as victims, along with the underlying belief in providential justice from English sensation writers and from Gaboriau. He picked up the disguise stuff from the Frenchman as well. Conan Doyle borrowed elements in Holmes' character from his own fantasies about medieval knights that he wrote up in *The White Company*, as well as some of the characteristics of the teacher and the physician. He didn't really invent any of these things—he just used them alone and in combination with great skill. And that made them popular. One can hardly blame others for following the same conventions as did Conan Doyle or for jumping on the Sherlock Holmes express. And follow they did, fortunate that Conan Doyle had prepackaged and made popular so many attractive conventions and was so prodigal and casual in his own creations that there were many, many threads to follow, to exploit, and to expand upon. A lot of those who followed were Americans who took to the detective story and used it for their own ends. And thereby hangs a tale.

3

Why Not Cops?

THE NAKED CITY

At the beginning of Julian Hawthorne's *Another's Crime* (1888), the narrator gives readers a behind the scenes look at New York's Mulberry Street police station.

> If you could put on the cap of invisibility and sit for twenty-four hours in the private rooms of Inspector Byrnes at police headquarters, you would see many strange sights. Representatives of every grade of the community pass through these mysterious portals during the day. All sorts of conditions of men, from the depraved pickpocket to the cultured millionaire; all varieties of the daughters of Eve, from the poor vulgar trull to the refined and lovely queen of society. Here meet youth and age, virtue and vice, industry and idleness, wise and foolish, good and evil. Strange events are there brought to light; life-histories, fantastic, tragic, comic, pathetic, romantic; crimes startling or sordid; human passions are there unfolded of every species—love, hate, revenge, avarice, self-abnegation, ambition, and despair, which is the death of all passion, good or bad.... All the contrasts of human existence, all its lights and shadows, appear in the Inspector's room, and disappear again, while you look on in your cap of invisibility [1–2].

If one wants to hear or tell stories, here is God's plenty: in 1888 there were two and a half million stories in that naked city, and there was Thomas Byrnes ("... at his desk, sits the Inspector, examining, weighing, deciding, investigating, advising, reproving, encouraging..." 2) who could tell all of them.

CHEESE IT! THE COPS!

The Inspector's role, though, would not have been a very old one. For 19th century America, policemen and police forces were new things, intended to be copies of two British innovations. The first was Robert Peel's invention of the Metropolitan Police of London in 1829, as "preventive police," police who would discourage crime by their uniformed presence.

The second innovation, occasioned by the fact that the preventive police hardly prevented crime, was the creation of a plainclothes detective force in1842—the year after Poe wrote "Murders in the Rue Morgue." As it had in Britain, in the United States the idea of establishing police forces met with protracted public debate in cities across the nation, debate about the corruption of the old system of constables and night watch, about the alarming increases in crime, about encroachment on civil liberties, about how much establishing a police force "on the English model" would cost, about how to organize it, and who would control it. Finally, police forces began to pop up across the country—Boston in 1838, New York in 1845, San Francisco in 1849, Baltimore in 1853, Philadelphia in 1854, and Chicago in 1855. None of it was easy, neither establishing the police forces nor creating detective divisions to investigate crimes that were not prevented. The addition of detectives invariably lagged behind the creation of uniformed police; thus it took Boston eight years (until 1846), and Chicago six years (until 1861) to add detective divisions to their uniformed police forces. And even after their creation, in some cases it took years before the detectives were properly organized. It is clear, for example, that while there were plainclothes detectives in the New York Police Department almost from its beginning, they were not efficiently or centrally organized until 1882 when Thomas Byrnes took over. And it wasn't easy keeping police forces running smoothly and efficiently either. In almost every city in the country with a police force, struggles for control of the department took place during the late 19th century. Sometimes these contests were between mayors and city councils; sometimes they were between city and state governments. None of them was very pretty. At one time New York City had two police forces, one appointed by the City and one by the New York State legislature. In Denver President Cleveland had to send Federal troops to keep a dispute between the governor and the city's police board from erupting in violence. Very little of this came to be reflected in the crime fiction of the time. In addition to the vexed problems police and politicians created for themselves, at the turn of the 20th century there were other problems for the cops—especially problems that concerned their public image —that seemed more immediate ... at least to writers of detective stories.

Take privacy, for example. In the debate about the creation of police departments in America (and in Britain), one of the chief concerns resided in the public's fear that the police would intrude upon their privacy. This was one of the reasons why the police wore uniforms and badges, and why jurisdictions resisted for a time the creation of plainclothes detective police. Fears about privacy and social propriety play significant roles in early American crime fiction; both serve as central concerns in *The Dead Let-*

ter and *The Leavenworth Case*. But these fears didn't just go away with the approach of the 20th century as police forces became regular parts of city life; they are there lingering in the background in turn of the century detective fiction. This goes from Ottolengui's "The police are bunglers anyway, and only make scandal and publicity" (*The Final Proof, or The Value of Evidence* 197) to Henry K. Webster's *The Whispering Man* (1909) with this jaundiced comment on the consequences of openness with the police:

> If I were to put this line of evidence into their hands, the first thing that they would do would be to take the whole Metropolitan press into their confidence, and fan the spark into a perfect blaze of scandal inside of twenty four hours [162].

In the same year Charles Walk makes an issue of openness and trust of the police in *The Yellow Circle* (1909):

> At last the party were brought face to face with the sole remaining expedient—the police.
> People of the class in which Miss Day and Mr. Gibbs moved usually shun police interference into their affairs as they would a pestilence. Indeed, are not the police the bulwark of their organization, the impregnable wall that stands between them and that dreadful monster, Crime, which haunts Society's frayed edges like a starving wolf skirting the sheep fold at dusk? A certain amount of intermingling between the monster and the police is, no doubt, necessary; but recognition of the guardian cordon from the other side is usually limited to the payment—or evasion—of taxes [22].

In spite of fears about privacy and social decorum, looking back at early American middle-class crime fiction, the police detective had pretty good odds of becoming a hero: it's what both Victor and Green move toward in their brushing up of the respectability of their police detectives. With Hawthorne the cop had achieved more than just social respectability—he'd become a pillar of society, a bulwark against the rushing tide of chaos, a larger than life, copper-buttoned, blue-coated hero.

So, what happened? The policeman as hero almost disappeared from American crime fiction between the 1890 and the First World War and continued as barely visible background furniture and convenient ending machinery until the late 1960s. How come? Weren't cops supposed to be heroes?

THE SHERLOCK HOLMES FACTOR

Sherlock Holmes has to bear a small part of the blame for taking the detective story away from the police. British writer Oswald Crawfurd made note of this in the Introduction to the American edition of his *The Revelations of Inspector Morgan* (1907):

> This collection of stories is an attempt to establish the professional detective police of my own country in that position of superiority to the mere amateur and outsider from which he has been ousted in contemporary fiction [vii].

Crawfurd hastens to add "What I have alleged, with knowledge of the British detective, I allege on good authority of the American detective." But nobody, it seems, listened. Following tradition, Conan Doyle repeatedly demonstrated how smart his hero was by showing how smart others weren't. One should recall here that up until comparatively recently, humiliation and abuse were considered worthy pedagogical techniques, and, after all, part of Holmes (via Joseph Bell) is a teacher. On top of that, contrasting the hero's intelligence with the stupidity of others was conventional practice in the incipient detective story. Conan Doyle is following a pattern that goes back to Vidocq's *Memoirs* where the hero gains acceptance, actually gets his job, by proving that all of the other police in Paris are inept and unresourceful. Poe picked this up and extended the contrast—thus not only is the Prefect a blockhead but so is the narrator—the difference being that one is good-natured and maybe, sort of capable, or at least willing to try to learn and the other is not. Conan Doyle copied this and forevermore the slow, but good-natured narrator has been called the Watson. And he did the same thing to the cops that Vidocq and Poe did—made them pig-headed, narrow-minded, and a bit dense. In *A Study in Scarlet*, cops, generically, come in for at least mild abuse when the great detective comments that

> Gregson is the smartest of the Scotland Yarders ... he and Lestrade are the pick of the lot. They are both quick and energetic, but conventional—shockingly so. They have their knives into one another, too. They are as jealous as a pair of professional beauties [Baring Gold I. 165].

And when Holmes and Watson arrive at 3 Lauriston Gardens to look at the crime scene, they meet Gregson and Lestrade (who Watson describes as "ferret like") and find both that the police have trodden the crime scene "like a herd of buffaloes" and that they have not the slightest clue about what happened there.

I.Q. TEST

Demonstrating that the hero is right and that others, particularly the police, are wrong became a pattern for those who wanted to jump on the

Sherlock Holmes bandwagon. And so bringing stupid, stubborn, ignorant policemen on the scene became a regular occurrence in American crime fiction before World War I. Thus, there's Samuel Hopkins Adams' bits of hyperbole—"The average town constable is appointed to keep him out of the imbecile asylum" (*The Flying Death* 94) and "The police ... with the characteristic stupidity of a corps of former truck-drivers and bartenders, decorated with brass buttons and shields without further qualifications dubbed detectives..." (*Average Jones* 15)—and Henry K Webster's more insouciant assessment of police intelligence:

> If the police go on exhibiting the same plentiful lack of wit during the rest of the case which they have shown to-night in the Pomeroy affair, I should say the murderer had a good chance to die of old age" [*The Whispering Man* 64].

There's Arthur McFarlane's comment on detective McGloyne—"... Oh no. [He's] just more than humanly stupid. And he tries to get away with it by playing Hell-roaring Jake to the gallery" (*Behind the Bolted Door* 5)— and finally there is Burton Stevenson's portentous "Grady isn't fit to head the detective bureau ... he's stupid, and I suspect he's crooked" (*The Mystery of the Boule Cabinet* 42). But more on that last part later.

You Know My Methods?

Like the Sherlock Holmes pieces, moreover, the problem isn't entirely that the police can't mentally measure up to the character playing the role of the detective hero, it's also that there's something wrong with the ways in which they approach problem-solving, with the ways they think or have been taught to think about how they are supposed to do their jobs. In the Holmes stories this notion of method supplementing, or substituting for, intelligence as a birthright comes in the Great Detective's gripes about Watson's focus on sensationalism as opposed to teaching lessons emphasizing method and logic when he tells his stories. In American crime fiction, sometimes the complaint is that the cops' lack of this same logic keeps them from solving the big crimes as in lawyer Richard Dallas' *A Master Hand* (1904):

> I was not disposed to altogether condemn police methods, for they are generally successful, if illogical, but I saw that in this case they were pursuing their usual course of first determining who ought to be the criminal and then securing the evidence to convict him; instead of, as seemed to me proper, developing first the evidence and reserving conclusions till it discovered the offender.
> I though the police method unfortunate, to say the least, for with the best intentions the exercise of unprejudiced judgment and the fair use of evidence

is made difficult where the case is 'worked up' upon a preconceived theory that a particular individual committed the crime [42–3].

And approaching crime this way, the cops are fit to solve only the most pedestrian of crimes: "In looking for illicit distillers and bootleggers, or Negroes charged with theft, he was in his element, but this sort of thing [real police work] was new to him" (*The Winning Clue* 8). More often, however, the problem with methodology has to do with the entrenched and traditional ways that police as an organization use to solve crimes. As a lead in to this attitude in fiction, we can start with fact—with the murder trial of William Henry in Brooklyn in 1895, a trial that relied heavily expert witness testimony about bloodstains. *The Washington Post* of August 4, 1895, under the headline "Science as a Sleuth: The Old-fashioned Detective Opposes it Vigorously," presents a literal version of police reliance on traditional methods:

> In speaking of science in the Henry case, one of the detectives who in the old days had been the right- hand man of Inspector Byrnes, when the latter was at the head of the central office, said that it would never secure a conviction. The famous thirty-third [sic] degree resorted to by Byrnes, he said, worked more surely with the average criminal than all the science in the world.

Just as it's there in fact, the notion of hide-bound official methodology is broadcast in the fiction of the period. Thus, in Richard Dallas' *A Master Hand* (1904) "The Inspector ... was little more than a machine, without much originality, and he worked on the lines dictated by experience and with the means and methods tried and available" (39). John Prentis in *The Case of Doctor Horace* (1907) takes some pains to point out the role of original thought in police procedure:

> In the detective corps of the Detroit Police there was one in whose soul it seemed as if there burned the fire of genius. He believed that he had seen a vision of something new. Hunter, the youngest man on the corps, had a youthful assurance to believe that he had found a different and a better way.... He felt that he had found a hitherto unused principle of criminology; a principle that in the dark and baffling mysteries of crime would bring a flood of light and the triumph of justice.... But while this idea grew in imagination, he had never yet the opportunity to put it to the test in reality. Hunter was a younger man, and enthusiastic, but more than these he was ambitious, and his duty was to obey orders. His chance of promotion lay in obeying orders faithfully, for that was the first principle of the department. He was the last man on the force and he was engaged only upon the routine cases of the regular docket. The Chief was not bothering about any new-fangled notions, and docket cases did not offer any field for original methods [66–68].

Responding to this kind of officialdom, one of Luther Trant's outbursts in, *The Achievements of Luther Trant* (1910) gives police technique historical perspective and makes the point that it has not advanced very far beyond what one finds in Hamurabi or in the sensation novel: "Five thousand years of being civilized ... and we still have the 'third degree'! We still confront a suspect with his crime hoping he will 'flush' or 'lose color,' 'gasp,' or 'stammer'" (2).

Criticism of outdated police technique usually fastens on Byrnes' "third degree." Thus, for Inspector Blake (a character in *The Shadow* [1913] who Arthur Stringer modeled on Inspector Thomas Byrnes) police problem solving and brutality mean the same thing. "So Blake believed in 'hammering' his victims. He was an advocate of 'confrontation.' He had faith in the old-fashioned 'third-degree' dodges" (49). Several years later Arthur McFarlane makes a similar point when his hero argues with a cop about old versus innovative police methods:

> In place of bullying, elephant-footed third degree, some time you may come to realize the possibilities of the 'confrontation'—the French are using it already—of auto-suggestion, of hypnosis, or even of a well-controlled trance and medium [*Behind the Bolted Door* 4].

While most turn of the century writers criticize the police for using outmoded methods, and use the 'third degree' as an example of such antiquities, a few actually confront what the 'third degree' actually meant: the nightstick, blackjack, rubber hose, brass knuckles, and bare fist. And even fewer are willing to posit that these demonstrate a sickness at the core of American law enforcement. One exception is when Josiah Flynt and Francis Walton give a satiric view of the third degree from the point of view of an expatriate American felon:

> I ain't stuck on England or the coppers here, but the coppers can't cut up with a bloke here the way they do in the States. 'Course they hammer me every now an' then when they take me to the station house, but that's just a habit they've got into. You see people over here won't let 'em do any hammerin' in the streets [*The Powers that Prey* 256].

And another is when Arthur Stringer in *Night Hawk* (1907) gives a more straightforward view when his hero observes "... that was the day in Chicago when we watched a patrolman club a mulatto stuss-worker on the head. The first sickening blow of the nightstick had turned my very soul over in its cage" (4).

As means of highlighting the outdated, outmoded, ineffectual method of the police, writers evolved several character patterns that center on the relationship between police detectives (and by implication the entire police as an organization) and the amateur or private detective hero. One followed up on the Holmes pattern of the cops going to the "consulting detective" when they need help, another enshrined competition (sometimes good and sometimes ill-natured competition) between the police and the hero as a means of defining both, and the last pattern represented what would become the fabled good cop bad cop scenario. In the former class we find friendly, tag-along police detectives like Mallory in Futrelle's Thinking Machine stories or McGraw in Burgess' *Master of Mysteries* (1912). These characters willingly admit that their mentors are smarter than they are, and they are not averse, either, from following their leads, and, in the end, from taking the credit for crimes solved mostly by someone else. In this context, writers like Charles Walk in *The Yellow Circle* adapt the good cop bad cop formula and make the aloof, by-the-book cop get things wrong and one who follows the lead and the leads of the civilian hero get things right. In American turn of the century fiction, however, the competitors—especially bullheaded, pig-headed, and arrogant cops—outnumber the cooperators. Thus readers often find recalcitrant police departments like the one in Clinton Stagg's *Silver Sandals* (1916):

> Of all the hundreds of policemen whom Colton knew, but a scant half dozen or so ever appreciated his ability or help. The others, with the superiority of professionals in all lines, went out of their way to confuse the blind man whenever possible [34].

That the genius detective, Thornley Colton, is a blind man who outthinks the police at every turn makes the police both stupid and mean.

A TOUCH OF CLASS

The majority of the police in fiction of the period are not only ignorant, pig-headed, witless, and stupid, but narrators also describe them as looking stupid—or looking coarse and brutish, which amounts to the same thing. This was, after all, very much the age of Lombroso, when character and appearance meant the same thing. Take, for instance, this copper from *Miss Madelyn Mack, Detective* (1914): "He was a short, stocky, roundheaded man with all of the evidences of the stubborn police bulldog, although the suggestion of any pronounced mental ability was lacking" (170). In *The Gray Phantom* (1921) Herman Landon portrays the entire personnel of New York's law enforcement community as being physically unappealing:

> Two policemen, one heavy and red-faced, the other lean and sharp-visaged, walked into the theater and stationed themselves beside the body with the air of zealots guarding the coffin of Mohammed.... They were followed by a puffy little man who let it be known that he was a deputy from the office of the chief medical examiner [23].

Handsome is, of course, as handsome does, so we have this peculiar simile from Anna Katharine Green's *A Difficult Problem: The Staircase at the Heart's Delight and Other Stories* (1900): "The man followed her in, sneaking and sneaking, like an eel or a cop..." (88).

All of this business about appearance ramifies in several directions. First of all, from the realistic and practical perspective, policemen then (and now) were usually big—the job literally and figuratively required cops to be robust individuals. But in turn of the century American crime fiction, since virtually none of it deals with violent crime in the streets, physical force or physical intimidation rarely becomes an issue. Instead, size and appearance usually connect with social status. Henry Webster makes this clear in *The Whispering Man* (1909) when the narrator can't tell the cops from the crooks:

> They were all in plain clothes, and with due deference to the personnel of the detective force, I am obliged to admit that it took me a minute or two to satisfy myself as to which of the other men sitting about in the room was the prisoner and which were the guardians of the law [48].

Inevitably, observing that an investigator does not look like a cop serves as a compliment—a compliment that always gets tied to class: upper class folks are slender, graceful, and their appearance reflects their intelligence. This is decidedly the case with the cop in James Hay's *The Winning Clue*:

> Here was no ordinary police-detective type. This man had neither square-toed shoes, nor a bull neck, nor coarseness of feature. About thirty-six years old, he was unusually slender, and as straight as a dart, a peculiar and restless gracefulness characterizing all his movements.... He gave the impression of having a brain that worked with precision and force of some great machine, a machine that never missed fire [103–4].

If a writer wants to have a cop who can keep up with the middle class characters who are typically central in the stories of the period, at least he should look like them. All of this boils down to the fact that in an awful lot in the fiction of the period class plays a significant role: typically bizarre circumstance embroils affluent people in crime that the working class police are called upon to solve but either find beyond their capabilities or solve it incorrectly. It's this situation in fiction and in life that Nelson Lloyd in *The Robberies Company, Ltd.* (1906) comments upon through head of the cartel of gentlemen crooks:

> It is a curious reflection on the present state of society that it should choose its protectors from the same class from which it gets its ditch-diggers and car-conductors. As a matter of fact, police work requires the same degree of intelligence as does the pulpit or the operating room. The policeman should be on a plane with the clergyman or the physician [169–70].

But facing up to this problem, the best that turn of the century fiction and turn of the century fact could come up with was the concept that the ideal police force should be led by a master-mind and should function like an army.

REVEILLE?

In Arthur Stringer's *The Shadow*, Blake, the Inspector Byrnes character, has a utopian vision of the police:

> ... the lamps of the precinct stations, the lamps of Headquarters, where the great building was full of moving feet and shifting faces, where telephones were ringing and detectives were coming and going, and policemen in uniform were passing up and down the great stone steps, clean-cut, ruddy-faced, strong-limbed policemen, talking and laughing as they started out on their night details. He could follow them as they went, those confident-striding 'flatties' with their ash night-sticks at their side, soldiers without bugles or banner, going out to do the goodly tasks of the Law... [108].

One can't have an army, however, without generals, the great minds who possess the knowledge and wisdom to direct the massed troops. Before World War I faith in this kind of leader was still possible, and until the Great Depression (or today), a lot of Americans believed in the organizing and elevating power of the captain of industry. As we have seen, both are metaphors that Hawthorne suggested to readers with his pieces about Inspector Byrnes. And then the Sherlock Holmes stories fastened the public even more firmly on the concept of the genius, that it took an uncommon intelligence to solve crimes. Indeed, this emphasis on the great man was the kind of thing that readers at the turn of the century also found in non-fiction about police. George Barton, for instance, who made part of a career out of writing about cops in books like *Adventures of the World's Greatest Detectives* (1900) and *Great Cases of Famous Detectives* (1913) centered his history of crime stoppers on the idea of the great detective. For example, in *Adventures of the World's Greatest Detectives* Barton featured cases solved by Chiefs James Brooks and John Wilkie of the Secret Service, Inspector Byrnes, Pinkerton, Chief Francis Kelly "Bank Detective," Captains Robert Linden and James Donaghy of the Philadelphia Police Department, and Captain P. D. O'Brien of Chicago. If the generals were out there solving crimes all the time, one wonders what the troops were doing, but that question doesn't come up. Instead, non-fiction encouraged the notion of the great and powerful superintending detective hero, and so, too, did fiction. One of the most complete descriptions of this sort of genius applied to organization in period fiction comes in Charles Walk's *The Yellow Circle* (1909):

> Inspector Swift was a very busy man. From his office at police headquarters he exercised a supervision over Williamsburg's detective force, distributed by means of branch stations over a wide area, that was well-nigh perfect. In fact, it was generally believed by his subordinates that the Inspector was omniscient, for certain it was that the least dereliction from duty, or negligence, occurring at any of the sub-stations was known at headquarters almost as soon as it happened.... Personally he was a large, handsome man some fifty-odd years of age, with iron gray hair and a white curling moustache which, together gave him an air of distinction, and an eye whose unwavering metallic regard stamped him as an individual of extraordinary force of character. However, unless deliberately called into play, the man's masterful personality was tempered by a courtly air and a polite manner of speech which marked his customary bearing [188–9].

The problem is that real police work is complex and corporate. It's hard to realistically make a supervisor into a popular hero because it's not the chief or the captain or the superintendent who actually does the detection or who catches the bad guys or who gets them to talk. Thus, Richard Dallas, the pseudonym of a former Maryland District Attorney, makes the problem with the police forces not one of execution but one of leadership in *A Master Hand*:

> ... what both departments [police and detective] should have and rarely possess, are men of exceptional ability, training, and broad education at their heads to plan and direct the work of their subordinates [39].

However well this might serve the public weal, a hero possessed of the same background, abilities and traits as the general or the captain of industry does not have much potential as an action hero of detective fiction. Nevertheless figures like Thomas Byrnes in life and in fiction served decades later as models for reformers like Sylvester and Vollmer when they tried to remake the American police force after World War I.

WHAT'S A POOR BOY TO DO?

Putting aside literary convention, one of the other things that took the police out of the running in the hero sweepstakes was the state of the art and science of detection at the turn of the 20th century: there was maybe some art but not much science. In spite of the contemporary, theoretical advances in what would become police science, it took a long, long time for newly discovered areas of forensic analysis to get down to the cops at the crime scene or the detectives looking at the bodies. This was true in fact—the movement to establish police department crime labs in America, for instance, didn't begin in earnest until 1930 when a group of Chicago businessmen financed ballistics expert Calvin Goddard's lab at Northwestern University—and it was also true in fiction. In most crime fiction before World War I there wasn't a whole lot that the police could do that the average, educated, upper-middle class man (and a few women) couldn't do. Most detection in life and in the books at the turn of the century depended on identifying or shadowing or talking to people to figure out who had motive and opportunity and anybody can potentially do that. But part of the significance of the emergence of the scientific detective story resides in the fact that that educated, upper-middle class individuals knew enough to fiddle with test tubes and reagents and could identify strange and curious things and the cops didn't. Thus Dallas' appeal for cops with "broad education" cited above. Indeed this is the first point that Pidgin makes in *The Chronicles of Quincy Adams Sawyer, Detective* (1912):

> Quincy, purely in the pursuit of his own inclinations, had made friends with the police inspectors and had entered upon an exhaustive study of police matters, a study to which many subjects in his school curriculum, as he early discovered, lent a wealth of information that was invaluable. For instance, he early made the discovery that, if one were able to deal out, in grudgingly small amount, scientific information concerning chemical analysis and kindred subjects, it was easy to secure in return information concerning the more ordinary points of police work [2–3].

All things considered, who was the intended audience of crime fiction at the turn of the 20th century, cops or educated, middle class people?

TRUE STORIES?

While there was a good deal of detective fiction published between the arrival of Sherlock Holmes in America and World War I, very, very few writers cared to use or even to mention the real world of crime or policing. There are a few, rare allusions to the acts or achievements of real policemen solving real crimes. Of course there was Inspector Byrnes who (in spite of the damage done to his reputation by the Lexow Committee hearings) is mentioned by name by several writers after Hawthorne. As seen above, he's brought into Arthur Stringer's *The Shadow* as the ultimately tragic (or pathetic) Inspector Blake and in *The Adventures of the Infallible Godahl* (1914) Frederick Anderson introduces a hot shot Deputy Byrnes of the NYPD. In *Master of Mysteries*, Gelette Burgess mentions Sergeant Petrosino, the celebrated head of New York's Italian Squad who was assassinated while on a fact finding trip to Italy. John Prentis gives a brief tip of the turn of the century hat to good government and policing in Detroit—"Detroit is a very law-abiding city; unseared with graft, unfamed in corruption, unmarred with slums. Lawlessness is unknown" (*The Case of Doctor Horace* 172). While Balmer and MacHarg don't refer to a specific hero policeman, their description of the Chicago Police Department suggests something akin to collective heroism, or at the very least problems of heroic dimensions for the police to confront:

> Harrison Street police station, Chicago, is headquarters of the first police division in the third city of the world. But neither London nor New York, the two larger cities, nor Paris, whose population of two million and a half Chicago is now passing, possess a police division more complex, diverse, and puzzling in the cosmopolitan diversity of the persons arrested than this district of Chicago [*The Achievements of Luther Trant* 51].

Just as turn of the century fiction makes only rare references to the successes and methods of real American police, it makes only occasional allusions to famous foreign police forces. Scotland Yard is a name dropped every once in a while, but, more often, it's the French police who get the nod. The popularity of the French cops no doubt rode in on Bertillon's coat tails—those of the inventor and invention of the universally adopted means of identifying individuals (doomed to oblivion by fingerprinting). Many, even most books about crime at the turn of the century mention Bertillon, his system of measurement or his *portrait parle*. Gallic, too, Robert W. Chambers' *The Mystery of Choice* (1897) and Arthur Hardy's *Diane and her Friends* (1914) are both set in France and feature canny and wise French police detectives. One of the most extensive paeans to the French connection with detection comes in Melvin Severy's *The Darrow Enigma* (1904):

> French detectives are the most thorough in the world, and I am about to make use of their method of instituting an exhaustive search. Each one of the squares formed by these intersecting strings is numbered, and represents one square foot of carpet, the numbers running from one to two hundred and eighty-eight. Every inch of every one of these squares I shall examine under a microscope, and anything found which can be of any possible interest will be carefully preserved, and its exact location accurately marked upon this chart I have prepared, which, as you will see, has the same number of squares as the room, the area of each square being reduced from one square foot to one square inch. You will note that I have already marked the location of all doors, windows, and furniture. The weapon, if there be one, may be very minute, but if it be on the floor we may be assured the microscope will find it. The walls of the room, especially any shelving projections, and the furniture, I shall examine with equal thoroughness, though I have now some additional reasons for believing the weapon is not here [www.gutenberg.org].

If turn of the century crime fiction makes little use of real policemen or police forces, it has just as little to do with real crime. Unlike Julian Hawthorne who made references in his novels to crimes that troubled the public mind (like Garfield's assassination) and patterned the main plots of his Byrnes books on real crimes, in what is, perhaps, a harbinger of the crime puzzle of the golden age of the detective story, writers at the turn of the century seldom use real crimes or criminals in any shape or form. While memories of the 1891 murders by Lizzie Bordon have survived now for more than a century, the case is invisible as far as contemporary crime fiction in America went. The same is true of the Ripper-like murder of Carrie Brown in 1891; it made lots of headlines in New York and abroad, but didn't have any impact on crime fiction at the turn of the century. Perhaps, like the Lizzie Borden axe murders, it was held to be too grisly for fiction. Not even the murder of Stanford White in 1906 made it into crime fiction. Crime fiction of the period only reflects real crime in singular instances like the allusions to Crippin's capture, effected by radio when he was in the middle of the Atlantic, in Arthur Train's *"C.Q." or, in the Wireless House* (1912). And maybe anarchists and the Mafia fall into the same category. A few writers manifest more than a passing interest in the Black Hand, Mafia, or Camorra. Thus in *The Net* (1912), Rex Beach presents the murder of a thinly disguised David Hennessy, Chief of the New Orleans Police Department, whose assassination on October 15, 1891 and reputed dying words ("the Dagos did it") led to the lynching of eleven Italian immigrants and a break in diplomatic relations between Italy and the United States. In the same year lawyer Arthur Train wrote an Italian book, *The Butler's Story, The Camorra in Italy, and an American Lawyer at Viterbo,* and The Mafia as a topic was also taken up by Arthur B. Reeve in "The Black Hand." The other perceived public menace, anarchists and bomb making, made an appearance in one of the episodes in Arthur Springer's *Night Hawk* and in Reeve's "The Bomb Maker." The single exception writers made in terms of the real world of crime and criminals was drugs. While the emphasis is consistently on those who use versus those who traffic in drugs, allusions to drugs and crime are legion in turn of the century fiction. One can find cocaine at the root of some of the evils, for example, in Stringer's *Night Hawk,* Adams' *Average Jones,* Vance's *The Lone Wolf,* and Burgess' *Master of Mysteries.* Arthur B. Reeve, in fact, returned to coke again and again—it looms large, for instance, in the short stories "The White Slave," "The Green Curse," and "The Opium Joint" as well as in his novel *The Ear in the Wall.* In fact, Reeve goes so far as to mention "the new dope law" in "The Bomb Maker."

Valentine's Day Massacre

Average Jones, Samuel Hopkins Adams' detective hero, forecasts that "Some day New York will find out that the 'finest police force in the world' is the biggest sham outside the dime museum business" (*Average Jones* 43). It didn't take until some day. Dishonesty, graft, became a major theme in American crime fiction almost as soon as it got off the ground—from the early 1890s onward. And since it was the largest city in the country with the largest police force and was the place where most books were published, graft meant the New York police and the New York police meant all police in the nation. All of this happened almost precisely when the American detective story was picking up the steam provided by the introduction of Sherlock Holmes in 1891. A lot of those two and a half million stories in Inspector Byrnes' Naked City had to do with dishonest cops working in a corrupt system. And the story that started at the Madison Square Presbyterian Church on February 14, 1892, was a doozy.

It was on that Valentines Day that Reverend Charles Parkhurst let loose from the pulpit, calling the Tammany Hall politicians "polluted harpies," and "a lying, perjured, rum-soaked, libidinous lot." But it wasn't just the politicos he went after; Parkhurst also blamed New York City's troubles on their "drunken lecherous subordinates." Mostly that meant the cops. As a result of his harsh words, Parkhurst was admonished by the grand jury's presiding judge for making but not substantiating his Sunday claims. And so the Reverend, his friend, John Erving, and private detective Charles W. Gardner began to prowl the city at night, documenting vice—going to brothels (female and male), gambling halls, saloons—and the collusion of the police with illegal activity. Gardner wrote it all up in his book *The Doctor and the Devil, or Midnight Adventures of Dr. Parkhurst* (1894). On March 14 Parkhurst took to the pulpit again, but this time his sermon was freighted with affidavits documenting both the prevalence of vice in the city and the dereliction of "the men whose one obligation before God, man, and their own consciences, is to shield virtue and make vice difficult." (www.oldandsold.com). There followed political and judicial maneuvers. Cops performed perfunctory raids and the citizen members of the Society for the Prevention of Crime tried to serve warrants on law breakers. It all culminated in the investigation of the Lexow Committee, so named because state senator Clarence Lexow presided over the committee's hearings, hearings financed by the citizens of New York after politicians blocked the $25,000 appropriated to fund the committee's activities.

CLARENCE AND TEDDY

Some of the evidence gathered by the committee reflected on police interference at the polls — not surprising because at that time joining the police force in New York and elsewhere depended exclusively on political patronage. But most of the testimony centered on uncovering systematic bribery, blackmail, and extortion. Out into the open came the fact that getting to be a policeman in New York was easy but not cheap: to be a patrolman one forked over $300, to be promoted to roundsman (i.e. supervisor of patrolmen) cost $500, but then things got steeper. To be made a detective sergeant cost $3,000 and candidates had to come up with $15,000 to make captain. Those, readers should note, are figures in 1890s dollars. The good part of the deal, however, was that cops didn't really have to earn the money to pay for their positions; they could and most often did simply extort it from business people, especially those in the vice business, in their precincts. Policy shops paid $15, saloons $20, pool rooms $300 a month. One madam testified that in aggregate she had paid the cops $30,000 to stay in business. A retrospective piece in *The New York Times* cataloged the extent of the extortion uncovered by the commission:

> The Lexow Commission ... took 30,000 pages of testimony and found: "The evidence of blackmail and extortion does not rest alone upon the evidence of criminals. It has been abundantly proved that bootblacks, pushcart peddlers and fruit vendors, as well as keepers of soda fountains, corner grocery men, sailmakers with flagpoles extending a few feet beyond the place they occupy, boxmakers, provision dealers, wholesale drygoods merchants and builders who are inclined to use the sidewalk, steamboat and steamship companies, those who give public exhibitions, and all persons who are subject to the police — all have to contribute in substantial sums to the vast amounts which flow into the station houses... ["Past City Inquiries Uncovered Graft," March 25, 1931].

That's a whole lot of people with no reason to respect the police, except, perhaps, as an efficient criminal organization.

Because of Lexow, cops lost their jobs and some went to jail. Inspector Byrnes had a hot time of it for a while but managed to retire without being actually charged with any crime. A reform administration took over the city and a new set of Police Commissioners moved in — one of them, Teddy Roosevelt, especially was dedicated to fixing the police force. To that end, Superintendent Roosevelt toured the city at night and came upon the other problem entrenched in the city's policemen, goofing off on the job. Jacob Riis in his *The Making of an American* (1901) describes one of his nocturnal jaunts with Teddy:

I laid out the route, covering ten or a dozen patrol-posts, and we met at 2 A.M. on the steps of the Union League Club, objects of suspicion on the part of two or three attendants and a watchman who shadowed us as night-prowlers till we were out of their bailiwick. I shall never forget that first morning when we traveled for three hours along First and Second and Third avenues, from Forty-second Street to Bellevue, and found of ten patrolmen just one doing his work faithfully. Two or three were chatting on saloon corners and guyed the President of the Board when he asked them if that was what they were there for. One was sitting asleep on a butter-tub in the middle of the sidewalk, snoring so that you could hear him across the street, and was inclined to be "sassy" when aroused and told to go about his duty [www.bartelby.com].

Although the New York Police Department still pays homage to Theodore Roosevelt, he soon left the post of President of the Board of Police Supervisors to pursue other opportunities. Whatever good he did was quickly undone. And before long Tammany politicians resumed their control of city hall and the police department. It is sobering to consider that the Knapp Commission of 1971 found some of the same things uncovered by the Lexow Commission in 1895. All told, in terms of graft and corruption, two formal investigations of the police bracket the period from the introduction of Sherlock Holmes in America to the country's entry into World War I: at the beginning there was the Lexow Committee Report (The Report of the Special Committee Appointed to Investigate the Police Department of the City of New York) of January 18, 1895, and at the end there was the Curran Committee Report (The Report of the special committee of the Board of Alderman of the city of New York Appointed August 5, 1912 to Investigate the Police Department) of June 10, 1913. This sort of atmosphere wasn't the sort designed to produce heroes.

While it pretty assiduously avoids real crime and criminals, occasionally crime fiction of the period makes references to the Lexow investigations. In 1902 Elliot Flower in *Policeman Flynn* gives what he would have readers believe is a fair and balanced view of the wave of reform to hit the city by portraying an honest, hard-working beat cop:

In this he is unique, but in many other respects he is typical of a certain class of policeman of whom the inhabitants of this city hear little. He is resourceful and honest; and if he were not it is probable more would be heard of him in the newspapers and police reports. A few rascally men on a police force can do a world of harm to the reputation of the whole body, and if they attain high rank they can demoralize a good part of it. Integrity is so important in those to whom is intrusted the enforcement of the law that there is a natural tendency to magnify the evils that are seen to exist, and the department is gauged by the worst rather than the best that is found in it. The men of the rank and file, as a rule, are faithful, earnest and reasonably clever. So, if Policeman Barney Flynn does not seem to you typical, you may rest assured it is because you know little of the police departments of great cities. It is the spectacular that gets in the lime-light of publicity, and faithfulness, persever-ance and honesty are not often spectacular, so we hear more of things we admire less; and hearing more of them, we gain the idea that they are the pre-dominating features of modern life [3–4].

Flower, however, follows this defense of the unsung heroes of the police force not with a heroic gang buster but with a series of comic vignettes about his hero, henpecked, docile, and pacific policeman Barney Flynn.

The following year (1903) Rodriguez Ottolengui in *The Crime of the Century* gives a tongue in cheek snapshot of the Lexow committee's impact on the city:

I s'pose you know, that since the Lexow Committee cleared up things, the town's been run like a Sunday-school. All the gamblin' places shut up tight, with rooms to let, eh [7]?

Following that ironic pot shot, the first half of Alfred Henry Lewis' *Confession of a Detective* (1906) presents the longest and most thorough review of Lexow. There Lewis presents the reminiscences of a character resembling Inspector Thomas Byrnes. They start off with

Every once in a while an investigating committee comes butting in from Albany, to go nosing on the trail of police graft. Inasmuch as the complexion of my politics—being all my life Tammany—isn't the Albany complexion, I'm regarded by these hayseed investigators as their natural prey…. The best behaved copper on the force, one having paid his three hundred dollars to become patrolman, his five hundred to be made roundsman, his three thou-sand to become detective sergeant, and his fifteen thousand to call himself Captain of Detectives, should be forgiven for saying that he has fairly earned his promotion…. I'll need full twenty years anyway to get my morals on an even keel, after playing thief taker for over thirty" [2–3].

The remainder of the first half of Lewis' book presents the hero's rise through the ranks and his encounters with politicians and violence at each step of the way. The second half of *Confessions*, oddly, contains several first class detective stories about almost Sherlock Holmes-class smart police detectives.

WHY NOT COPS?

If things worked according to the way they are supposed to work, at the turn of the 20th century when writers discovered that writing detective stories was fascinating, enjoyable, and—roll the dice—sometimes profitable, they should have made the policeman into a hero. It's just so logical: take crime, add individuals professionally engaged in preventing or detecting crime, and it equals the detective story. Right? Except it didn't work out that way. It didn't work out that way, first, because literary convention has always made the outsider or the amateur the hero, the one who finds the facts, the one who saves the day, the one who solves the puzzle. It's a convention as old as the epic and it's one that applies equally to Vidoq, Poe, Gaboriau, Conan Doyle, and the other founders of the form. They knew that there would be no problem or puzzle if the brains and resources to figure it out were already available in the community. In this context, the police were those resources available to the community that didn't have what it took to solve the problem or understand the enigma. So strike one.

The next roadblock to the police as potential heroes was historical. In America, as elsewhere, police and police detectives were new things, parts of organizations that neither they nor the culture had yet completely figured out. Society, for example, hadn't altogether decided whether the police were for order or for law or maybe even for both. The 19th century view of the role of the police tended toward the former. Thus this retrospective look at changing attitudes toward heavy-handed police tactics in *Adventures of the Infallible Godahl*:

> The old deadline, relic of the days of a great policeman, has long since passed into history as a police institution in the Maiden Lane district. The public did not take to the idea of a squad of plainclothes police telling a man in which direction he might walk the free streets of the city, no matter what the record of that man might be… [105–6].

What a great deal of the fiction of the period makes clear is that the often brutal methods the police devised and practiced to establish order were ineffectual in coping with complicated crime or with crime among any but the lowest elements in the society. And nobody wants to read about them. Strike two.

Historical, too, is the ignominy cast over the profession by the sensational revelations about the corrupt practices of police officers, especially New York police officers. Forget Victor, Green, and Hawthorne's attempts to make police heroes respectable. After 1894 and the Lexow hearings, for a long, long time, American crime fiction made the blanket assumption that most or all cops were corrupt. All of them were on the take, whether it was in New York or San Francisco, in the big city or the country town. Consequently, there are very, very few writers at the turn of the century who chose to picture police in any positive way. Some writers, as noted above, bring in the apprentice, side-kick cop to work with the genius amateur or private detective. Indeed, the four stories featuring Inspector Val and

Sergeant Sorg in Lewis' *Confessions of a Detective* and Prentis' novel *The Case of Doctor Horace* co-staring Detroit detective Hunter serve as exceptions to the rule that news about police corruption imposed on American crime fiction. Strike three.

There were enough strikes against the police in literature and sometimes in life at the turn of the century to retire an entire side. On the question of intelligence, for instance, we have seen all the allusions to dumb cops. By no coincidence, one of the Lexow revelations was that some candidates for the force were tacitly permitted to have others take the police department's intelligence test for them: "There does not seem any obstacle to the appointment of candidates [for jobs as policemen] ... though they be both intellectual and physical weaklings" ("Pulls and the Police," *New York Times*, June 10, 1894). And, too, the issues of social status and education loomed large in the view of turn of the century writers. Middle class readers wanted to read about sophisticated, urbane, middle class heroes and knew that, to the detriment of everyone, this sort was unlikely to be found in the ranks of the boys in blue. And they didn't really want to read about real crime. Reading about real crime was what got moralists like Anthony Comstock all lathered up about crime fiction. Legislators in state assemblies were still introducing anti-dime novel "Comstock" bills after the turn of the century, but they did acknowledge that there was now good detective fiction and bad detective fiction. Thus the dilemma faced Assemblyman Charles Carrier in drafting the "anti–dime novel bill" he introduced in Albany in 1905:

> A bill which provides for the suppression of the novels of Conan Doyle and other well-known writers of the higher class of detective fiction would hardly receive the indorsement of the legislature. Yet it is very hard in a bill to draw a line between detective fiction of that kind and the kind which is devoured by the youth of the country with such direful results ["Anti–Dime Novel Bill," *New York Times*, February 7, 1905].

From this perspective, an acceptable read would be about Mrs. Somebody's stolen emeralds, maybe, or even about the wealthy industrialist found shot in his Wall Street office. It would be one that talked a lot about logic and solving puzzles. And it would never descend to depict real crime like the murder of prostitute Carrie Brown, strangled and disemboweled in an East River flop house on Shakespeare's birthday in 1891, or use as a model the story of those eighty-one whacks that Lizzie Borden delivered in Fall River, Massachusetts on August 4, 1892. Those were for the police, not for the detective story.

4

The Scientist Hero?

IN THE BEGINNING

Even if social and literary conventions didn't take them out, the police took themselves out of the running in the contest to determine who was going to be the hero of the developing detective story. There were, however, other candidates. Along with the cops, another emerging profession offered a potential hero to the detective story—the scientist. It may be surprising to some, but the professional scientist is a relatively modern phenomenon, one that began about the same time that police forces began. The mid-1800s marked the creation of lots of milestones in the history of science from Darwin setting sail on the *Beagle* to Pasteur figuring out what germs did. Both cause and effect, the enthusiasm created by all of the life altering discoveries moved people and institutions to approach science in a new way, and as a consequence, governments and universities created the professional scientist. In this light, one should recall that it was not until the founding of Johns Hopkins University in the 1870s that organized advanced study of anything was possible in the United States. Where once there was only the physician and the amateur enthusiast who dabbled in science, by the end of the 19th century there was the biologist, the chemist, and the physicist. And then the end of the century saw the beginning of behavioral sciences and the emergence of the psychologist, the criminologist, the sociologist, and that hybrid of medical and behavioral sciences, the psychiatrist or, as they were then, the alienist.

WHEN BODIES FLOAT

No doubt about it, a kind of science was there at the beginning of the detective story. It was there because science played a conspicuous and vital role in the interplay between ways of knowing—the clash of rational and irrational worlds—that makes gothic fiction gothic. Scientists, albeit misguided ones, figure prominently in gothic fiction—just consider, for instance, *Frankenstein* or, later, *Dr. Jekyll and Mr. Hyde.* Poe knew all about this. And, in part, it's why he put what could be (and surely should be) called science into his detective tales. Not, however, science as the threat like that found in Shelley or Stevenson, but science as an efficient and even interesting means of triumphing over the mundane, as a really modern Prometheus ... unbound. Thus, while it's not the showiest part of the story, the solution to the carnage in "Murders in the Rue Morgue" relies on the hero's observation, classification, and knowledge of the natural world: Dupin finds the most illuminating clue in one of the corpse's fingers, determines that it's hair—but not human hair—and knows that it's orangutan's hair. On top of that, he refers the narrator to state of the art science by giving him a passage in Cuvier about orangutans to read. This, essentially, shows in an abbreviated and sketchy way science at work and demonstrates acquisition of, possession of, and application of knowledge about the natural world. This kind of science was the sort of thing Poe and his contemporaries could find illustrated at the Peale Museum of Natural History in Philadelphia, at emerging zoological gardens (the zoological society of London was founded in 1826), or in "cabinets" of stuffed animals on display at schools and colleges. They were the contemporary ways to observe and to know the variety and the intricacies of the natural world. And that's an essential part of Dupin's talent: he knows. And without his discovery and recognition that it's orangutan hair, the whole case goes Pfft. There's even more science in "The Mystery of Marie Roget." In some ways (actually for want of a compelling solution) Poe focused on science in his second Dupin story. "Marie Roget" contains a long discussion of the physics and chemistry that explains how corpses behave when they decompose in bodies of water, as well as Dupin's pointers on how to argue methodically and scientifically. Here science doesn't provide the kind of plot surprise it does in the first story, but it serves as part of the build up of evidence of time of death that will lend support to the hero's final conclusion. Oddly (or significantly), Poe didn't use any details from what used to be called physical or natural science in the best of his detective tales, "The Purloined Letter." Indeed, in that piece the uninspired and mechanical use of scientific method (i.e. the seemingly meticulous and microscopic search made by the police) comes off as second best to Dupin's flash of creative genius. In the non-Dupin piece "Thou Art the Man," however, Poe returned his detective stories to focus on science and scientific method when he introduced the use of ballistics (albeit Paleolithic ballistics) as evidence. Very much in accord with the times, moreover, the use of science, the details of the discovery of and analysis of material evidence, while important, does not end the cases that Poe sets forth for his readers. It is all "circumstantial evidence," and the ultimate determination of guilt or innocence has to wait for direct, human confirmation. Thus the conclusions wait for the confession of the orangutan's owner in "Murders in the Rue Morgue," and for Goodfellow's confession in "Thou Art the Man."

Victor, like Poe, used what she thought of as science in *The Dead Letter*. Part of the rage for science in the 19th century led to the creation of sciences that ultimately weren't—the build up and canvassing for pseudo-sciences like mesmerism or phrenology. One of these was the "science" of chirography that, in *The Dead Letter*, Mr. Burton has acquired through "patient study and unwearied observation, with naturally quick perceptions." That way of knowing is vital to his solution to the case. Unlike Victor, however, Green largely ignores science in *The Leavenworth Case*. Indeed, one of her purposes was making it a lawyer book, pursuing a different kind of logic for her hero. As seen above, in the Inspector Byrnes books Hawthorne focuses principally on sensation with a bit of routine police work, especially shadowing, thrown in. Insofar as they reflect on police science, they are antique curiosities. In *A Tragic Mystery*, for example, Inspector Byrnes has his men scour the city for a pistol of a same caliber as the bullet extracted from the murder victim and when a suspect is discovered to possess such a weapon, it is used as a definitive sign of his guilt. It is, nonetheless, manifestly unfair to judge these works on the basis of their science or whether their heroes function as scientists.

All of these early writers, especially Poe, wrote before the real explosion of science and technology that occurred at the end of the 19th century. Insofar as it exists in their fiction, their science is either elementary or jejune. Furthermore, the evidence upon which their stories turn has to be seen to be believed—by characters and readers alike. Neither the writers nor their contemporaries knew about the hidden world—they had no concept of the volumes that fingertips or blood could speak to the cognoscenti at the turn of either the 20th or the 21st century. And in one sense, it didn't make a whole lot of difference. A retrospective glance at the genre is proof enough that detective stories don't really have to have science in them at all and detectives don't have to be or behave like scientists. Sure, that's easy to say now, but it didn't look that way at the turn of the century. Then it looked like science could figure anything out and the scientist was going to be the one to do it. And that wasn't just in the realm of nature, it applied to social problems, too. And so it came to pass that writers at the turn of the century turned to science. They did it because, as popular fiction, interest in science and technology ran very high at the time. They did it, too, because science yielded them new ways to make their detective stories work and new clothes for their heroes to wear.

SOMETHING IN THE AIR

During the last quarter of the 19th century, what can be called a rush of enthusiasm for science and technology swept across Europe and especially across America. In the U.S., particularly, science received large scale public recognition and financial support for the first time ever. Even the fiction makes comments on this. Thus in Albert Dorrington's *The Radium Terrors* (1911) we learn that "America is the place where the million-dollar men encourage science..." (165) and Balmer and MacHarg's Luther Trant pays a visit to a psychology laboratory (perhaps modeled on Hugo Munsterberg's lab at Harvard) with a major donor to the university in tow in "The Man Higher Up." In the U.S. Edison and Tesla made electricity into more than a thrill in a savant's entertainment. Count von Zepplin in Germany and in North Carolina the Wright brothers mastered the air. At Princeton, in 1873, a scientific school was organized at the University, and similar institutions popped up across the nation. Then 1876 saw the opening of Johns Hopkins University with its six internationally famous scholars, including Ira Remsen, the father of organic chemistry. In every one of the sciences—astronomy, biology, chemistry, geology, medicine, and physics—in the 1880s and 1890s discoveries were posted almost daily. Perhaps more importantly, the practical results of science for the first time lit up city streets, cured diseases, and sent words flying first across thin wires and even through thin air.

HOORAY FOR SCIENCE!

If at the turn of the 20th century science became the big new thing, the hoped for revolution that promised to change the human condition, then the detective story decidedly unfurled its banners and took its cause to the streets. Thus the physician-lawyer hero of Melvin Severy's *The Darrow Enigma* (1904) says

"All of us men of science have felt something, however little, of this, and I believe, as a class, scientists transcend all other men in their respect for absolute truth." He cast another one of his searching glances at me, and said quickly: "This is precisely why I am going to confide in you and rely upon your assistance in a matter, the successful termination of which would please me as much as the discovery of an absolute standard of measurement" [www. gutenberg.org].

The trial testimony of the expert witness scientist in George Allan England's *The Greater Crime* (1917) makes even more grandiose claims for science:

"Gentlemen," said he, "these are not matters of sentiment, but of science. Science knows neither good nor evil. She knows only facts. No criminal has yet been able to commit a crime without leaving certain traces which the eye of science can detect. The old saying 'Dead men tell no tales,' has become false. He who depends on it in murdering depends on a fallacy.

"Today the murderer has to reckon with the chemist, the physicist, the Roentgenologist, and other scientists, including the Bertillon-measurement expert, the fingerprint analyst, the expert blood-tester and many others. Between them and the way of the transgressor has become hard indeed" [137–8].

"All of this," said he, "leads up to the statement that science, taking no cognizance of morals, right or wrong, can infallibly be depended upon to protect all those human concepts. Her proofs, gentlemen, are indisputable. She cannot lie. Her truth is absolute" [140].

Strong stuff. There was flat out hero-worship too. Thus Arthur B. Reeve, alluding to the actual turn of the century scientists who used themselves as subjects of their own experiments, repeatedly talks about the scientist as martyrs. Thus this from "The Poisoned Pen" (1913)

"Would you taste an unknown drug again to discover the nature of a probable poison?" asked Craig.

"I don't know," he answered slowly, "but I suppose I would. In such a case a conscientious doctor has no thought of self. He is there to do things, and he does them, according to the best that is in him. In spite of the fact that I haven't had one hour of unbroken sleep since that fatal day, I suppose I would do it again."

When we were leaving, I remarked: "That is a martyr to science. Could anything be more dramatic than his willing penalty for his devotion to medicine?" [www.classicreader.com].

And this from "The Germ of Death" (1913):

"It is the spirillum Obermeieri," said Kennedy, "the germ of the relapsing fever, but of the most virulent Asiatic strain. Obermeyer, who discovered it, caught the disease and died of it, a martyr to science" [classicreader.com].

But their readers didn't particularly want martyrs. What the turn of the century public wanted was active, manly (it *was* the turn of the 19th century after all) heroes and for science to eradicate, or, at the very least, infallibly and inevitably detect crime. The notion about science's infallibility when applied to crime, in fact, became a minor theme in contemporary journalism. It appeared in newspaper pieces, like two that appeared in *The Washington Post* in 1895: "The Camera in Crime: Wonderful Results Obtained by a German Chemist" (September 29, 1895) and "How Blood Will Tell: Many Mysteries Will Now be Explained" (November 11, 1895). And it was this kind of faith and optimism that led the magazine *Current Literature* in 1911 to publish a piece entitled "Why the Great Scientist will Supersede the Great Detective."

If the promise of science in the real world never could live up to this kind of expectations, detective story writers could, and a number of them turned to the scientist or the physician as their heroes. A lot of readers know about Arthur B. Reeve's polymath scientist, Professor Craig Kennedy, introduced in book form in 1912, but there were other scientists. There is Dr. Berkeley in Richard Slee and Cornelia Pratt's *Dr. Berkeley's Discovery* in 1899. As noted above, there's Melvin Severy's Maitland, introduced in *The Darrow Enigma* (1904). Balmer and MacHarg's *The Achievements of Luther Trant* (1910) starts off in a university psychology laboratory, and Francis Lynde's Scientific Sprague says that "I'm down on the Department of Agriculture pay-rolls as chemistry sharp" (9) in his 1912 debut. And there enough contemporary physician heroes to staff a small HMO. There's a selfless, philanthropic doc co-hero in Adams' *The Flying Death* (1908), and in the same year James Barnes introduced a physician hero in *The Clutch of Circumstance*. There's a medico in charge in Will Irwin's 1910 *The House of Mystery*, another in George F. Butler's *The Exploits of a Physician Detective* (1911), and (introducing the new specialty) the hero of Arthur McFarlane's *Behind the Bolted Door* (1916) who is an alienist. Even with characters who are not physicians or scientists by profession, everybody, it seems, has a lab. Astro, the fake medium detective in Burgess's *Master of Mysteries* (1912), has a lab: one of the book's illustrations, in fact, shows him in what looks to be a lab coat holding up a test tube. Hanshew's Cleek navigates a lab pretty expertly for a reformed burglar, Futrelle's Thinking Machine has both an alphabet soup of academic degrees and a laboratory to which he occasionally repairs, and in McIntyre's Ashton-Kirk's mansion

> An open door gave a glimpse of a second apartment with bare, plaster wall, fitted with tables covered with sheet lead and cluttered with tanks, grotesquely swelling retorts, jars, and other things that make up a complete laboratory [*Ashton-Kirk Investigator* 26].

Hugh Weir's woman sleuth Madelyn Mack (1914) goes into a dissecting room, and her female predecessor, Frances Baird, in Reginald Kauffman's *Miss Frances Baird Detective* (1906) carries a microscope and testing apparatus for blood stains around in what can only be a most capacious purse. In Pidgin's *The Further Adventures of Quincy Adams Sawyer and Mason Corner Folks* (1909) the hero's idea of a good time is "… to spend to-morrow in the laboratory making toxic analyses" (375).

But turn of the century writers—or most of them—had no wish to create only sunshine scientists. They wanted them to be, indeed needed them to be authentic. Part of this they made happen by basing their narratives on real scientific facts or using authentic scientific instruments and methods. More of that in a bit. Another way writers created science verisimilitude in turn of the century fiction came from the fact that they were inveterate and purposeful name droppers. Allusions to scientific people and things litter period fiction. Practically every author mentions Bertillon, his measurements or his *portrait parle*: that's *kinderspiel*. But they almost never stop there. During the course of his stories, Arthur B. Reeve alludes to the Reichert test, the Weil cobra venom test, as well as to Freud, William James, Tesla, DeForest, Lombroso, and the Society for Psychical Research: that's just scratching the surface. In *The Achievements of Luther Trant* Balmer and MacHarg's hero not only cites Freud (and Jung, too), but also hauls in prominent psychologists practicing in the U.S.: Fritz and Munsterberg at Harvard, and Jastrow at Wisconsin. A number of writers point readers to Lombroso's *The Female Offender* (1903). Thus, in "The Scarlet Thread," for example, the Thinking Machine says "I know nothing about women myself … but Lombroso has taken that attitude" (58), and in Arthur Stringer's *Wire Tappers*, the female lead says "Yet I feel I have none of the traits of the Female Offender" (66). In *The Mystery of June 13th* Severy, too, brings up Lombroso's work on women offenders, and then he piles on a bunch of other names: Topinard, Sappey, Quetelet, Dwight, Naegele, Rollet, Manouvrier, Humphrey, Hrdlicka, Cunningham, Vierodt, Tylor, Quain and Wilson. All of them, one assumes, real scientists. Miscellaneously, turning period pages, these guys turn up: A.P. Brown, Lechanarzo, Davina Warrerson, Zancray ("the French psychologist who's been making a study of crime…" *Behind the Bolted Door* 46), Goddard at Yale, Binet, Prince, William James, Bromig ("the Berlin alienist," *Night Hawk*, 27), and Captain E.N. Windsor, bacteriologist. Few people then or now have ever heard of most of them. That's the point: they're not there to be familiar, they're there to add weight and authority and the ambience of real science. They're there so that what the hero says goes, absolutely and without question. And so are the gizmos.

GADGETS

Although by a long shot Arthur B. Reeve was not the sole laborer in the scientific detective story vineyard, he was certainly the most persistent and well-known. What made him famous was all of Craig Kennedy's instruments. The revelation of the malefactor's identity at the end of each of the short stories depends upon the operation of some kind of machine. Playing off of the contemporary enthusiasm for the telephone and the radio, a number of Reeve's stories turn on Kennedy using some sort of sound amplification, transmission, or recording device. While Reeve may call one of Kennedy's instruments a "detectaphone," a lot of what he does with his gadgets boils down to what came to be known as bugging or wiretapping. The other large class of things that Reeve's scientist-detective drags around with him serves to enhance vision. Thus readers watch Craig Kennedy using a stereoscopic microscope, a camera lucida, and a "telectrograph" (a device for the transmission of photographs) in "The Forger." In other pieces they see or hear about motion picture cameras, spectroscopes, cytoscopes, right-angle cameras, cameras with fish-eye lenses, and even, in "The Invisible Ray," television. Joining a number of other writers who use them, Reeve also introduces medical instruments with strange names designed to measure heart function and respiration—thus the plethysmograph, sphygmomanometer, sphygmograph and, in "The Sybarite" the electrocardiogram. Along side these tongue-twisting marvels, in "The Scientific Cracksman" Reeve even introduces his readers to the wonders of the electric drill. What all of these devices do does not matter as much as the way they do it. Most of the gadgets that Reeve introduces, after all, have become either commonplace or, like all of the eavesdropping equipment, illegal. What counts is that in the stories Reeve makes Kennedy use his scientific devices the same way magicians would use their props. Kennedy's gizmos all come in black boxes whose function the operator explains, but only after they have done surprising, wondrous things. In addition to working in the stories like magic tricks, the machines also fulfill one of the most ardent dreams of science: the removal of the human element and the production of absolute truth.

But as with the name dropping, stories with too much scientific bias ran the risk of too many names, too many devices, too many theorems that would have had readers shopping for another form of diversion pretty quickly. What some of writers realized was that the most important role for science in detective fiction wasn't in the science *per se* or even in trying to make scientists (with apologies to all scientists then and now) into interesting and memorable characters, but in making their stories work.

THE HOWDUNIT

One of the most fundamental things that Poe invented for the detective story was its signature narrative time structure. Starting with "The Murders in the Rue Morgue," detective stories don't begin at the beginning; they begin in the middle—after the crime (or enigma) has occurred. So in Poe, readers start with the narrator and Dupin out for a midnight stroll in the streets of Paris. After the middle, detective stories then proceed to delve into the beginning, presenting an attempt to understand what actually happened in the past. Thus Dupin and the narrator listen to witnesses' testimony, examine the crime scene, collect evidence, and set a trap for the culprit. And finally they get to the end in the present when the truth and the consequences of the crime are dealt with. The sailor shows up and verifies Dupin's surprise revelation about the beginning: the orangutan did it. While the showiest part of the detective story, writers and readers both hope, is that final startling revelation about who did it, building and articulating the machinery that makes that surprise work and holding off the surprise while at the same time maintaining the reader's interest is its most important part. Both the detective story and the romance or sensation novel rely on the enigmatic core—most often the seemingly inexplicable facts of a crime—and the surprise revelation of the truth. One of the places where the detective story departs is that the explanation of tragic and baffling events needs to be not only surprising but also consistent, logical, rational, and real. Rather than doing things like lobbing in a lost cousin at the end, it's in presenting the facts of the crime and investigation consistently, logically, rationally, in accord with reality, and in an interesting fashion that the hard work of writing a detective story resides. And that's precisely where the new and robust interest in science at the turn of the century helped out. It gave writers new ways for imaginary crimes to be committed, new ways that they could be detected, and new ways to satisfy and fulfill their readers. On top of the conventional readers' justification emphasized by the Sherlock Holmes stories—reading detective stories means exercising one's logic—the scientific detective story adds to the justification about teaching logic that of teaching interesting, even vital facts.

WHO'S THERE?

One of the most arresting photographs in Thomas Byrnes' *Professional Criminals of America* (1886) shows the walrus mustached Inspector watching as four burley plainclothesmen wrestle with a furry criminal in order to get him into the proper position for his mug shot to be taken for the files and then for Byrnes' book. The caption is "Why Thieves are Photographed." The first time Inspector Byrnes appears in crime fiction, in *The Great Bank Robbery*, before he comes on stage Hawthorne couples his name with that photograph and with his Rogues Gallery. One of the reasons why Hawthorne began with the Rogues Gallery lay in what would soon become detective fiction's fascination with its practical solution to some really basic questions, questions like: how can one tell one person from another? how can one tell whether people are who they say they are? and how can one document anyone's past without knowing who they are? There are some other real posers about identity, but they fall under the heading of metaphysics (something detective fiction shuns) or psychology (something that comes in later). Figuring out physical identity is complicated enough, and the turn of the 20th century saw what can be seen in retrospect as a brief flare up of identity system wars, conflicts that fought for victory in police forces, in the courts, and in detective fiction.

If science begins with observation, measurement, classification, and verification of natural phenomena, then that's what the late 19th century search for means to infallibly determine identity was—in spades. It started off with Byrnes' use of an instrument, the camera, to aid in observation— a principle of which Francis Bacon would have been proud. Accurate, sometimes embarrassingly so, as they may be, photographs have a short shelf life because people age and can choose to change their appearances— just as detectives did when they worked in disguise. While Byrnes and his cops were snapping what came to be called "mug shots," the French had been working on a system that was believed to be an infallible way to identify individuals—the Bertillon system. The Paris Police officially adopted it in 1882 and Major R. W. McClaughry, warden of the Illinois State Penitentiary introduced it to the U.S. in 1887. It seemed like a good idea at the time. But it wasn't simple:

> Bertillon took measurements of certain bony portions of the body, among them the skull width, foot length, cubit, trunk and left middle finger. These measurements, along with hair color, eye color and front and side view photographs, were recorded on cardboard forms measuring six and a half inches tall by five and a half inches wide.
>
> By dividing each of the measurements into small, medium and large groupings, Bertillon could place the dimensions of any single person into one of 243 distinct categories. Further subdivision by eye and hair color provided for 1,701 separate groupings [http://criminaljustice.state.ny.us/ojis/history/bert_sys.htm].

As noted above, allusions to Bertillon and Bertillonage in turn of the century fiction are legion. Reeve summons up the Frenchman and his method in practically every other Craig Kennedy story. Mr. Keen, tracer of lost persons, in Robert Chambers' novel of the same title (1907), bases his record-keeping method on Bertillon: "... my tables, containing six hundred classified superficial phenomena peculiar to all human emotions, have been compiled and scientifically arranged according to Bertillon's system" (186). In the expert testimony included in England's *The Greater Crime* Dr. Nelson includes "the Bertillon-measurement expert" with those who "make the ways of the transgressor hard indeed." Carolyn Wells targets not just Sherlock Holmes, but Bertillon's "speaking likeness," or "portrait parle" in her 1912 syndicated burlesque entitled "Sure Way to Catch Every Criminal. Ha! Ha! Sherlock Holmes, 'Raffles,' Arsene Lupin, M. Lecoq, Carolyn Wells and Other Infallible Detectives Test the New Scientific 'SPEAKING LIKENESS' Discovery." Oddly, enthusiastic references to Bertillon and Bertillonage continue in American detective fiction well into the 1920s—see, for instance, Frederick Anderson's *Book of Murder* (1930) or Cleveland Moffet's *Through the Wall* (1928). What we have here is classic cultural lag, because by 1928 the Bertillon system's weaknesses had been amply and indisputably demonstrated and it had been replaced by a newer, surer way of identifying individuals.

TEETH, EYES, HANDS

The search for that newer, surer way of identifying individuals forms a minor thread in turn of the century detective fiction, one that both ties in to a topic of contemporary scientific interest and becomes a means of embellishing the fictional detective's searches. One of the earliest examples of an alternate to Bertillon occurs in Rodriguez Ottolengui's "The Phoenix of Crime," reprinted in his *The Final Proof, or The Value of Evidence* (1898). A dentist by profession, Ottolengui anticipates a technique that remains a standard in forensic investigations:

> In these days of advanced dentistry, the people of this country have been educated up to such an appreciation of their dental organs that, from the highest to the lowest, we find that people habitually saving their teeth by having them filled ... it is a common practice among dentists to register in a book of record all work done for a patient. In these records they have blank charts of the teeth, and on the diagram of each tooth, as it is filled, they mark in ink the size and position of the filling inserted [125].

And he furnishes a plate of a dental chart to top off the description.

If, in the manner of gadget science fiction, Ottolengui anticipates the future, Gelett Burgess does too in "The Heir of Soothoid" from his *The Master of Mysteries*. In that piece the hero predicts the retinal scan when he determines the identity of rival claimants to a patent medicine fortune by looking into their eyes with an ophthalmoscope because "I can tell a great deal from the eye, as much as from the palm or the voice" (225). Not the palm but unique vein patterns on the back of the hand serve the detectives as means of identifying people in Arthur B. Reeve's "The Invisible Ray" and Clinton Stagg's *Silver Sandals* (1916). While that one had no future, at least they were at the right part of the body.

THE MOVING FINGER WRITES

Fingerprints as an infallible method of identification was a concept that occurred to many people at the end of the 19th century—it occurred to Herschel, Faulds, Galton, and a few other inquiring minds. Edward Henry's system of classifying fingerprints came into official use in Britain in 1901 and in the following year Dr. Henry DeForest introduced it as a practice of New York's Civil Service Commission. In 1902, in fact, Bertillon himself used a fingerprint as the sole evidence to solve a murder case (www.criminology.fsu.edu/faculty/nute/history). The death of measuring body parts a la Bertillon and the demonstration of the preeminence of fingerprinting was the case of the two Will Wests. The booking officials at the Federal Penitentiary at Levenworth, Kansas in 1903 began processing a new arrival named Will West and in so doing discovered that another prisoner named Will West already resided with them. Looking at their records, the two not only had the same names but they also looked alike and had almost identical Bertillon measurements. But they had different fingerprints. That closed the case on Bertillon and opened what has become universal adoption of fingerprinting as an absolutely dependable method of identification.

Even before the century turned, fingerprinting fascinated writers. In what may be its first appearance in fiction, fingerprinting became the scientific *deus ex machina* that Twain used to bring home the tragedy in *The Tragedy of Pudd'nhead Wilson* in 1884. Certainly after 1900 most detective story writers make casual, passing reference to fingerprints, and writers about gentleman burglars, like Frank Packard note that crooks know all about fingerprints and how damning they can be as evidence. So entrenched they became that Edgar Rice Burroughs used them in *Tarzan of the Apes* (1914) to demonstrate that the ape man is really Lord Graystoke.

Because one of the evolving tenets of detective fiction was its dedication to accuracy, it became difficult for writers to avoid mentioning fingerprints. At the same time, however, another one of the tenets of the emerging genre was the need for surprise. So almost as soon as fingerprints gained wide official and public recognition, some enterprising writers felt the need to try to figure out how to get around them, to use them as part of the patented detective story surprise. Thus in 1912 Pidgin puts in a mummified finger used as a stamp to leave misleading fingerprints to baffle Quincy Adams Sawyer, detective and his readers. The next year, in a Sherlock Holmes burlesque by A. Conning Goil ("Latest—Desiccated Detective Stories, Boiled to the bone," *Los Angeles Sunday Tribune*, April 27, 1913), the detective, Shirley Combs' startling discovery is that the culprit had "… skinned the hand of his [deceased] friend and put the skin upon a glove which he took care to wear when cracking cribs." After the war, in the 1920s, there were even more fake fingerprint stories making the rounds, for example there's Hammett's "Slippery Fingers" and Evelyn Johnson and Gretta Palmer's "Finger Prints Can't Lie." Within a decade, then, fingerprinting went from being the hot new thing to being a humdrum and mundane part of police routine, and because of that it lost much of its allure to detective story writers. The same thing happened with blood.

Blood will have Blood

Blood has always been the primal, most powerful, and universal sign of crime. But nobody understood much about blood until the beginning of the 20th century. And, unlike fingerprints, one can't tell a whole lot about what a blood stain or sample means by just looking at it with the naked eye. Before the 20th century the most pressing issues about blood with respect to the medical jurisprudence had always been determining 1) whether any rust colored stain was blood, 2) if it was blood, whether it was human blood, and 3) whether it could be connected to any specific individual. In Poe's day none of those questions could have been answered, but at the turn of the 20th century more was learned about blood than was learned by all of accumulated history. In 1900, for instance, Karl Landsteiner discerned that human blood was not all the same but came in types—he labeled them A and B blood types and his associates found types AB and O. In that same year German scientist Paul Uhlenhuth invented the precipitin test based on the discovery that the blood of different animals had one or more characteristic proteins. Shortly thereafter, in 1905 at the University of Pennsylvania chemist Edward Reichert discovered that crystalline of structures for blood proteins were unique to each species and that these could be determined using what came to be called the Reichert test.

Even before the turn of the century writers of detective stories began to include references to blood and blood science in their fiction. Thus back in the days when all science could do was microscopically measure corpuscles, Robert Chambers in *The Mystery of Choice* (1897) includes an episode in which a local druggist in provincial France performs an apparently routine (but unnamed) test to determine the source of a blood sample and finds an in it anomaly: "The little chemist of Quimperle came up at that moment, rubbing his glasses with a colored handkerchief. 'Yes, it's human blood,' he said, 'but one thing puzzles me: the corpuscles are yellow'" (96). In one of the Thinking Machine stories, "The Flaming Phantom," there's another country pharmacist, this time in America, who conducts an unspecified blood test off stage and determines that the blood the "ghost" splattered about the supposedly haunted house wasn't human but canine blood. As the characteristics of the scientist became more pronounced in them, it became routine for fictional detectives to do their own tests on blood. As noted above, Frances Baird carries a microscope and blood testing kit around with her and Anna Katharine Green's Violet Strange reads bloodstains better than the police in "The Intangible Clue." As early as 1903 and Ottolengui's *The Crime of the Century*, Mr. Barnes hypothetically explains that blood evidence was a gimmie for the prosecution in criminal cases:

> "The prosecution says, 'Prisoner, there is blood on your garments!' Prisoner foolishly replies, 'That is not blood, but rust, or if blood, it is chicken blood!' Then the expert stalks in and testifies, 'It is blood'!" [13].

As was his wont, Arthur B. Reeve became the turn of the century's leading lay preacher on the subject of blood tests, explaining in detail how they worked and touting their effectiveness. Of course, right before readers' eyes rabbits suffer so that Craig Kennedy can conduct blood tests, like the Reichert test he does in "The Blood Crystals." In the stories Reeve cites Reichert, Uhlenhuth, and the "... minute, careful, and dry study of the blood of human beings and of animals" published by the Carnegie Institution ("The Silent Bullet"). All told, Reeve sees blood science a potential evidentiary philosopher's stone:

> It has even been suggested that before the studies are over photographs of blood corpuscles may be used to identify criminals, almost like fingerprints. There is much that can be discovered already by the use of these hemoglobin clues. That hemoglobin, or red colouring matter of the blood, forms crystals has been known for a long time. These crystals vary in different animals, as they are studied under the polarizing microscope, both in form and molecular

structure. That is of immense importance for the scientific criminologist ["The Blood Crystals" www.classicreader.com].

In practical terms, however, blood evidence in Reeve's stories and those of a number of other writers (see George Allan England's "The Case of Jane Cole" for example) sometimes simply distills down into unadulterated racism:

> Probably you didn't know it, but "In fact, they have been able to reclassify the whole animal kingdom on this basis, and have made some most surprising additions to our knowledge of evolution. Now I don't propose to bore you with the details of the tests, but one of the things they showed was that the blood of a certain branch of the human race gives a reaction much like the blood of a certain group of monkeys, the chimpanzees, while the blood of another branch gives a reaction like that of the gorilla. Of course there's lots more to it, but this is all that need concern us now.
> "I tried the tests. The blood on the handkerchief conformed strictly to the latter test. Now the gorilla was, of course, out of the question—this was no Rue Morgue murder. Therefore it was the negro waiter."
> "But," I interrupted, "the negro offered a perfect alibi at the start, and—"
> "No buts, Walter. Here's a telegram I received at dinner: 'Congratulations. Confronted Jackson your evidence as wired. Confessed'" ["The Silent Bullet" classicreader.com].

In spite of all of the attention writers devoted to blood evidence in turn of the century fiction, in reality it didn't turn out to be the philosopher's stone or the elixir or even anything close to providing definitive help in the detection or the solution to crime. Practically speaking, it might be of some conceivable help to know that a crime was committed by a human being, but even narrowing that individual down to one having the rarest blood type, AB, meant narrowing suspects down to .04 % of the U.S. population, or in 1900 to 3,043,760 people. The test, in effect, finds not the needle in the haystack but another haystack in the haystack. Blood, of course, provides another piece of circumstantial evidence, but in Arthur B. Reeve and a few other turn of the century writers it becomes something more than that. Because of the way it's presented in the fiction, blood evidence becomes conclusive. It's presented by a scientist around whom the writer has constructed an air of infallible authority. And at the turn of the century that authority in American detective fiction doesn't come from the fact that the detective hero is an eccentric genius a la Dupin or Holmes but is a genius certified by academic achievement and attainment. Thus Craig Kennedy is Professor Kennedy, the first achievement of Luther Trant is earning the respect of his psychology professor, Samuel Hopkins Adams grounds Average Jones' solutions and conclusions in the fact that he went to Hamilton College, and Jacques Futrelle makes his hero not only Professor Van Dusen, but also adds Ph.D., L.L.D, F.R.S., and M.D. after his name. And, as noted above, the authority of this new brand of detective does not rest simply on their credentials, but on their use of scientific methodology—the citing of authority and the conducting of experiments with magical machines that produce marvelous results.

THE OLDEST SINS THE NEWEST KIND OF WAYS

Was a time in crime fiction that killing was a simple business. There wasn't a whole lot of variety: it was hands, or blunt instrument, or edged weapon, or firearms. A few foreign aristocrats dealt in exotic poisons and forever after gave Italians a bad name for it. But until the 19th century, the means of death dealing were pretty limited, like the lead pipe, candlestick, rope, knife, pistol options of the board game Clue. One of the things that Poe clearly had in mind with his creation of the detective story was embellishing the means of death, making it the focus of the enigma and the primary focus of the detective's investigations. Nobody, after all, can figure out what caused the carnage in the old lady's apartment in the Rue Morgue. Poe, then, had the motive but not the opportunity to concentrate on grounding the detective story on new and original means of killing people—he had no way of knowing of the myriad means of delivering death that science would discover, because at the turn of the 20th century science and technology in fact afforded seemingly endless new ways to extinguish life. And detective story writers jumped right on this. They provided novelty—and stories built of surprise need novelty—and they provided the most essential element in making the scientist a hero: make the problem one only a scientist can understand and explain.

BETTER LIVING THROUGH CHEMISTRY

During the 19th century things like arsenic or carbolic acid or chloroform, or cyanide were easy to come by. Opium, in the form of laudanum, could be found in most households and cocaine was ubiquitous, eventually finding its way into the secret formula of a popular soft drink. One of the consequences of this is that an even a quick scan of period newspapers turns up lots of incidents of accidental poisoning and suicide by means of poison. But the papers of the time do not report many murders committed by the same means. Maybe they just weren't detected, or, more likely, maybe there weren't many reported because there weren't many. Most of the available poisons were easily detected either by horrendous symptoms or by post mortem examination. As early as 1836, for instance, arsenic could be detected by the test devised by James Marsh in that year. Closer to the turn of the century, however, a whole class of newly discovered chemicals—many of which were virulent poisons—became the rage—at least in detective story circles. The first time readers meet Sherlock Holmes, in fact, he's messing about with "the latest vegetable alkaloids" (a class that includes compounds like atropine, hyoscine, scopolamine, ephedrine, nicotine, strychnine, caffein, and curare). Not only were poisons in the news because of these discoveries, the awareness of poisons had other ramifications as well.

People began to pay a lot more attention to poisons and what they did or could do. First, an interest and specialty in forensic toxicology developed—originally in France where tests began to be invented to detect the presence of some of the new class of vegetable alkaloids. Also, in the realm of dangerous chemicals and drugs, at the turn of the century in the United States the publicity run up and lobbying about the dangers of chemicals and drugs began that would eventually lead to the enactment of the Pure Food and Drug Act in 1906, the legislation that regulated, among other things, alcohol, morphine, opium, cocaine, heroin, chloroform, cannabis indica, chloral hydrate, and acetanilide. In the judicial realm, too, changes came about that focused on the need to provide for the public more sophisticated and reliable protection from death from unnatural causes. Thus, medical examiners began to displace coroners as the officials responsible for certifying deaths and the cause of those deaths. For most of the 19th century in the U.S. that function was exercised by elected coroners and coroners' juries. Frequently they had minimal educations and no scientific training. Jurgen Thornwald's *The Century of the Detective* quotes a 1914 report on New York City's coroner that ends up playing on what seem to be the public's fears about poisons and prisoners:

> … the elected coroner in New York City represents a combination of power, obscurity and irresponsibility which has resulted in inefficiency and malfeasance in administration of the office…. So far as the activities of the coroner's office in New York City are concerned, infanticide and skillful poisoning can be carried out with impunity [153].

Detective fiction of the period uniformly pictures coroners as puffed up buffoons with an unerring instinct for accusing innocent people. The answer, of course, was to replace the elected lay coroner and coroner's jury with an appointment of an individual with the proper credentials to make valid scientific conclusions in certifying deaths and their causes. In this

Boston led the way by replacing the city's elected coroner with a physician Medical Examiner in 1877. All of these things focused on the issue of death from unnatural causes and of all unnatural causes put poison right up on the top of the charts.

While there seems to be no evidence that a wave of poisonings swept across the nation at the turn of the 20th century—in fact, the reverse seems true—detective stories of the period make it seem like there was. A quick survey of contemporary detective fiction finds people done to death, not by the old fashioned arsenic of popular lore, but by exotics like atropine, cacodyl (arsenic trioxide), carbolic acid, chloroform, cocaine, curare (woorali), cyanide of potassium, hydrogen cyanide (prussic acid), donine, hyoscyamine, morphine, narceine, narcotine, nicotine, nitric ether, nux vomica, promaine, and ricin. All of these lethal compounds serve writers in a variety of ways. First of all, writers intend the hero's possession of specialized scientific knowledge to make him or her both smarter and more authoritative than anyone else in the story—particularly the police and elected officials. Science, scientific terms, and scientific tests and devices, in effect, serve as an alternative to argument, because their "proofs" are unassailable—or are supposed to be unassailable. Another purpose that poisons serve in detective fiction at the turn of the century is they are used to scare readers. Take this description of prussic acid from *The Darrow Enigma*:

> "Your Honour," Maitland replied, "it is the most fatal of all poisons known to chemists. It is also called cyanhydric, and, more commonly, prussic acid. An insignificant amount, when inhaled or brought into contact with the skin, causes immediate death. If a drop be placed upon the end of a glass rod and brought toward the nose of a live rabbit he will be dead before it reaches him" [www.gutenberg.org].

Finally, using poisons and other modern means of delivering death makes the villain smarter—a worthy opponent to the scientist, genius hero.

OTHER UNNATURAL SCIENCES

The most evil people one encounters in turn of the century detective fiction use diseases—diseases hot off the press—for their own ends. Perhaps the first of this ilk is Dr. Medjora in Ottolengui's *A Modern Wizard* (1894). There detective Barnes discovers that Medjora murdered his wife with diphtheria bacillus and Ottolengui carefully links this diabolic means with contemporary science news: "You forget, or you did not know, that the bacillus of diphtheria was not discovered until Klebs found it in 1883, and the fact was not known until Loffler published it in 1884" (414). On a wider scale, in 1911 Albert Dorrington's *The Radium Terrors* Asian villains cause radiation sickness and extort money from the wealthy by withholding treatment until exorbitant medical fees are paid. Indeed, radiation as alternately evil and good became twin themes in period detective fiction, appearing in Reeve's "The Deadly Tube" and "The Ghouls," Futrelle's "The Lost Radium," Ottolengui's "A Shadow of Proof" and Hanshew's "The Divided House." On the bio-medical threat side, Reeve also introduces bubonic plague germs in "The Germ of Death" and one of Butler's stories ("The Tragedy at the Colonial") turns on Meniere's disease, a condition indicated by episodic hearing loss, dizziness, tinnitus, and a sense of pressure in the ear. But on the life sciences side, there is more. If Conan Doyle has his speckled band of unknown genus, American writers of the period had their own fauna designed to make their plots work and give their readers the creeps. But they were real. Hence, there are red dot spiders (Adams), cobra venom (Reeve), the mynga worm (Hanshew), and (the crossword puzzle favorite) tsetse fly (Reeve again and Butler) lurking, waiting to be discovered by the detective.

Physics, or more properly technology (if technology is physics with a patent), makes an emphatic appearance in period crime fiction along side biology and chemistry. Thermite gets a lot of play; it's a safe cracking innovation demonstrated in Stringer's *The Wire Tappers* as well as Reeve's "The Diamond Maker," *The Ear in the Wall*, and *Constance Dunlap*. Patented in 1895, thermite is a mixture of powdered aluminum and powdered iron oxide which, when ignited in a flash one is unlikely to forget reaches a temperature of whopping 4,500 degrees Fahrenheit. At lesser temperatures, Reeve (in "The Steel Door") and Stringer (*The Wire Tappers*) both introduce oxyacetylene welding and Severy in *The Mystery of June 13th* has arc welding, both techniques introduced at the turn of the century. While they represent older technology, the notorious practice of using explosives to make political points at the turn of the century comes into a number of works—usually those associated with anarchists or the Mafia. See, for example, Reeve's "The Black Hand," and Burgess' "The MacDougal Street Affair" for Mafia related bombings and "The Adventure of the End and the Beginning" in Stringer's *The Night Hawk* for anarchists. The newly invented automobile serves as the basis for the conundrum in Futrelle's "The Phantom Motor," and plays an important role in Reeve's "The Green Curse," as well. One of the cleverest of the new technology stories is "The Man Who Flew" in Lewis' 1906 *Confessions of a Detective*, a story in which an airship plays an integral and surprising role.

SO WHAT HAPPENED?

What with all of the success and celebrity of science and technology at the turn of the century, it looked like scientists should have had a pretty good chance of taking over the hero's spot in the developing detective story. Except that they didn't. And they didn't for several discernable social and literary reasons. Let's try the social ones first.

Scientific detective stories of the period operated on the assumption that science provided undisputable answers to complex crime problems, that it proved beyond a shadow of a doubt what happened. Except that's not what happened in the real world. One of the vexed issues of turn of the century jurisprudence was that of the expert, scientific witness. Justice Learned Hand, in fact, wrote a treatise on the subject: *Historical and Practical Considerations Regarding Expert Testimony* (1900). What happened (and continues to happen) in American courtrooms was the spectacle of dueling experts. As documented in James C. Mohr's *Doctors and the Law, Medical Jurisprudence in Nineteenth-Century America*, the most famous trials of the period that turned on forensic evidence often became well-publicized contests of our chemist versus your chemist. Thus the Henry case cited on the topic of the third degree in the last chapter serves as an example. *The Washington Post's* headlines go

SCIENCE AS A SLEUTH
The Old-fashioned detective opposes it Vigorously,
HENRY CASE AN EXAMPLE
Expert Testimony on a Few Faded Blood Stains Relied Upon to Secure
Conviction—Easily Contradicted by Other Experts [August 4, 1895].

Ottolengui's detectives in *Final Proof* written at about the same time note the same problem:

> Yes, but did you ever see a trial when the expert witnesses were called, that equally expert witnesses did not testify to the exact contrary [30]?

The perception that science could not win clear-cut victories in the court room, then, didn't do a whole lot to support its infallibility in either fact or in fiction.

There's also the fact that scientific discoveries and advances in technology have a notably short shelf life, especially technology. Arthur B. Reeve's excitement and enthusiasm about Kennedy using an electric drill is a case very much in point. And for all of Reeve's and other writers' conviction that a machine could detect lies, the results of such machines have never been admitted into courts in the United States as evidence. It might be noted, too, that evidence obtained by electronic eavesdropping, another one of Reeve's favorites, is also inadmissible in U.S. courts. And the blood tests much ballyhooed by period writers have long ago been superseded by others.

And then there some things about scientists that didn't fit what was going on on the literary side of things. First off, making a character's principle attribute being a scientist has a number of disadvantages, the principal one is that single minded dedication to abstruse and solitary study may be admirable but it's not something capable of a lot of embellishment, at least for the lay reader. Polymaths like Holmes excite interest, while pure scientists don't. And that's why so many of the period heroes are scientists plus, plus lawyer like Maitland or plus professor like Van Dusen. The other principal minus on the side of science is the way it's handled in period detective fiction is often exclusionary or at least not participatory. Thus, in a review of *Her Other Self* in the *Washington Post,* the writer zeroes in on the difficulty of using science in fiction:

> As a rule, an incursion into abstract science for material to weave into a romance is a fruitless task. It was successful in the hands of Bulwer, of Poe, and Stevenson, but few outside of these [March 25, 1905].

Not only that, in the scientific detective story readers just have to accept that tests prove what they're said to prove and that stuff like, for instance, hyoscine does what the expert says it does. This kind of reader/writer relationship, it turns out, ran counter to the one invented by Poe and then gradually picked up until it became the main feature of golden age detective fiction. The one where the reader is allowed and even encouraged to try to figure things out along with the detective hero.

5

New Science and Pseudo Science

NEW WORLD, NEW SCIENCE

The 19th century saw the first real advances in the application of the natural and physical sciences to the solution of crimes. In the middle of the century Alfred Swaine Taylor set about to categorize and explain the medical and the legal aspects of physical evidence in his *Medical Jurisprudence* (1843). This became a standard reference work, beginning a new era of scientific examination of evidence, establishing new standards for medical testimony, and inspiring a robust medical jurisprudence movement in America, one that led to publications such as John James Reece's *Text-Book of Medical Jurisprudence and Toxicology* (1884). In quick succession, too, at the end of the century the scientific study of identity began with Bertillon's invention of anthropometry, and then emphatically with Francis Galton's *Finger Prints* (1892). When human affairs went terribly wrong and crimes occurred, by the end of the 19th century the advancement of science made it possible to explain what happened—at least some of the time. But those same sciences were completely clueless when it came to doing the most important things—predicting who was likely to commit a crime or explaining why bad things happened: why people committed immoral or illegal or anti-social acts in the first place. There was only the old explanation: sin drove people to commit evil deeds. But one rarely finds this Newgate solution proffered either by those who thought about crime or by those who took to writing the new detective story. Instead late 19th century thinkers and, in turn, late 19th century fiction writers began to look for new ways to explain why individuals turned to crime.

Criminology, as it came to be known, began to provide new sets of answers to the problem of identifying those who were likely to commit crimes. Essentially begun with the publication of Cesare Lombroso's *Criminal Man* (*L'Uomo Delinquente* 1876), the last quarter of the century saw a spate of publications that undertook to examine the same question—what kind of people commit crimes? Thus there were works like Ferri's *Criminal Sociology* (1884). Havelock Ellis' *The Criminal* (1889), Green's *Crime: Its Nature, Causes, Treatment, and Prevention* (1889), and Carr's *Insanity in Criminal Cases* (1890). In 1893 Austrian jurist Hans Gross considered not only the collection and interpretation of physical evidence, but also concentrated on the mind of the criminal as well as the minds of the investigator and judge in his *Handbuch fur Untersuchungsrichter, Polizeibeamte, Gendarmen (Criminal Psychology: A Manual for Judges, Practitioners, and Students* U.S.1911). In its introduction Gross sketches his purpose:

> Of all disciplines necessary to the criminal justice in addition to the knowledge of law, the most important are those derived from psychology. For such sciences teach him to know the type of man it is his business to deal with. Now psychological sciences appear in various forms. There is a native psychology, a keenness of vision given in the march of experience, to a few fortunate persons, who see rightly without having learned the laws which determine the course of events, or without being even conscious of them. Of this native psychological power many men show traces, but very few indeed are possessed of as much as criminalists intrinsically require. In the colleges and pre-professional schools we jurists may acquire a little scientific psychology as a "philosophical propaedeutic," but we all know how insufficient it is and how little of it endures in the business of life. And we had rather not reckon up the number of criminalists who, seeing this insufficiency, pursue serious psychological investigations [www.gutenberg.org].

Amassing knowledge of psychology, however, wasn't just something that needed to be applied to criminals and criminal justice. It could be applied to everyone and almost everything and during the last part of the 19th century the new discipline of psychology took off, especially in the U.S where Americans developed a real fascination with both the theory and the scientific machinery of the new ways of looking at why people do what they do. Thus, in 1883 the first psychology laboratory in the country was established at Johns Hopkins University, in 1888 J. McKeen Cattell became America's first professor of psychology at the University of Pennsylvania, and in 1896 Lightner Witmer established a clinic of psychology at the University of Pennsylvania, the first such clinic in America and perhaps in the world (geocities.com/Athens/Delphi/6061/en_linha.htm#-600). In the 1890s, too, S.S. McClure hired Harvard's newly imported psychology whiz, Hugo Munsterberg, to write pieces on crime and psychology for his new magazine. And, of course, Freud loomed large, very large. But we can repress that for the time being.

BUMPS

If at the end of the 19th century science and technology gave detective story writers a broadening stream of clever and novel ways to finish off that body in the library, there also evolved new explanations for the central problem of what kind of people do bad things and why they do them in the first place. Understanding these issues and stamping out crime would be a lot easier, of course, if one could tell the innocent from the guilty by simply looking at them. That's what Austrian physician Franz Joseph Gall (1758–1828) had in mind when he started looking at what the uninitiated called the bumps on people's heads. He came up with the notion 1) that moral behavior as well as all the other character traits resided in different parts of the brain, 2) that they developed differently in individuals, 3) that the skull conformed to the particular shape of those parts, and 4) that, presto, one could read character by looking at the shape of a person's skull. Gall's discipline, tagged "phrenology" by British physician T.I.M. Forster in 1815, held that "benevolence" was centered in one specific section of the brain, and that defect in that particular area (reflected in the shape of the skull) was a pretty good sign that one had at least a potential felon on one's hands. Largely debunked by the end of the century, phrenology, nonetheless, made at least a few cameo appearances in turn of the century detective fiction. As late as 1911, George Butler, who as a medical doctor should have known better, brings phrenology into one of his detective's, Dr. Furnivall's, cases. There the physician detective looks at the portrait of a young man and pronounces that

> The brain is large at the base, as compared with the upper superior convolutions of the cerebrum, especially the upper frontal lobes at the seat of the facilities of benevolence and veneration. The development immediately over the eye shows perception in a marked degree, and the fullness of the eyes themselves means a flow of language—words, words, words, to such an extent that a superficial observer, or one who loved the speaker, would believe him much deeper and more accomplished than is the case. The forehead, in the recession of the upper superior convolutions, indicates also this same lack of benevolence [*Exploits of a Physician Detective*, 195–6].

This diagnosis—one that readers could follow on one of those plaster heads with numbers painted on it—the narrator tells us, is one that "has become so famous among physicians and phrenologists." Several years later John McIntyre, perhaps now aware that it was both old fashioned and bunkum, gave phrenology a transitional twist in *Ashton-Kirk Special Detective* (1914). There the genius, polymath, amateur detective sets up a clue early in the novel by more or less casually alluding to "The studies of that ingenious old empiric of Antwerp, Gall":

He had all to do with them [skulls] in this particular regard, though his system was later much amplified by Spurzheim and the Englishmen George and Andrew Combe. His idea was that the skull's development followed that of the brain; that certain parts of the brain stood for certain faculties; if the brain were large in this faculty the skull would show it. And in that way we were to have a very convenient method of judging the character of a particular person [96–7].

And indeed it is the shape of his skull that marks the villain in the novel. But he has that particular type of skull because he's a throwback:

… the man in the rolling chair, Alva, is a 'throwback'; that his deformed head is an assertion of the old Aztec strain; that if this deformity had anything to do with the fiendish character of the Aztecs, it might naturally be supposed that it had some effect on him [276].

The villain's skull shows him to be a villain and atavism explains why his skull looks so odd. What McIntyre does here is to begin with Gall and end with Lombroso.

THROWBACKS

Toward the end of the century and the erosion of faith in physiognomy as a science, Cesare Lombroso took over the attempt to figure people out by just looking at them—or, actually, by cutting them up and classifying what he saw. Lombroso's *Criminal Man* held that handsome does as handsome is—attractive people aren't criminals; misshapen ones are, and biology is destiny. Based on autopsies and examination of a number of criminals, the Italian physician thought that he had identified a catalog of physical attributes (or stigmata as he labeled them) that, taken together, were signs of one kind of criminal, the born or atavistic criminal. These anomalies included having too much hair, fleshy and protruding lips, a sloping forehead, a receding chin but large jaw muscles, extraordinarily large or very small ears, long arms but short legs, and general facial asymmetry. For Lombroso these were the tell-tale marks that identified the individual as an unevolved being, one who resembled humanity's simian forbearers and who therefore lacked the evolutionarily acquired benefits of civilized humanity. These were the guys who committed crimes. For a time Lombroso was hot stuff both in Europe and in the U.S. . One finds plenty of commendations of his ideas in turn of the century journalism, both learned and not so learned.

But there's not a lot of Lombroso in the developing detective story—particularly in American detective stories. There are, as seen above, a couple of tongue in cheek allusions to Lombroso's *The Female Offender* in the fiction of the period, but comparatively few to his central work, *Criminal Man,* the book that lays out the whole business about atavism and stigmata. Arthur B. Reeve, for instance, who inclines to snap up every scientific fact, theory, or gizmo making the rounds and then add it to the collection he recites again and again in each of his stories, makes only one reference to Lombroso. Thus, in "The Green Curse" Kennedy finds Lombroso's books in the lair of a crazed anarchist:

> On an ink-spattered desk lay some books, including Lombroso's "Degenerate Man" and "Criminal Woman." Kennedy glanced at them, then at a crumpled manuscript that was stuck into a pigeonhole. It was written in a trembling, cramped, foreign hand, evidently part of a book, or an article [www.online-literature.com].

Rare in the detective fiction of the period, references to Lombroso are also seldom seen in contemporary fiction about criminals. Perhaps the most pointed one comes in Alfred Lewis' *The Apaches of New York* (1912) where readers get a glance at the habitués of the Chatham Club:

> Those citizens of Gangland assembled about the Chatham Club tables would have made a study, and mayhap a chapter, for Lombroso. Speaking generally, they are a stunted litter, these gangmen, and seldom stand taller than five feet four. Their weight wouldn't average one hundred and twenty pounds. They are apt to run from the onslaught of an outsider. This is not perhaps from cowardice; but they dislike the exertion of fighting, and unless it be to gain money or spoil, or a point of honor is involved—as in their duels and gang wars—they back away from trouble [126–127].

JUST SAY NO

The main reason why there are so few references to Lombroso in the early detective story—one would like to believe—was that his ideas about identifying criminals were so completely and fundamentally wrong. Physical attributes have no connection to one's observance of the law or moral conduct. This was emphatically demonstrated in scientific literature of the time, and it was pretty quickly accepted that statistics can (and in this case do) lie. Indeed, before the turn of the century in Julian Hawthorne's combination of fiction and fact in *The Great Bank Robbery*, America's number one policeman displays the New York Police Department's collection of photos of felons and informs readers by implication that Lombroso's ideas about criminal types are just so much banana oil. Looking at photos of real criminals

> You will think … that you have seldom seen an equal number of intelligent, respectable, self-satisfied persons. Nothing diabolic, nothing brutal, no signs of corroding anxiety or secret agony [9].

There was not just the issue of accuracy involved in rejecting Lombroso as a means of drawing characters in detective fiction, there were other reasons—some of them having nothing to do with whether Lombroso was right or wrong. First of all, turn of the century criminologists didn't deal so much with individuals as with what they identified as and believed to be a class—the criminal class. European criminologists wanted to find a biological determinant for felonious behavior while at the turn of the century American academics, journalists and politicians increasingly and vociferously wanted to blame crime not on biology but on what vile social and economic conditions can do to individuals. Thus we have the works of journalists like Jacob Riis and the muckrakers as well as fiction like Josiah Flynt's *The Rise of Roderick Clowd* (1903), Flynt and Walton's *The Powers that Prey*, Lewis' *The Apaches of New York*, and Stringer's *The Under Groove*. Then there are egalitarian rebuttals to the idea that one can tell a criminal by just looking at him or her. This, while not precisely egalitarian, becomes explicit in the spate of gentleman crook stories at the turn of the century. The heroes of these stories walk like toffs, talk like toffs, but practice the arts of the yegg and second story man. Not much on heredity or environment here. Not only that, unlike Raffles, who served as the inspiration for all of the American gentleman burglars, the American variety is inevitably a democrat. On the topic of judging people according to their appearance, for example, Frank Packard's Jimmy Dale, America's preeminent gentleman burglar, says

> "Oh, I dare say there's a lot in physiognomy Carruthers…. Never studied the thing, you know—that is from the stand point of crime. Personally, I've only got one prejudice: I distrust, on principle, the man who wears a perennial and pompous smirk—which, strictly speaking, isn't physiognomy at all. You see, a man can't help his eyes being beady or his nose pronounced, but pomposity and a smirk, now…" [*The Adventures of Jimmy Dale* 61].

Added to this, the developing detective story chose, in fact had to choose, not to deal with what Lombroso and his followers called the criminal class. It was what all of the detractors of dime novel detectives inveighed against. So distancing itself from the kind of criminal popularly associated with the dime novel trumped the critics who saw reading about crime as morally debilitating. Thus, in order to cement its hold on middle class readers, the emerging detective story simply chose not to deal with actual criminals—or with actual crime. That was the stuff of the dime novel and the *Police Gazette*.

The last, most pressing reason for the avoidance of Lombroso was that, as its conventions evolved, with his notions about biological determinism, the detective story just can't work. They undermine its basic elements. While the detective short story as created by Poe exists principally as a presentation of a genius' intellectual *tour de force* and pure sensation novels can get away with presenting slouching, beetle-browed, obvious villains, the new detective story (especially the new detective novel) increasingly depended upon a structure that 1) involved proving the hero's competence—something hard to do if everyone knows the bad 'uns when they see them; 2) involved shifting suspicion among a number of suspects—presenting a cast of *middle class* characters, many or even all of whom could have committed the crime; and 3) ignoring conscience or providence as active agents of justice It's why detective novels came to be called whodunits. If one can tell who's a criminal by simply looking at hairline or chin or ears or by nervous twitches, where's the suspense? Where's the game? Where's the story? Nowhere.

RACISM

Just because the turn of the century detective story distanced itself from Gall, Lombroso, and their particular brands of biological determinism, doesn't mean that pseudo science, bias, and prejudice played no role at this particular stage in the development of the form. For one thing, fiction of the period was flagrantly racist. When Africans or African Americans appeared—which was not very often—race as inevitably identifies them as criminals as Lombroso's physical stigmata would have identified a born criminal to a believer. Almost. Jean Webster's *The Four Pools Mystery* (1908), for instance, piles stereotype on stereotype when the murderer turns out to be a scary, itinerant, chicken stealing black man. In "The Tin Box" episode in *The Exploits of a Physician Detective*, where another African American is a murderer, Dr. Furnivall tells bystanders that

> I have settled on what seems, so far, the only possible fact, and am looking for a man who is large, for she so described him, brutal, because of his methods; densely ignorant, for reasons that will appear in his confession, probably a foreigner or negro of the lowest stamp. I incline to the negro because the woman noticed that he had an odd gait—so many of them have great feet and wear ungainly shoes run down at the heel, and walk with visible effort... [81–82].

In George Allan England's short story "The Case of Jane Cole, Spinster" the detective pins the murder of Jane Cole on an African American both because of a blood test and because "… I had to bear in mind the negro psychology. The [murderer's fear of a] black cat was the real factor, you see" (*World's Best Detective Stories* IV, 157). One could add that at least these characters are not the first upon whom suspicion is cast, nonetheless, unlike Lombroso's ideas, racism would play a role in American detective fiction for a long, long time. One exception to all of this occurs in *Alias the Night Wind*. In that novel the hero, beleaguered by a corrupt police force, escapes with the aid of an African American servant and finds refuge at the home of an African American physician, perhaps the first such character to appear in American fiction.

DEADLIER THAN THE MALE?

There is little need to establish that making pronouncements about the nature of women and women's roles in the home and in society flourished during the 19th century. Almost in their entirety these were, by turns, dogmatic, bizarre, tyrannical, and downright wrong. Coincidence it may have been, but it may be worth noting that the golden age of the detective story corresponded in America and in Britain with changes in the roles of women that happened after World War I. For the modern detective story to develop, writers and readers alike had to accept 1) that women possessed no privilege when it came to the processes of the law, 2) that anyone (including any woman) could be a detective and 3) that anyone could have committed the crime under consideration, not just an assembly of slack-jawed males. Turn of the century fiction made some progress on women as detectives—more on that later. In the main, however, not a lot of ground was gained in the equality of the sexes as criminals. There was, to be sure, the precedent of Lizzie Borden and the admonition of Kipling's refrain in his 1911 poem of the same title, "the female of the species is deadlier than the male." And there was Lombroso's work on women criminals. In fiction, Jacques Futrelle includes a candid observation about women and cites *The Female Offender* in his story "The Scarlet Thread" when the Thinking Machine echoes a Lombrosean sentiment:

> "The subtler murders—that is, the ones which are the most attractive as problems—are nearly always the work of a cunning woman. I know nothing about women myself," he hastened to explain; "but Lombroso has taken that attitude" [57–8].

But even though Kipling, Lombroso, and Futrelle's Professor say that women can be pretty dangerous propositions, in American detective fiction at the turn of the century it's just not true. In fact with respect to the role of women in the mystery, not many changes had been made since the sensation novel of the mid 19th century. Therefore, in turn of the century fiction, everyone was after women's money, or, more correctly, their family's money. The stolen inheritance comes up again and again in period fiction. Here's a partial list: Adams' "The Million-Dollar Dog," Gelett Burgess' *The Picaroons*, Futrelle's "The Problem of the Cross Mark," Green's "Problem VI: The House of Clocks," Mary Roberts Rinehart's *The Man in Lower Ten*, Burton Stevenson's *The Holladay Case*, and Charles Walk's *The Yellow Circle*. These and more contemporary stories center on saving a woman's inheritance. There are even a few, rare, plucky women who try to steal inheritances—as in Futrelle's "The Superfluous Finger" in which a woman has a finger amputated in order to impersonate a real heiress. But she was probably put up to it by men. And if it's not their money, it's their jewels—women in any number of turn of the century detective stories serve principally as owners of rare, opulent, and very expensive jewelry that can be stolen or misplaced—it might be noted here that Cartier may have invented the story of its curse to interest Mrs. Evelyn Walsh McLean, of Washington D.C in the Hope diamond in 1910 While the detective story of the period rarely treated women as villains, gentleman crook stories provided a larger potential stage for women as criminals, but even there sentiment colors female characterization. Thus while a mysterious, off-stage woman directs the Gray Seal, Jimmy Dale, in his criminal exploits, her motives come from the sensation novel theme of the stolen inheritance. Even Arthur B. Reeve's Constance Dunlap, who begins as a promising confidence woman, pretty quickly changes into an amateur detective. While all of the links between women and the transmission of wealth looked backward to the sensation novel, the other popular dilemmas for women in period detective fiction looked ahead to the 20th century. But it's hard to decide whether it's better to play a part in an economic myth or to be seen as crazy, because that became the lot of many women characters in turn of the century detective stories.

TAKE THAT BOBBY PEEL

The way in which Anglo-American law defined crime and criminals was changed decisively and permanently on January 20, 1843. That's the day Daniel McNaughton went gunning for Prime Minister Robert Peel and by mistake shot and killed his private secretary, Edward Drummond. Brought to trial, the medical witnesses summoned by both the defense and the prosecution all agreed that McNaughton was insane, and the jury returned a special verdict that sent McNaughton to an asylum and not the gallows. This verdict contributed to two things. First it gave rise in both British and American jurisprudence to the adoption of what came to be called the McNaughton Rule, i.e. the principle that a person is legally sane unless it can be proved that "at the time of committing the act, the accused was laboring under such a defect of reason, from disease of the mind, as not to know the nature and quality of the act he was doing or, if he did know it, that he did not know what he was doing was wrong." Just as importantly, it gave rise to new attitudes toward defining and treating mental illness. In short, it gave rise to modern psychiatry. Thus Andrew Roberts finds decisive evidence linking the McNaughton case and the growth of psychiatry in the medical literature of the time:

> [The] ... trend in The Lancet to focus on establishing psychiatry as a science can be traced back to that momentous occasion when it suspended judgement on McNaughton for a week. On 18.3.1843 an editorial dealt with the issues arising directly from the trial. The scientific spin-off began the next week when "Some further considerations on insanity, in its relation to jurisprudence" induced a seven column lead editorial on the "study of mind" as "part of the science of medicine." The editorial called for more empirical rigour in phrenological investigations, accurate classification of mental phenomena, and precise and logical definitions (Lancet 25.3.1843 pp 936–939). In June 1843 an article citing McNaughton as its cause examined the theory behind moral management and argued for "obtaining a correct knowledge of the principles of psychology in daily medical practice [Lancet 3.6.1843 pp 349–350] [http://www.mdx.ac.uk/www/study/mhhglo.htm#psychiatrist].

Interestingly, McNaughton and its ramifications in law and in medicine occurred in the same decade that Poe invented the story that made crime into an occasion for thought rather than an occasion for punishment meted out in the theater of God's judgment. While in some sense, fiction about crime in its depiction and analysis of aberrant human behavior has always been about psychology, it wasn't until psychology and psychiatry began to be recognized as regular and accepted fields of study that the crime story could turn into the detective story. Thus it happens that in the middle of the 19th century the cornerstones of detective fiction relied more on what we would now call psychology than what we would call police work. Poe, it's pretty clear, cared more about the association of ideas and our neglect of the obvious than he did about crime, and in *The Moonstone* (1868) the theft of the diamond is better explained by a psychologist or psychiatrist than by a policeman. Times they were changing. And it wouldn't be long before detective story writers shifted to give psychology and psychiatry a whack at detecting and even preventing crime.

OH BRAVE NEW WORLD

Just as turn of the century detective story writers unfurled the banners of science and technology, they also became apostles of psychology and psychiatry. And Edwin Balmer and William MacHarg made themselves into psychology's most ardent prophets. Even before they introduce their hero, Luther Trant, in action, Balmer and McHarg tell their readers that psychology and its methods are going to be the Rosetta Stone that enables society to read the human mind and exact real justice:

> Though little known to the general public, they are precisely such as are being used daily in the psychological laboratories of the great universities—both in America and Europe—by means of which modern men of science are at last disclosing and defining the workings of that oldest of world-mysteries—the human mind.
>
> ...
>
> If these facts are not used as yet except in the academic experiments of the psychological laboratories and the very real and useful purpose to which they have been put in the diagnosis of insanities, it is not because they are incapable of wider use. The results of the "new psychology" are coming every day closer to an exact interpretation. The hour is close at hand when they will be used not merely in the determination of guilt and innocence, but to establish in the courts the credibility of witnesses and the impartiality of jurors, and by employers to ascertain the fitness and particular abilities of their employees [*The Achievements of Luther Trant* foreword].

But Balmer and McHarg were not alone in their evangelizing. Even before Luther Trant made his debut, Cleveland Moffett in *Through the Wall* (1909) looked into the future and predicted the utility and perfection of psychology in enacting justice:

> A kind-eyed, grave-faced man was this, who, for all his modesty, was famous over Europe as a brilliant worker in psychological criminology. Bertillon had given the world a method of identifying criminals' bodies, and now Duprat was perfecting a method of recognizing their mental states, especially any emotional disturbances connected with fear, anger, or remorse [328].

Seven years later Arthur McFarlane in *Behind the Bolted Door* had no doubts about the role of psychiatry:

> And the Doctor had seized upon the occasion as a chance to explain once more why the "new medicine"—the "newest medicine"—psychoanalysis, must in the scientific future become the sole and logical medium for the detection of crime [2].

THE DOCTOR WILL SEE YOU NOW

And so it happened that a few writers at the turn of the century made psychologists or psychiatrists their heroes. George Butler's Dr. Furnivall from *The Exploits of a Physician Detective* fits in here. While a few of Furnivall's cases turn on strictly medical facts, in most of them he uses hypnotism to probe the minds of witnesses and suspects. Certainly the most familiar contemporary psychologist detective is the aforementioned Luther Trant. Balmer and McHarg entitled their book the "Achievements" versus the "Adventures" of Luther Trant in order to emphasize the importance of what their hero does as they trace his career from an undergraduate psychology department's wunderkind to celebrated private consultant specializing in crime. To that vocation he brings not magnifying glass or false moustache but a new attitude—"I read from the marks made upon the minds by a crime, not from scrawls and thumbprints upon paper" (88)—and also a variety of fancy instruments with long Greek names. Joining Furnivall and Trant as heroes who specialize in the arts and sciences of the mind, Dr. Lanehan the hero of McFarlane's *Behind the Bolted Door* is "Among neuropaths a name fast becoming international" and so is the villain of that novel. There's an alienist who helps expose a fake spiritualist in Wells Hastings and Brian Hooker's *The Professor's Mystery* (1911), and one who is the victim in Henry K. Webster's *The Whispering Man*. To these academically certified practitioners one needs to add most of the detectives of the period because most of them are well versed in the literature and methodology of the discipline. The heroes in Futrelle, Moffett, Reeve, Severy, Walk, Henry Webster—in fact in almost every hero in the turn of the century library—at one time or another acts like a psychologist. And that would mean...?

It's Greek to Me?

One way that writers make their detectives act like psychologists or psychiatrists is that they make diagnoses. To begin with, simply the fact that they make diagnoses—label and classify the reasons why a person committed a crime—signals a new attitude toward crime and criminals: it's not sin or weakness, it's an illness that made him do it. On top of that, when detectives do label the causes of criminal behavior, they use psychological terminology. When Poe invented the detective story there were not a whole lot of ways to describe mental illnesses. In 1844 a Royal Commission on Lunacy identified eight "principal forms of insanity": Mania, Dementia, Melancholia, Monomania, Moral Insanity, Congenital Idiocy, Congenital Imbecility, General Paralysis of the Insane, and Epilepsy (www.mdx.ac.uk/www/study/mhhglo.htm#psychiatrist). The list surely wants in precision. Turn of the century detectives had far more numerous and precise terms to use. In Henry Webster's *The Whispering Man*, for instance, the murder victim suffered from "Degenerative Recurrent Hypomania." In *The Master of Mysteries*, Astro, the detective, finds a case of Disassociated Personality, and Edith Buckley turns her novel *The Snare of Circumstance* on a Jekyll-Hyde Multiple Personality Disorder. Dr. Furnivall pinpoints "Religious Insanity" as the motive for the first case in *The Exploits of a Physician*. Samuel Hopkins Adams in *The Flying Death* has recourse to the somewhat vague "Murderous Mania," but Severy gives his readers both psychiatry and foreign words when he rings in *mania transitoria* and the *folie circulaire* in *The Mystery of June 13th*. Arthur B. Reeve gives readers both the Greek and the English with the case of pyromania in "The Firebug." And in "The Vanisher" he introduces "suicidal mania." Epidemics of kleptomania and somnambulism sweep through turn of the century fiction. But more of that in a bit. These diagnoses have a number of implications for detective fiction. One is that psychology provided turn of the century writers with a new arsenal of behaviors to describe and motives to ascribe to the characters in their detective stories. Just as importantly, it provided them with an additional way of demonstrating their hero's genius. Thus the psychological diagnosis falls into the same category as the discovery of the unusual scientific or medical fact that lies under the crime: it depends on knowledge attained only by extensive specialized education and accessible and applicable only by the genius.

AND THEY HAVE GREAT TOYS

Hand in hand in a number of turn of the century stories the articulation of psychology or psychiatry employs scientific techniques or instruments along with the tongue twisting diagnostic terms. There are simple tests that require only a stop watch like the word association test that both Luther Trant and Craig Kennedy use to ferret out the truth. But machines presented more allure to the psychologist detective than a timed verbal examination. Thus Reeve's narrator tells his readers in "The Scientific Cracksman" about keeping up to date in the gizmo department:

> Neither of us was unfamiliar with the process, for when we were in college these instruments were just coming into use in America. Kennedy had never let his particular branch of science narrow him, but had made a practice of keeping abreast of all the important discoveries and methods in other fields. Besides, I had read articles about the chronoscope, the plethysmograph, the sphygmograph, and others of the new psychological instruments [www.-online-literature.com].

And building on the period's faith in science and technology, those articles held out the promise that the fallible, human element could be eliminated in both the criminal and the detective. Thus we get Maitland in *The Mystery of June 13th* discoursing on the application of machines to criminal testimony:

> There are in every human organism, certain processes which are affected by the emotions, quite independent of the will. Just as fear checks the flow of saliva, so do the inner emotions impress themselves upon the circulation of the blood. If, now, we can find some way of observing the changes in the circulation of a criminal, we shall be able, no matter how calm and indifferent he may outwardly appear, accurately to gauge the conditions of his internal emotions. Several instruments may be used for this purpose, among them the cardiograph, kymograph, hemadynamometer, sphygmograph, sphygmophone and hematachrometer [524].

What he's really talking about here, what Severy, and Reeve, and a couple of others are talking about in their detective stories is the lie detector.

TELL THE TRUTH

> "What's the great idea?" he said laughing. "Some scientific machine? Do we have bands round our wrists which register guilty heart-beats? There is such an invention, isn't there?" *The Murder of Roger Ackroyd*

A lot of people at the turn of the century thought that science could and would make it possible to tell when someone was lying. Efforts to create instruments that could do that began in 1875 with Italian physiologist Angelo Mosso who showed a correlation between emotions and blood pressure and pulse rate. In 1895 Lombroso constructed a machine called a hydrosphygmograph that did just that and he used it in an Italian trial (www.argo-a.com/eng/history). In 1915, at Harvard psychologist William Moulton Marston—who worked with Hugo Munsterberg on the application of psychology to crime detection—devised a lie detecting machine based on blood pressure. A more complex instrument capable of continuously recording blood pressure, respiration, and pulse rate was devised in California by medical student John Larson in 1921. But fiction beat them all to the punch.

As early as 1905 American detective story writers used lie detectors for dramatic effect in their stories and proselytized on their behalf. Thus Melvin Severy gives readers an impassioned trial speech on the virtues of the sphygmograph (an instrument that records arterial pulse) in sorting out the truth in *The Mystery of June 13th*:

By the use of the sphygmograph M. Voisin exposed a sham epileptic in Paris by showing his sphygmogram bore no resemblance to that of a true epileptic before and after a fit; and Enroco Ferri refers to a case where the sphygmograph showed that a person accused of a theft was innocent of that particular theft, but was guilty of another of which he had not even been suspected. He cites also a case where the same instrument established the innocence of a man condemned to death. You will perceive that the sphygmograph has already proved its efficiency in the domain of criminology [524–525].

Without the big words or fancy machine, Jacques Futrelle's detective uses pulse to figure out who's telling the truth in "The Motor Boat" published in *The Sunday Magazine* on September 9, 1906. In his 1909 novel *Through the Wall*, Cleveland Moffett gives an extended demonstration of psychological tests including magic lantern pictures shown to a suspect while he is hooked up to a primitive sphygmomanometer (blood pressure cuff). The whole topic of lie detection had become familiar enough so that by 1909 Charles Walk could make it a subject to light banter:

There's a contrivance recently invented by some college professor ... that I'd like to try on Cullimore. It's a lie detector; with its aid one can plumb the bottomless pit of a chap's subconscious mind, and fathom all the mysteries of his subliminal ego. You set some wheels going, the chap lays his hands on a what-you-call-'em, and then you proceed to fire some words at him. It's like a game [*The Yellow Circle* 69].

In the 1910 collection *The Achievements of Luther Trant*, Balmer and McHarg present an aggressive demonstration of a plethysmograph (a device used to measure the changes in the volume of the whole body during respiration, changes in the chest volume due to blood flow or respiration) and a Pneumograph (a device used to monitor breathing, sometimes used to describe a simple chest wall movement detector with a length of large-diameter tube tied around the chest) to get the truth out of a the man higher up in a story with that title. Finally, in *The Silent Bullet* collection Arthur B. Reeve published two stories that turn on Kennedy's use of instruments to detect lies: "The Silent Bullet" and "The Scientific Cracksman." But, in the real world, there was a problem with all of these psychology department gadgets.

At the murder trial of James Alphonso Frye his defense lawyers asked the court to admit expert testimony with respect to a systolic blood pressure deception test and even offered to conduct that test on the defendant in court. They were turned down. On December, 1923, in Frye v. The United States of America, the U.S. Court of Appeals in Washington D.C. agreed with the lower court and held that such evidence was not admissible in court (http://psychlaw.stanford.edu/expert_cases.html). And just as lie detectors disappeared from American court rooms, they disappeared from detective fiction. If machines and detective fiction weren't going to be very congenial bedfellows, diagnoses and story telling would get along a lot better. And somnambulism and kleptomania are cases in point.

A GREAT PERTURBATION IN NATURE

Sleep walking is one of the most frightening phenomena one can confront. It raises questions about identity, free will, and other weighty issues. Somnambulism, real and imaginary, was much in the public eye at the turn of the century. Partly this came from the pseudo science of mesmerism—a practice that labeled hypnotic states "artificial somnambulism"—partly the increasing popularity of spiritualism with mediums nodding off into trances had something to do with it. On top of these, the immense popularity of George du Maurier's novel *Trilby* (published serially in *Harper's Monthly* in 1894) made somnambulism a hot topic. This was so much the case that contemporary newspapers jumped all over any story that had the least thing to do with sleep walking. A piece in *The New York Times*—on September 11, 1881—makes a telling point about the combination of sleepwalking, crime, and fiction. It recounts a crime committed in Paris in which a young man attached one Mme Desvallieres:

> It was afterward ascertained that this young scoundrel of 18 years of age entertained a criminal passion for Mme. Desvallieres's daughter, a girl of 13. To gratify this passion he stole a key to the apartments, and, as he states, stabbed the girl's mother, purposing to "render her insensible" and get access to the girl's room. He was sentenced to eight year's penal servitude. The reading of trashy feuilletons seems to have led him astray, as also to have suggested his pretense when first arrested that he had acted under the influence of dreams or in a state of somnambulism.

In part, all of this contemporary fascination with somnambulism influenced detective story writers at the turn of the century, and so did the literature of psychology and psychiatry, manifested in studies like William Hammond's 1881 *On Certain Conditions of Nervous Derangement, Somnambulism, Hypnotism, Hysteria, Hysterroid Affections*. Across the board sleep walking was a hot topic.

One consequence of its popularity was that somnambulism had a part to play in lots of turn of the century detective fiction. It's there in Green's *Doctor Izard* (1895) as well as in her Violet Strange stories; Twain uses somnambulism in *Tom Sawyer, Detective*, and so do John Kendrick Bangs in *Paste Jewels* (1897), Rodriguez Ottolengui in *The Final Proof*, Mary Roberts Rinehart in *The Amazing Adventures of Letitia Carberry*, Gelette Burgess in *The Master of Mysteries*, and Louis Vance in *The Lone Wolf*.

Indeed, the whole of Arthur Stringer's *The Night Hawk* occurs while the hero-narrator is in what amounts to somnambulistic state. All of this represents a lucky convergence of events in the real world (the repeated instances of sleep walking in the press), with scientific study of the subject by psychologists and psychiatrists, with well-known literary conventions that associated somnambulism and crime. In this respect there is the convention of bad sleep walking—somnambulism reflecting unexpiated guilt, embodied most prominently in Lady Macbeth's midnight rambles; and there is also the convention of good sleep walking established by Collins in *The Moonstone.* Turn of the century writers used them both. Indeed, in *Doctor Izard* Anna Katharine Green uses bad sleep walking and in Violet Strange's episode of "The Dreaming Lady" she introduces good sleep walking. Both kinds of somnambulism call upon the detective to be adept in psychology and psycho therapy—the latter typically demonstrated in the means used to recreate the prevailing conditions and the state of mind of the sleep walker. Further, the advantage of the *Moonstone* pattern lay in the fact that it enabled writers to construct stories that appear to involve crimes and criminal behavior but that end with the kind of exoneration acceptable to a genteel audience. This demonstrates a kind of higher wisdom possessed by the detective as one who can, in effect, decriminalize problems. That's harder to do with the other mania at the top of the turn of the century hit parade of psychic aberrations, kleptomania.

NICE SHINY THINGS

Kleptomania was first described and named by Matthey, a Swiss physician in 1816. He identified the mania as "a unique madness characterized by the tendency to steal without motive and without necessity" ("Shoplifting as Moral Insanity" *Journal of Macromarketing.* 24.1. June 2004. 9). Perhaps almost by definition a disease of the wealthy, Kleptomania attracted a good deal of interest in the professional psychiatric literature of the 19th century. Like somnambulism, kleptomania also held a fascination for contemporary newspapers and their readers. Take this random sampling of headlines of the 1880s on the topic from *The New York Times*:

KLEPTOMANIA OR WHAT? [October 16, 1882]
PILFERING FROM STORES
Kleptomania and Mere Theft—How Much is Done by Women—Why Merchants Do Not Prosecute [March 4, 1883]
A MANIA FOR STEALING
Something to which Jewelers have become Accustomed [July 1, 1883]

AN INSATIATE KLEPTOMANIAC
A Woman Who Practices Shoplifting Just for Fun [December 12, 1885]

Unlike other mental illnesses, kleptomania possessed an attractive combination of sensation, high society, mental illness, and chicanery.

It also held out allure for detective story writers. A lot of writers did kleptomania stories. Wardon Curtis has one in *The Strange Adventures of Mr. Middleton* (1903), and one of *The Exploits of a Physician Detective* is "The Kleptomaniac." The title story in Anna Katharine Green's *Golden Slipper and Other Problems for Violet Strange* (1915) is about the disease. Jacques Futrelle's "The Problem of the Auto Cab" is about kleptomania and so is Arthur B. Reeve's "The Kleptomaniac." Arthur Stringer combines it with picking pockets in the first episode of *The Night Hawk* and Ottolengui uses kleptomania in *The Final Proof.* In addition to being a topic of considerable contemporary interest, kleptomania possessed other advantages for turn of the century writers. For one thing, it enabled them to treat crime in a completely different manner than they would face with what would soon become the detective story's central dilemma, murder. Across the board, period detective writers treated kleptomania as an illness and not a crime. Take, for example, the symptoms and diagnosis from Curtis' *The Strange Adventures of Mr. Middleton*:

> She has, oh, she has become a kleptomaniac. With every luxury, with her fine home on the Lake Shore Drive, with all her father's wealth, and no want money can gratify, she takes things. In her circumstances it is out of the question to call it stealing. It is a mania, a form of insanity [51].

As with the character who gives the above speech, describing herself under the guise of "I have a friend who …," writers acknowledge that the compulsion to steal also involves a measure of self-disgust. Thus the kleptomaniac in Green's "The Golden Slipper" laments that

> A curse has been over my life—the curse of longing I could not combat. But love was working a change in me. Since I have known Captain Holliday—but that's all over. I was mad to think I could be happy with such memories in my life. I shall never marry now—or touch jewels again, my own or another's. Father, father, you won't go back on your girl! I couldn't see Caroline suffer for what I have done. You will pardon me and help—help—[28].

And that help part is significant, too. Just as the fiction recognizes kleptomania's status as an illness, it also prescribes neither jail nor opprobrium but therapy. It's what Craig Kennedy orders in "The Kleptomaniac" and several years earlier Dr. Furnivall demands the same thing in *The Exploits of a Physician Detective*:

> "The whole difficulty is as much your fault as hers. Kleptomania is a disease, and should be treated as such. It sticks out all over her."

"All I want is the diamond," he said, adding quickly, "and to know how she managed the business."
"We will arrange that on one condition—"
"The $1,000?" he interrupted, with irony.
Dr. Furnivall went on:
"It is that when you have received this information and recovered the stone you will call the physician for your wife that I shall name for you" [247].

In spite of its status as an illness, kleptomania produced some of the zaniest plots in turn of the century fiction. Thus, for example, the kleptomania episode in Stringer's *The Night Hawk* involves a young woman who has an artificial third arm to facilitate her picking pockets, and, anticipating Michael Innes, "The Kleptomaniac" in *The Exploits of a Physician Detective* revolves around training a monkey to steal and eat rock candy in anticipation of his stealing and eating a diamond.

BACK TO THE DRAWING BOARD

In spite of or because of the grasp that scientific criminology and abnormal psychology had on turn of the century detective fiction, neither the criminologist nor the psychologist was going to take over as the new hero of popular fiction. With criminology, the causes for this are a bit clearer than they are with the psychologist: the criminologist didn't succeed as a hero because biological determinism took it, as it were, on the chin at the turn of the century. Phrenology had been debunked in the 19th century and pretty early in the 20th century Lombroso became passé—often supplanted by the findings of early sociologists with respect to the impact of growing up in the fetid living conditions of the slums and being schooled by the chaos of the streets. Likewise the enthusiasm for machines and the role that they could play in the detection of crime ran squarely into the Frye decision and the subsequent exile from the legal process imposed on lie detectors. Cut adrift from science and the courts, criminologists didn't have a whole lot to offer detective fiction after the First World War.

That was not the case with the psychologist. One of the problems that arose regarding the psychologist as hero of the detective story was that psychology became too easy. While even talking intelligently about medicine or chemistry demands a fair degree of expertise unavailable to the uninitiated, that is superficially not the case with psychology or psychiatry. At the turn of the century psychology unintentionally provided diagnoses and labels that were easy, too easy, to attach to individuals who committed crimes. That meant that anybody could name someone else a pyromaniac or kleptomaniac. And if on one hand 1) symptoms of mental illness are simple to spot, and 2) anybody can spot them, the result is no real problem and no real problem solver—no suspense and no skill—and no detective story. On the other hand, psychology and psychiatry also made things too hard for the middle class popular genre into which the detective story was developing. There was all of that sex business. While there are a few innocuous allusions to Freud in the detective fiction of the period, they avoid mention of the substance of his works. That kind of psychology emphatically lay far outside the pale of popular fiction. But there was a more fundamental problem with the emerging behavioral sciences. They take as a part of their province the diagnosis and ultimately the treatment of complex and often disturbing facets of the human behavior—predation, sadism, and a whole lot of other things that people don't even want to think about. In times bygone, in times before McNaughton, crime and punishment were a simple equation. They, in effect, cancelled each other out; for God or for society, judicial decision and punishment cancelled out the crime. But what happens when medicine and therapy replace punishment? What happens when the criminal believes there has been no crime? What happens when medicine or therapy can offer no hard and fast answer, no time-table, no cure? Restiveness with the non-judgmental objectivity of the behavioral sciences often brought about the kind of plea for definitive moral judgment seen at the end of Thomas Harris' *The Silence of the Lambs*:

> At least two scholarly journals explained that his unhappy childhood was the reason he killed women in his basement for their skins. The words crazy and evil do not appear in either article [357].

Faced with issues like these, at this crucial stage in its development, the detective story chose to be entertainment and not an encounter with the dark side of human nature.

6

Journalists and Journalism

On November 17, 1872 the *New York Times* carried a story about a mutilated human body divided between two barrels found floating in Boston's Charles River.

> The remains were speedily identified, and we then expressed a hope that, with so plain a case, the Boston detectives would prove themselves ... by speedily discovering the murderer, and obtaining the necessary evidence of his guilt. All that we hoped for has been promptly and fully achieved, but rumor has it that we owe the result to the enterprise of journalism rather than to the skill and devotion of those officers who are liberally paid for devoting themselves to such tasks.

The story goes on to explain how two reporters "of a Boston newspaper" did all of the detecting and handed their conclusions and proofs over to the police. The headline for the story is "Journalism as a Detective Agency" and the piece ends with this observation:

> As our detective service is at present constituted, it is of little value in its legitimate sphere, and society is fortunate in having some guarantee for the detection of criminals in the skill, enterprise, and rivalries of reporters.

Sounds pretty good for reporters' chances to take over the role of hero in the detective story.

READ ALL ABOUT IT!

All of the ingredients were there to make the reporter the hero of the detective story at the turn of the century. After all, the late 19th century was the Golden Age of Journalism in America. In part, like the revolution in science, medicine, and psychology it was fueled by new technology. Printing, something that had hardly changed since Gutenberg, changed radically: the 1880s saw the invention of not one but two automated type setting machines (the one by Merganthaler and the one by Paige that cost Mark Twain his fortune) and they changed the way books, magazines, and newspapers were made. Just as the linotype made setting type easier, so did F.E. Ives' invention of half tone engraving in 1886 make the publication of pictures simpler and that opened the way both for more photos in newspapers and for the illustrated magazine—magazines like *The Strand* in Britain and *Leslie's* in the U.S. Everything in the world of publishing got not only easier, cheaper, and faster, it became more immediate, too. On February 13, 1877 the *Boston Globe* published the first story reported by telephone and Marconi's wireless passed its first test in 1900 by relaying news of the America's Cup yacht race off Sandy Hook, New Jersey to the press. In addition to all of the new technology, there were a variety of new ideas that aided in the creation of the 11,314 newspapers in the United States in 1880, at least one of which had a circulation of a million copies a day by the turn of the century. There was S.S. McClure's invention of syndication—of buying and selling stories to multiple papers across the country. Along with syndication came the advent of modern advertising, a phenomenon that allowed both newspapers and magazines to sell their product for less than it cost to produce it. At the same time, there was the creation of the network of reporters and telegraph lines that made up the Associated Press to supply news from across the country and eventually the world. By the middle of the 19th century Horace Greeley's *New York Tribune* was sold coast to coast and, for the first time, gained a national and eventually international readership. And newspapers caught the attention of academe: in 1875 Cornell University offered a certificate (but no courses) in journalism and the University of Missouri offered the nation's first collegiate journalism course (History of Journalism) in 1878 (http://inventors.about.com/library). With or without the college courses, the turn of the century also saw the emergence of reporters like Richard Harding Davis who attained the status of celebrities. Related to the appearance of the star reporter, at the turn of the century there emerged newspaper entrepreneurs, editors and publishers dedicated to rising circulation (and profits), and to do so they not only printed the news but also made it happen by stirring things up—thus James Bennett of the *New York Herald* sent Stanley to Africa on his Livingston hunt and the term "yellow journalism" was coined for William Randolph Hearst and Joseph Pulitzer who used banner headlines, illustrations, and sensational stories to create the furor that led to the Spanish American War. Progressives, reformers, muckrakers also found in the press a choice instrument with which to expose corruption in business and politics. But before looking at them, newspapers and newspaper reporters staked a small claim on the role of the hero in the detective story.

ALL THE NEWS THAT'S FIT TO PRINT

In Henry K. Webster's *The Whispering Man* (1909) one of the main characters sees the press not only as the enemy of genteel society but also the foe of efficient law enforcement:

> If I were to put this line of evidence into their hands, the first thing that they would do would be to take the whole Metropolitan press into their confidence, and fan the spark into a perfect blaze of scandal inside of twenty four hours [162].

This complaint is a familiar one to readers of detective fiction. In 19th century sensation novels like *The Dead Letter*, part of the point of the way the plot works is to keep the family's misfortune and suffering out of the public eye. The model of justice is a paternalistic one of the family or the village that takes care of its own problems 1) because they can do it better than others, and 2) so that they do not need to admit their shortcomings to unsympathetic outsiders. Crime, in this context, is both nobody else's business as well as something that needs to be hidden from view for the welfare of the public because of its potential to unbalance readers' moral equilibrium. This was the reason for Anthony Comstock's crusade against dime novels, *The Police Gazette*, and crime reporting in general: Comstock and his adherents believed that discussion of crime, *any* discussion of crime, was the first step toward moral dissolution and criminal debauchery. It was also the reason that William Randolph Hearst warned his editors and reporters, "Don't use the words 'murder,' 'scandal,' 'Divorce,' 'crime,' and other rather offensive phrases when it is possible to tell a story without them" (Crawford 231). Like the police, then, the press stood as unwelcome intruder in early detective stories. Moving into detective fiction of the 20th century, the press with its potential to debase the morals and taste of its readers and to foment social embarrassment changes into the press as an impediment to efficient and effective law enforcement—the reporter who gets in the way or who compromises an investigation by revealing too much, not about the persons or families involved but about the evidence or the ongoing investigation. For a brief time at the turn of the 20th century, however, reporters were neither perverse voyeurs nor bumbling blabber-mouths. For a brief time they had a chance to be the heroes of the detective story.

Turn of the century newspapers began to focus readers' attention on crime both as an individual and aggregate phenomenon: major papers covered individual cases of crime not only in their own cities, but from places elsewhere in the country as well as abroad. Cited elsewhere have been news stories from *The New York Times* from the turn of the century that not only reported crimes in New York City but also crimes from other cities at home and abroad—like the piece about the French youth and the trumped up story about somnambulism he told the gendarmes. In addition to crime and court reporting, in New York City, at least, during the mid-1890s newspapers dedicated a great deal of space covering the revelations of the Lexow investigations and detailing the corruption of those the city had employed to protect and serve its citizens. In the aggregate, 19th century newspapers in every major American city periodically ran editorials about the frightening increases in their city's crime rate. Then, in 1904 *The Chicago Tribune* took on the entire nation and compiled statistics on the number of homicides in the U.S. from 1881 and 1902 discovering, not surprisingly, that there were more in 1902 than twenty years earlier. Side by side with news from the police blotter or the courts or the legislative investigative committees, newspapers ran stories about Sherlock Holmes and other fictional detectives and commentary about the detective story as a literary form. S.S. McClure started all of this, of course, by selling Sherlock Holmes stories to just about every major newspaper in the land. And when the Holmes stories ran out, papers looked for their own, home grown detective stories. It's why Jacques Futrelle invented the Thinking Machine for *The Boston American*. And it's why even *The New York Times*, a paper that refused to run comic pages when all of its competitors did, published serial detective stories like Howard Fielding's *A Secret of the Heart*—the first installment of which appeared on March 14, 1896.

Part of this had to do with crime, but part of it also had to do with fiction. Thus William Randolph Hearst also urged his editors to use the techniques of fiction to make true crime more engaging and less potentially morally corrosive for their readers:

> Murder stories and other criminal stories are not printed merely because they are criminal, but because of the *mystery*, or the *romance*, or the *dramatic qualities* in them. Therefore, develop the *mystery*, or the *romance*, or the *dramatic qualities* ... [quoted in Crawford 231].

KNIGHT RIDERS

Increasingly, as publishers and editors saw the role of their newspapers as not simply reporting events but as promoting the public weal through campaigns and crusades—like the Pulitzer and Hearst agitation against Spain or the Hearst papers' periodic protests and warnings about drug use. If these crusades were begun in publishers' or editors' offices, the knights who carried them out were the reporters. Indeed, at the turn of the century news reporters began to see their job as more than a job but as a profession, as a high, very high calling. One can see this documented in *The Ethics of Journalism* (1924) where Nelson Crawford reprints 16 codes of ethics established either by journalists or by their newspapers at the turn of the century. They all take the idea of public trust very seriously and this is manifested in two ways: first, in the pledge to avoid vulgarity ("The physiology of conception and childbirth and all matters relating thereto will not be discussed in the [Seattle] *Times*" [Crawford 235]), and then in the vow to rigorously and objectively seek the truth. Thus this *The Kansas City Journal Post*'s credo:

> There are two sides to every story. GET BOTH.
> The best story is simply told and told simply.
> Be truthful.
> Get the facts.
> The Journal Post will play its politics on the editorial page. Write political stories impartially.
> Treat religious matters reverently.
> The Journal Post's ideals are high—truthfulness, toleration, fairness, decency, and cleanliness.
> ALWAYS VERIFY NAMES!
> [Crawford 237]

Given that one of the facets of the Sherlock Holmes stories that critics felt separated them from vulgar dime novels was their emphasis on logic, reason, and methodical thinking, journalists' emphasis on thoroughness and impartiality seemed to fit right in. It is small wonder, then, that when the detective story was on the lookout for a new hero the reporter made a pretty good candidate. And so reporters had a chance for the starring role.

REPORTERS AS DETECTIVES

In the detective stories of the turn of the century reporters play a number of significant roles. The first, and most natural, of these was that of the narrator, of the Watson character. American fiction was never quite comfortable with the idea of a physician having the kind and variety of leisure necessary to just hang around with the genius detective to say nothing of taking the time off to follow him (or her) on cases. On top of that, there was the issue of authority—it was and is not a pleasant prospect to think of those responsible for one's physical health as dullards. Lawyers were an alternative. The law and, by easy extension, crime was the lawyer's business. And, in fact, there are a fair number of lawyer-narrators from *The Dead Letter* and *The Leavenworth Case* onward. More on them later. But as Watsons, reporters were as good as or better than lawyers. Following the news, shadowing the famous and infamous, rushing to the scene of the crime, and interviewing everyone at the scene, after all, was their business. And so was serving their community—even before the crusading days of Hearst and Pulitzer—by follow-up reports on the causes and consequences of crime. So in the fiction of the period one finds a number of reporters playing the Watson role. Futrelle's Thinking Machine has Hitchinson Hatch, Arthur B. Reeve's Craig Kennedy has Walter Jameson and Hugh C. Weir's Madelyn Mack has woman reporter Nora Noraker. Although not the narrator, Waldemar, editor-owner of the *Universal*, plays second fiddle in the Average Jones stories. Each performs all of the traditional duties of the Watson character—friendship and admiration, small practical assistance, befuddlement when confronted with complex problems—with the added feature of doing their jobs, of writing up the means and ends of detection as well as describing the person and actions of the public figure of the great detective for the edification of the newspaper reading public—and for their employers. Then, too, since doing this was their profession, reporter-Watson characters avoided the label of sycophant that American satirists so often pinned on the real Watson.

Moving up the detective food chain, in fiction of the period reporters sometimes serve as what can perhaps be called co-detectives in a number of stories. After he has been set aright about the role of women, the newspaper editor in Leroy Scott's *Counsel for the Defense* (1912) ably assists lawyer Katharine West and her private detectives in winning the day. Harris Haines of *The New Era* adds insight and common sense to the proceedings before his death in Adams' *The Flying Death*. Mr. Terence K. Patten of the *Post-Dispatch* pops in at the end of Webster's *The Four Pools Mystery* to find the facts and set folks straight. There's a subsidiary detective in *The Whispering Man* who was not only a policeman but also a reporter and who makes his living as an artist. In the last two instances the writers use the reporter, in effect, as the *deus ex machina*—the character who, when all of the clues seem exhausted by the narrator-detective and all seems hopeless and befuddled, drops in, sees the truth, and sets things right. Finally, moving into the realm of the full-fledged detective hero, reporters play that role in Buckley's *The Snare of Circumstance*, Roman Doubleday's *The Hemlock Avenue Mystery* (1908), and in the title story about the newsroom boy detective from Richard Harding Davis' collection *Gallagher* (1891). The most influential reporter detective of the period, however, was not American but Gaston LeRoux's Joseph Josephson, "Rouletabille," introduced in *Le Mystère de la chambre jaune* (*The Mystery of the Yellow Room*) translated in 1908:

> The boy-faced reporter speedily made himself many friends, for he was serviceable and gifted with a good humour that enchanted the most severe-tempered and disarmed the most zealous of his companions. At the Bar cafe, where the reporters assembled before going to any of the courts, or to the Prefecture, in search of their news of crime, he began to win a reputation as an unraveller of intricate and obscure affairs which found its way to the office of the Chief of the Surete. When a case was worth the trouble and Rouletabille—he had already been given his nickname—had been started on the scent by his editor-in-chief, he often got the better of the most famous detective [www.online-literature.com].

American writers, however, did acknowledge that reporters had skills.

SINGULAR GIFTS

Even when reporters appear only as incidental or background characters in detective stories, turn of the century writers tend to treat them with the same kind of glowing optimism expressed toward the scientist or psychologist as the new modern hero. Thus, in *The Snare of Circumstance*, a grumpy old man lectures the hero on the virtues of journalists as opposed to those of professional detectives:

> "There you are!" the old man interrupted, stamping his foot. "There you are! Like all young fools. Never to know your best gifts and so to slight them. Talk about your experience measured against that of a professional detective! Bah! How many detectives concern themselves about the hair-line of accuracy? How many professional detectives analyze? How many are capable of deducing a proposition without forestalling a conclusion? Now can you understand why it is you that I want for the work?" [*Snare of Circumstance* 4–5].

The narrator of Roman Doubleday's *The Hemlock Avenue Mystery* expounds on the hero's gifts that are appropriate to both the reporter and the detective:

> Percy Lyon had a natural gift for human nature, as some people have for music or for mechanics. Unconsciously and instinctively, he could read character, and as with all instinctive knowledge, he was utterly unable to say how he reached his conclusions. His judgment had so often proved to be truer than appearances that it had surprised even himself. His success in his newspaper work depended almost wholly upon this gift. In news as news he had little interest, and he often chafed at the routine drudgery of his assignments, but when his work was to "write up" some one, whether it was a drunken tramp arrested for disorderly conduct, a visiting diplomat surrounded by mystery

and red tape, a famous actress or an infamous trust president, he was in his element [27].

Burton Stevenson combines praise for reporters' conviviality with the altruistic substance of their profession:

> Long before I reached my rooms I heard the clatter of voices and caught the odor of various qualities of tobacco. They [reporters] were lolling about over the furniture, telling stories, I suppose, and they greeted me with a cheer when I entered. They were such jovial fellows that it was quite impossible to feel angry with them—and besides, I knew that they were gentlemen, that they labored early and late at meager salaries for the pure love of the work; that they were quick to scent fraud or trickery or unworthiness, and inexorable in exposing them; that they loved to do good anonymously; remaining utterly unknown save to the appreciative few behind the scenes [*The Holiday Case* 90–91].

In addition to the dedication to truth and skepticism that Stevenson talks about, reporters in the detective fiction of the period have a lively and active distrust of authority, especially the police. Thus, for example, in *The Flying Death* the heroic reporter generalizes on the inability of the police to see the obvious: "Anyone except a Central Office detective would have had the sense to know that the letter was written to bear out a grudge. They never should have arrested him" (45–46). In *The Mystery of the Boule Cabinet* the narrator centers the contrast between the police and the press on imagination:

> Godfrey himself had been accused more than once of a too-luxuriant imagination. It was, perhaps, a realization of this which had persuaded him, years before, to quit the detective force and take service with the *Record*. What might have been a weakness in the first position, was a mighty asset in the latter one, and he had won an immense success [solving crimes] [25].

And a number of writers vaunt the reporter's superior knowledge of crime, the streets, and criminals versus that of the police. Thus with respect to the newsroom's boy Gallagher's knowledge of the real world, Richard Harding Davis' narrator says that:

> ... his was rather the work of the criminal specialist, and his morbid interest in the doings of all queer characters, his knowledge of their methods, their present whereabouts, and their past deeds of transgression often rendered him a valuable ally to our police reporter, whose daily feutilletons were the only portion of the paper Gallagher deigned to read [*Gallagher* 6].

Jean Webster broadens out street knowledge to a special, inborn habit of mind and uses physiognomy to convey the virtues possessed by the archetypical reporter:

> His face was the face one feels he has the right to expect of a newspaper

man—keen, alert, humorous; on the look-out for opportunities.... It was not only wide-awake and intelligent; it was something more. "Knowing" one would say. It carried the mark of experience, the indelible stamp of the street. He was a man who has had no childhood, whose education commenced from the cradle [*The Four Pools Mystery* 5].

Looming large in the reporter's professional character is the action imperative demanded by publication deadlines. Along with correct and decisive thinking, for newspaper reporters thinking on one's feet and making split second decisions stands as a necessary virtue. This is one of Gallagher's assets in the first story in Richard Harding Davis' collection where, all in a day's work, the hero spots the disguised murderer, arranges to have him arrested, gets a scoop about a bare-knuckle prize fight and, chased by police and incensed cabbies, makes it to the paper in the nick of time for the next day's edition. But perhaps the most interesting quality possessed by reporters is the value they place on telling stories. Thus reporter Haynes in *The Flying Death* attributes his success in solving an off-stage case to his ability to distinguish a true story from one that is false: Haynes and not the cops knows that the accused "... saved himself by telling a straight story, even though it seemed damaging, where most men would have tried to lie" (45).

THE MAGAZINE BOOM

Reporters at the turn of the century not only worked for newspapers, they also worked for magazines. If the turn of the 20th century was the newspaper's golden age, it was also the golden age of magazines in America and Britain. The sudden success of magazines at that time depended on the same technological advances that boosted newspaper circulation into the millions: the linotype, half-tone engraving, advertising, national distribution by rail, and an increasingly literate and educated reading public—a reading public created both by universal free education and by the Morrill Act of 1862 which established Land Grant colleges in every state to teach agricultural science "... *without excluding other scientific and classical studies.*" On top of these things, the popularity of magazines increased because of the growth in middle class leisure time. And so there was a bi-weekly parade of new titles hitting the magazine stand, the railroad station, and the U.S. Mail. It, of course, was the phenomena that brought *The Strand Magazine* to readers on both sides of the Atlantic. But just as important for American detective fiction were the magazines that became the center of what Teddy Roosevelt would later call "muckraking":

Cosmopolitan (founded 1886), *Collier's* (founded 1888), *McClure's* (founded in 1893), *Everybody's* (founded in 1899), and *The American Magazine* (founded by disaffected members of *McClure's* staff in 1906). It is surely worth noting here that two of the most prominent of these magazines, *Collier's* and *McClure's*, were also the American magazine publishers of Sherlock Holmes' exploits.

McClure's Magazine usually wins the prize as the center of the investigative reporting that eventually gained the muckraking label. S.S. McClure's mission for his new magazine was "… to deal with important social, economic, and political questions; to present the new and great inventions and discoveries; to interpret the conquests of science; to advance great moral enthusiasms; to remove the barriers of the intellectual life; to promote the well-being of childhood and youth; to give the best in literature; and, above all, to achieve an unforgettable charm and vitality in all its undertakings" (http://tarbell.alleg.edu/mc2.html). McClure published the most important work of the most important journalists of his day; indeed, in publishing them, McClure made them the most important journalists of their day. There was Lincoln Steffens with his "Enemies of the Republic," March, 1904; "Rhode Island: A State for Sale," February, 1905; "New Jersey: A Traitor State," April, 1905; and "Ohio: A Tale of Two Cities," July, 1905 and all of the other pieces that would become *The Shame of the Cities* (1904). Ray Stannard Baker came from Chicago to contribute "What the United States Steel Corporation Really Is." November, 1901; "The Right to Work," January, 1903; "Reign of Lawlessness," May, 1904, "What is Lynching?" January, 1905; and "How Railroads Make Public Opinion," March, 1906 (http://www.spartacus.schoolnet.co.uk). Between 1902 and 1904 *McClure's* carried the serialization of Ida M. Tarbell's classic *History of the Standard Oil Company*. From the very beginning, as noted above, McClure showed a vigorous interest in crime and detectives. Indeed, McClure himself possessed many of the elements that made the detective story the detective story at the turn of the century. There was his wide-ranging interest in science and technology including the uses of photography, his interest in the emergence of criminology (seem in *McClure's Magazine* running Ida Tarbell's pieces from Paris on Bertillon as well as his publishing and editorializing about crime statistics) his interest in psychology manifested in his hiring Harvard psychologist Hugo Munsterberg (author of *On the Witness Stand* 1908) to write about crime and criminals for his magazine, his commitment to reform and progressive political causes, and his fascination with the detective story: McClure, after all, was responsible for the newspaper syndication of the Sherlock Holmes stories and "The Final Problem" ran first in America in *McClure's Magazine*.

THE MUCKRAKERS

With a number of writers of the period, it's difficult to tell whether muckraking or the detective story came first. Samuel Hopkins Adams, creator of the Average Jones, wrote a series of articles in 1905 and 1906 for *Collier's* about patent medicine frauds. These became the foundation for the book *The Great American Fraud* (1906) and, in turn, the book and the articles gave impetus to the drive to pass the country's first pure food and drug legislation in 1906. George Allan England, whose novel *The Greater Crime* (1917) focuses on issues of scientific detection, evaluation of evidence, and expert witnesses also wrote *The Air Trust* (1915), a book that

> ... is the result of an attempt to carry the monopolistic principle to its logical conclusion. For many years I have entertained the idea that if a monopoly be right in oil, coal, beef, steel or what not, it would also be right in larger ways involving, for example, the use of the ocean and the air itself. I believe that, had capitalists been able to bring the seas and the atmosphere under physical control, they would long ago have monopolized them. Capitalism has not refrained from laying its hand on these things through any sense of decency, but merely because the task has hitherto proved impossible [www.guttenberg.org].

Policeman Flynn (1902), a series of humorous vignettes about a duty-bound Irish-American policeman, was an odd precursor to Elliott's Flower's *The Spoilsmen* in 1903, a novel about corruption and political chicanery in Chicago. Creator of Miss Frances Baird in 1906, one of the first women agency detectives, Reginald Wright Kaufman also wrote about prostitution in *The House of Bondage* (1910). Alfred Henry Lewis who made novels both out of the venality of police and the underworld wrote also about New York politics for *Cosmopolitan* as well as a series of articles for the same journal in 1908 on the control of politics and politicians by businessmen entitled *The Owners of America*. And finally, Francis Lynde, creator of chemist detective Scientific Sprague, wrote a novel about graft entitled *The Grafters* (1904). All of this more than suggests that for some writers at least at the turn of the century detective stories and working for the public weal through the medium of exposes or investigative reporting went hand and hand. Indeed the link between the detective story and the investigative reporter is a unique bias in American detective fiction, one that goes back to Poe. Poe, it should be remembered, in addition to being the inventor of the detective story also worked as an editor and reporter. As an editor for *Graham's Magazine* Poe challenged his readers to play cipher games with him and earlier, as a stringer for *The Southern Literary Messenger* he unmasked the secret of a popular attraction, Maelzel's chess-playing automaton. Poe, granted, never quite had the public weal in mind in his journalistic endeavors, but the writers at the turn of the century did believe that progress was possible and that, as difficult as it might seem, they could change the world—or at least let a lot of people know that it needed changing. Nonetheless, there's a perceptible difference in tone between the muckrakers' journalism and their detective fiction. The heroes in their detective stories, for instance, interestingly enough, are rarely reporters. Even Adams' hero Average Jones has only a tangential connection with newspapers—as a lark and then as a profession he reads and collects the ads they run. And their personalities tend toward the aloof and insouciant. Scientific Sprague, for example, is a friendly background character until at the end of each story there's a call for clear thinking. There is a related kind of double perspective in Lewis' *Confessions of a Detective* in that it contains some stories about a very corrupt policeman and others about an honest and very brainy one who solves bizarre crimes. While subject to occasional bouts of Adams' outrage, Average Jones is the kind of glib talking sophisticated character that would become the norm in detective fiction after the war—except that he's more aware of irony. What seems to have been the case with the muckrakers is that their detective stories, rather than being an escape from their serious concerns about the state of the nation, became an alternate approach to those problems, one that sought to avoid the unbridled zeal and unfortunate prudishness too often associated with American reformers, and instead tried to teach through entertainment rather than through polemic. And this makes turn of the century fiction—or one branch of it at least—significantly different from the golden age detective story as it developed after World War I in Britain and then in America. That variety of detective fiction took wealth and conservative social values for granted and imaged a world that was self-satisfied and never changing. The muckrakers at the turn of the century didn't write that kind of fiction.

They Had Issues

While they do not present them as vociferously as they do in their nonfiction or their fiction overtly targeted at the Big Boys and the Big Issues, nonetheless a number of writers at the turn of the century made clear in their detective fiction where their sympathies lay and what the broad outlines of their social agendas were. Take the lobbying that went on before the adoption of pure food and drug legislation. Reflective of the interest and interests that led to the Harrison Narcotics Act of 1914 (a measure that made cocaine and heroin controlled substances, available only by prescription), a lot of period stories deal in one way or another with cocaine, morphine, opium, or heroin, either in brief allusions or as factors contributing to a character's criminal actions. Arthur B. Reeve, for one, used drugs repeatedly either in the background or the foreground of his Craig Kennedy stories. On the pure food side, Samuel Hopkins Adams was very much in the vanguard of lobbying, and Adams, as one might expect, uses the issues associated with the pure food and drug movement by bringing in corrupted meat and the Canned Meat Trust in "The Red Dot":

> "Ah," he commented, "the Canned Meat Trust. What have you been doing with them?"
> "Sold them a preparation of my invention for deodorizing certain by-products used for manufacturing purposes. Several months ago I found they were using it on canned meats that had gone bad, and selling the stuff" [*Average Jones* 42].

Adams also briefly looks at the drug side of pure food and drugs with the pathetic patent medicine millionaire in ""Open Trail" who must turn to Average Jones to rescue and rehabilitate his wayward son. Gelett Burgess in "The Heir to Soothoid" from *The Master of Mysteries* also gives readers a retrospective look behind the scenes at the cynicism of quack medicine and the evils of its advertising:

> "Biggest fake on earth," said the colonel, "and the most remunerative. My old uncle invented it, you know. Conceived the brilliantly vile idea of doping ordinary chicle with a tincture of opium and making chewing gum of it. 'It soothes the nerves,'—I should say it did! 'Children cry for it,' and all that sort of thing! It's monstrous, of course. It ought to be suppressed by law, and it's only a question of time when this pure-food agitation will knock it out of business. It's a crime against civilization..." 329

Another one of the Progressive Era's signal concerns was the treatment of children. The National Child Labor Committee, organized in 1904 pioneered the techniques of mass political action, including investigations by experts, the widespread use of photography to dramatize the poor conditions of children at work, pamphlets, leaflets, and mass mailings to reach the public, and sophisticated lobbying. Along with discussion about the police and about crime and the nature versus nurture debate, welfare of children is one of the other important social issues interwoven in Ottolengui's *The Crime of the Century*. In that novel Leroy Mitchel, millionaire newspaper owner, philanthropist, and amateur detective, notices a newspaper headline—BRUTAL TREATMENT OF A CHILD—and spends part of the rest of the book seeking to promote an abandoned child's health and security. The health and welfare of the poor became an issue in other detective novels as well. The subject of Settlement Houses (a movement begun by Jane Adams in 1889 that included advocating for and helping immigrants adjust to life in the United States) enters incidentally in McFarlane's *Behind the Bolted Door* with a red herring about eager young people soliciting a philanthropist's contribution to such an institution. Aiding the poor and downtrodden, however sometimes is a struggle of almost biblical proportions, as in the physician hero's exertions described in Adams' *The Flying Death*:

> There came a week of terrible heat when the tenements vented forth their half-naked sufferers nightly upon the smoking asphalt, and the Angel of Death smote his daily hundreds with a sword of flame. Dick Colton fought for the lives of his people... [4].

What this kind of concern also amounts to in some of the detective fiction at the turn of the century is an occasional flash of consciousness about the difference between the rich and the poor. Most often it occurs in books about underworld characters, characters, after all, who are pretty directly descended from Robin Hood. There's a contrast between the rich and poor in the juxtaposition of Jimmy Dale's alternate identities as the suave clubman and the down and out doper Larry the Bat in *The Adventures of Jimmy Dale*. Anderson's rogue hero Godahl, too, is aware of the social and moral influence of money:

> Godahl, swinging his cane with a merry lift, picked his way up the crooked street under the Elevated to Wall Street. To the east the Street was lined with grimy warehouses; to the west it was lined with marble. To the west was the heart of gold. Godahl turned west. Every window concealed a nest of aristocratic pirates plotting and scheming for more gold. In the street the hoi polloi were running errands for them, enviously cognizant of the silk hats and limousines of their employers. Gold bought everything with invisible lines of force radiating on all sides [*Adventures of the Infallible Godahl* 164–5].

The entire issue is the focus of Nelson Lloyd's *The Robberies Ltd* (1906) where the author creates an organization of suave, sophisticated, efficient robbers that believes that materialism is the root of society's ills and the root also of idleness. They believe that both should be displaced by an active appreciation for ideas, study, and art.

Indeed there's a minor theme in the fiction that declares that money not only corrupts but also undermines the most basic individual right—the right of the law's protection:

> Legal processes," interrupted George, "operate chiefly against the poor and the innocent. Indeed, the law is anything rather than the poor man's friend" [*The Mystery of June 13th* 139].

Demonstrating the netherworld of statute law that further disinherits the meek from money, power, or influence, became the principal object of Melville Davisson Post in collections like *The Strange Schemes of Randolph Mason* (1896). In that collection of short stories as well as its successor, *The Man of Last Resort, or The Clients of Randolph Mason* (1897) Post not only flays capitalists and cartels—there is the magnate of "the shoe trust" in "The Plungers of Manhattan"—but uses as an underlying thesis the notion that the law does nothing to protect the individual. Here Post begins with the dark side of Blackstone's *Commentaries*:

> The machinery of criminal jurisprudence cannot be used for the purposes of redressing civil wrong, the distinction being that, by a fiction of law, crimes are wrongs against the State, and in order to be a crime the offense must be one of those wrongs described by the law as being against the peace and dignity of the State. If, on the other hand, the act be simply a wrong to the citizen and not of the class described as being offenses against the State, it is no crime, no matter how injurious it may be or how wrongful to the individual ["Woodford's Partner" 141–142].

And he winds up with the conclusion that justice for individuals is chimerical. Josiah Flynt Walton and Alfred Hodder's *The Powers that Prey* documents the abuse of the law from another angle, and one of the achievements of Luther Trant was to use psychology to even the judicial playing field between the rich and the poor:

> "But it's some advance, isn't it Rentland," he asked, "not to have to try such poor devils alone, but, at last, with the man who makes the millions and pays them the pennies—the man higher up?" [*American Rivals of Sherlock Holmes* 168].

Building upon the inequity of the law, there is a sub-set of books about shyster lawyers, such as the one with the longest title is *The Confessions of Artemas Quibble: Being the ingenious and unvarnished history of Artemus Quibble, Esquire, One-Time Practitioner in the New York Criminal Courts, Together With An Account of the Diverse Wiles, Tricks, Sophistries, Technicalities, and Sundry Artifices of Himself and Others of the Fraternity, Commonly Yclept "Shysters: OR "Shyster Lawyers," as Edited By Arthur Train Formerly Assistant District Attorney New York County.* But lawyers have always been easy targets for critics and satirists. Businessmen weren't such common targets in a society that set so much store on ambition and success. But they commonly assumed the role of the unsavory character or even the villain in turn of the century detective fiction. Thus an embezzling bank president is behind all of the bumps in the night in Mary Roberts Rinehart's *The Circular Staircase* (1908) and a coven of bankers intends to steal the heroine's fortune in Burns and Ostrander's *The Crevice*.

Thus economics and politics were more frequent and arguably more important subjects than the health and welfare commentary that turn of the century writers brought into their works. Most specifically, there was Ida Tarbell's target, the Standard Oil Company. In *The Mystery of June 13th* Melvin L. Severy has a lot to say about it and about John D. Rockefeller. First there is the overview:

> The world's idea of a business man today is John D. Rockefeller, but there is a greater one coming. Mark the trend of affairs. The Standard Oil is getting the iron clutch on everything. Light, heat, transportation, food, banks, trust companies, insurance companies, public utilities; they are all in its hands. It controls mines and railroads; the legislatures and the colleges; the bureau of statistics and the press; the courts and the central government. It poisons the child in the primary school with little, sugar-coated pellets marked "patriotism" and attaining to Caligula's wish, clutches its fingers around the one throat of humanity.... I tell you, Standard Oil is winding itself, like a huge python, about the waist of the human race, and when it gets ready for the final squeeze there'll not be a whole bone left [53].

And then there is the perverse personal application of Ida Tarbell's *History of the Standard Oil Company*:

> I fancy what's good enough for John D. is good enough for us. Now, the Standard Oil has built up such a power that it is today able to challenge our most fundamental democratic institutions. Standard Oil is the quickest known solvent for the ink of our National Constitution, and the best legislative lubricant yet invented. The Standard Oil history is my mercantile bible, and John D. Rockefeller is my prophet [154].

Complaints about corporations in the detective fiction of the period fall into two categories: production and promotion of adulterated and dangerous products and restraint of trade. And so readers found detective stories like those cited above that focused on impure, inefficacious, and dangerous food and drugs. Into the latter category fall all of the stories that concentrate on monopolistic practices—on trust and implicit need for the kind of trust busting that became one of Teddy Roosevelt's issues. All of the Scientific Sprague stories, for instance, concern the Eastern Conglomerate's attempts to gain control of the Nevada Short Line Railroad's routes and rights of way—the same general topic that Lynde took up in *The Grafters* and that lies behind the murder in *The Millbank Case*. *The Further Adventures of Quincy Adams Sawyer and Mason Corner Folks*, too, concerns the evil practices of the railroads. And one of the most commented upon evil practices of the railroads and other corporations was manipulation of the stock market. This is one of the central motifs in all of Charles Stringer's books. In *The Wire Tappers* high finance and bunco fall into the same category:

"Yes, they call it high finance. But it's about as legitimate on the whole as the pea and thimble game I used to watch in up at the county fairs in Canada. In other words, Frank, when we carry on in our particular line of business cleanly and decently, we are a hanged sight more honest than those Exchange manipulators" [168–9].

Malignant forces coerce Stringer's heroes into tapping telegraph wires in order to gain unfair advantage in the market—as they do in *The Wire Tappers* with respect to news affecting the market for cotton futures.

More heinous than monopolistic practices and their attendant market manipulations was graft—the buying and selling of politicians to serve the needs of special interests rather than the needs of the public. Judging from the detective fiction of the turn of the century, there was a lot of that going on. Period stories that center on political corruption are relatively plentiful. In *The Confessions of a Detective*, Lewis' narrator both presents chapter and verse on police corruption but also maintains that the cops aren't alone and that graft is universal:

> Graft? You want me to give you a sort of graft-map, do you? There wouldn't be room on Manhattan Island to draw one. There's no limit to graft; it's everywhere.... Every department—Street, Dock, Water, Building, Park, Health, Lighting, each has its line of graft [72–3].

But more often focus concentrates on the lack of regulation and corrupt legislatures. In *The Further Adventures of Quincy Adams Sawyer* it's the railroads who call the tune in spite of an honest governor's best efforts

> The private secretary laid some papers on the governor's desk. The first one that he examined conferred certain valuable privileges, in perpetuity, upon a corporation without requiring any compensation for the franchise. The property thus alienated from public use had been paid for by the people's money
> ...
> "Send for Senator Dowling. I must see him immediately."
> His Excellency thought, "how can the people's so-called representatives give away the property of the people so indiscriminately? It would not do to mention it without proof, but I am convinced that all such public robberies are for private gain."
> ...
> "How will prices be regulated?" was the Governor's query.
> "As they have always been," replied the Senator brusquely. "Supply and demand–"
> "And by combinations called trusts," added the Governor.
> [16–17]

And in Adams' "The One Best Bet" the gambling interests have bought their own legislature:

> "The sport of kings—maintained on the spoils of clerks," retorted Average

Jones. "'To improve the breed of horses,' if you please! To make thieves of men and harlots of women, because Carroll Morrison must have his gambling game dividends! And now he has our 'representative' legislature working for him to that honorable end!" [2].

It's not only corporations and legislative bodies that have been tainted by corruption. Whole areas of the country are tarred with the brush of graft. Thus in *Scientific Sprague* we get this assessment of a western community:

That Mesquite project is another of the grafts that are continually giving the country a black eye, Jack. It's 'bunk,' pure and simple. Everybody who has ever been in the Mesquite knows that you couldn't raise little white beans in that disintegrated sandstone! [199].

Indeed, reading turn of the century detective fiction sometimes portrays contemporary America in the same light as a third world country would be portrayed today—a place in which money and its resulting power dominate all facets of life from the deliberations about national policy to the wholesomeness of what is put on the dinner table. And, in fiction at least, cleaning up the mess was one of the detective's responsibilities. Thus Hornblow includes graft busting on "Never-Fail Kayton's" resume in *The Argyle Case* (1913):

He made possible the prosecution of graft scandals in New York City; he ferreted out the truth about ... frauds in Florida and Michigan; he waged a merciless war on all police corruptionists, railroad thieves, and bribe-taking legislators [38].

When Our Deep Plots Do Pall

As a consequence of a number of turn of the century writers' commitment to the general and specific objectives of the progressive movement—the muckrakers—one finds a number of period stories that revolve around civic or corporate graft and corruption. Thus Arthur B. Reeve's story "The Campaign Grafter" and his novel (or connected series of short stories) *The Ear in the Wall* both concentrate on political corruption: the former is an attempt to use a doctored photograph to disparage Wesley Travis:

... a comparatively young man a lawyer who had early made a mark in politics and had been astute enough to shake off the thralldom of the bosses before the popular uprising against them. Now he was the candidate of the Reform League for governor and a good stiff campaign he was putting up [www.classicreader.com].

And *An Ear in the Wall*, likewise deals with a reform politician bedeviled by the illegal practices of a political machine. In Adams' "The B-Flat Trombone" there's an attempt to use an infernal machine to dispose of a political enemy and, recalling that the memories of the assassination of two presidents were relatively fresh, in "One Best Bet" Average Jones saves a reform governor from being shot. Indeed, Adams' detective inherits his millions from a grafter relative with sole proviso that he live in New York for 5 years so that he will "squander his unearned and undeserved fortune, thus completing the vicious circle, and returning the millions acquired by my political activities, in a poisoned shower to the city..." (3). Burgess' political blackguards use drugs to detour an aggressive D.A. from prosecuting corrupt politicians in "The Trouble with Tulliver" episode from the *Master of Mysteries*. Balmer and McHarg introduce malevolent financial powers that persecute the hero in *The Blind Man's Eyes* (1916) and focus on corrupt and illegal business practices in "The Man Higher Up." All of the short stories that make up *Scientific Sprague* focus on the hero and his friend Maxwell (the manager of the Nevada Short Line Railroad) and their attempts to fend off the persecution of an Eastern Conglomerate. Lynde's *The Grafters* also deals with illegal practices of railroad companies. In *Counsel for the Defense* Leroy Scott makes the villain a private company that will stop at nothing to gain control of the public water works. Severy invents a villain intended to be a model of all that can be evil about business and business people. Arthur Train's McAllister exposes a stock swindle and in "McAllister's Data of Ethics" makes a small gesture in behalf of the working poor. Hugh C. Weir's "Cinderella's Slipper" turns on the murder of a senator's aide to prevent the exposure of illegal business practices.

In any number of ways muckraking came as a welcome addition to the repertoire of techniques accumulating around the developing detective story. It, in effect, was something old and something new. As something old, the detective story with its plot, characters, and theme based on muckraking was really just a new breed of sensation novel. One of the traditional problems with the sensation novel resided in the fact that it's inhospitable to male heroes: they can't be persecuted and suffering innocence and retain what the 19th century saw as the essential features of manliness. But when the much advertised power and reach of cartels, trusts, and monopolies replace Grimsby Roylott, Count Fosco, Uncle Silas, and all of the other Victorian villains, suffering their crimes and persevering in an enterprise in which many victories were pyrrhic became something that made a character, male or female, into a hero. The something new part of the equation was that at the turn of the 20th century a number of editors, publishers, and readers wanted journalists and journalism to advance the progressive (i.e. muckraker's) addenda. And since in life the investigative reporter acted as a detective in bringing to light corporate and political felonies, fiction about heroes who did the same became more than welcomed. But it didn't last.

So What Happened?

As appropriate as they seemed for the role, reporters never really made the grade as heroes in turn of the century detective fiction. They did pretty well playing second fiddle, acting as Watsons, but even when they occasionally do act the star turn in the story they're often not on the job—they're on vacation or on leave. The muckrakers, after all, were journalists and they knew that reporters don't work for themselves, and that their editors, at least in stereotype—even at the turn of the century—were demanding and exacting taskmasters. That meant that in the reality that the writers knew only too well, reporters who worked on deadlines had little time to hang around talking to people or following leads. If a reporter was going to be a detective hero, there needed to be some way around his or her job. Thus in *The Snare of Circumstance*, for example, Elmer Bliss leaves his job at the *New York Sphere* in order to devote himself to being a detective because he can't be a detective and do his day job too. Added to these practical difficulties, there was social stigma attached to reporters. It was similar to that attached to the police: no matter what advances had been made, neither cops nor reporters was acceptable in polite company and nobody really wanted to talk to them anyway. Part of this had to do with the old theme of scandal, but as one moves into the new century, a lot more detective fiction had to do—at least in terms of ambience—with life in the world of the affluent. And, aside from all of the high-minded talk about reporters' dedication and vocation, they were also often portrayed as spirited, lighthearted (albeit very smart) fraternity boys. They were depicted as the crowd waiting at the doorstep, waving their hands and shouting intrusive questions. And in that they were hardly the sort that the millionaire (or his wife) would turn to to solve their problems.

In regard to reporters, it is interesting to note that when muckrakers turned to detective fiction, they did not turn to the reporter as the detective. In one way or another, their heroes are all free agents—Average Jones is independently wealthy, Balmer and McHard's Luther Trant has his own agency and Lynde's Scientific Sprague seems to be on perpetual vacation from his job with the federal government. Harvey O'Higgins's case may be illustrative. O'Higgins was a progressive writer who had paired up with reformer Ben B. Lindsey to write *The Beast* (1910). In the mid teens he wrote a series of a Horatio Alger–style boy detective stories collected as *The Adventures of Detective Barney* (1915). After the War he created a second detective hero, a lawyer turned private detective, who appeared in *Detective Duff Unravels It* (1929). The first series has little in the way of social agenda and seems emphasize entertainment. The second collection of short stories regained some of the old progressive zeal—most of the stories feature Duff in contact with the rich as villains with the hero relying on psychology and demonstrating that wicked acts generally boil down to a weakness fostered by one's upbringing. The point here, perhaps, is both that O'Higgins chose not to feature a writer—a reporter or journalist—as his detective either before or after the war, that his post war stories use a more professional detective hero, and that whatever social comment exists in the series is far more diluted than was the muckrakers' norm in their heyday.

This seems to reflect an opinion like the one voiced at the turn of the century by Tammany Hall's Boss Crocker who is reputed to have said "Our people could not stand the rotten police corruption. They'll be back at the next election: they can't stand reform either." The same thing happened on a more elevated political level. In the 1890s when he was a New York City police commissioner after the Lexow revelations broke, Theodore Roosevelt was an active and articulate reformer, an ally of Jacob Riis and other investigative journalists. But in 1906 when David Graham Phillips wrote "The Treason of the Senate" for *Cosmopolitan* then President Roosevelt believed that there could be too much of a good thing. He took a character's name from Bunyan's *Pilgrim's Progress* and applied it to journalists who asked too many questions: "muckrakers." Asking those questions went out of style. And so did the issue-related detective story. Symbolic of that change, *McClure's Magazine* went out of business and sold its allied publishing house. But before the publishing house went out of business it ran the contest for detective story writers that marked the beginning of the golden age of the detective story in the U.S. The winning novel written by two cousins had no social comment but plenty of appeal to those who liked to solve puzzles and play games. It was Ellery Queen's *The Roman Hat Mystery*.

7

The Private Eye

The private detective as hero. It was a natural and obvious move. After all, there was the gallopingly popular model of Sherlock Holmes in fiction—he was a private investigator, sort of—and there was also Allan Pinkerton who told the reading public how good he and his agents were. It all sounded easy and obvious. But it wasn't, quite.

THE EYE OPENS

Like police, private detectives don't have a very long history. They were a French invention. Eugene Francois Vidocq, whose memoirs had something to do with Poe's creation of the detective story, invented the profession after his politics got him kicked out of his job as the first chief of the Paris *Brigade de Sureté* (Brigade of Security). Out of work, he offered the same services he provided as a police detective to the public for a fee when he established the original private detective agency, *Bureau de Renseignements* (Office of Intelligence) in 1832. Living amid turbulent and unstable social conditions, as the first private detective, Vidocq possessed qualities that would become forever identified with private eyes: he was a reformed felon, an ex-policeman, a skilled thief taker, and a clever, tireless self-promoter who always landed on his feet. Other than the felon part, he sounded a bit like Allan Pinkerton.

At the beginning of the 19th century, as in Britain, what law enforcement there was in the United States rested on antique institutions created to meet the needs of a feudal, agrarian culture. There were elected constables and the allegedly volunteer community members of the watch. Readers of Shakespeare know that even in the sixteenth century both offices were filled with well-meaning, ineffectual mental defectives who were more often wrong than right. And if this kind of peace keeping and law enforcement didn't work well in 16th century England, neither the institution of the constable nor that of the watch had much of a chance of preventing or detecting crime in the U.S. with its tangle of political jurisdictions, ethnic and racial tensions, burgeoning cities, readily available firearms, and constitutional commitment to privacy, and individual rights. Indeed, it was the multiplying examples of the inefficiency and corruption of the system of elected constables that moved the country's major cities to create police forces in the middle of the 19th century. In almost every case, however, those police forces were manifestly inadequate to serve and protect the citizens of their cities—the original Chicago "day police," for example, consisted of only nine officers. Even as the new police forces were being put in place, entrepreneurs, often ex-constables, set themselves up as private investigators. In 1845 Gil Hayes set up shop as a private detective in New York, and others offered their services as detectives in cities across the nation—private detective offices opened in St. Louis in 1846, Baltimore in 1847, and Philadelphia in 1848.

WE NEVER SLEEP

But all of this served as prelude to Allan Pinkerton's arrival on the scene.

> In his position as part of the municipal police force of Chicago Mr. Pinkerton saw the evil of political influences in the thwarting, detection, and punishment of criminals. He conceived the idea of an independent organization, free from these influences, and, with Edward L. Rucker, an attorney of Chicago, established in 1852 "Pinkerton's Detective Agency" [Obituary, *New York Times*, July 2, 1884].

Over the years Pinkerton prospered. He and his agents saved President Lincoln from assassination when he first traveled to Washington, solved the Adams Express Company robbery, rooted out the Molly McGuires, and chased down Butch Cassidy and the Sundance Kid. Indeed, the Pinkertons had a hand in a lot of the 19th century's most well-known criminal cases. Of course it didn't hurt his initial prosperity that the President of the United States was, like Allan Pinkerton, a Republican from Illinois. And it also didn't hurt that Pinkerton had a flair for self-promotion—from the creation of the unblinking eye, "We Never Sleep," company logo to the series of ghost written novels about the exploits of Pinkerton and his agents like *The Expressman and the Detective*. Added to all of this, Pinkerton professed to operate according to a set of business ethics, many of which ran counter to the practices of the police and other private detectives. Two of Pinkerton's rules would echo through thousands of private eye novels in years to come: 1) the agency would not take cases on speculation but charged a daily rate, plus expenses, for its services, and 2) the agency would not accept divorce cases. Indeed it was as much Pinkerton's success as the inefficiency and corruption of contemporary police forces that made the private detective a household word at the turn of the twentieth century. And all of this, together with a dramatic increase in both wealth and crime, violent and otherwise, and the creation and success of dime novel detective stories after the Civil War, led to what amounted to a glut of private detective agencies and private detectives. Few important court cases from the mid 19th century onward proceeded without the testimony of private detectives. And wanting dependable police forces, private detective agencies routinely provided security for merchants—from 1894 to 1909, for example, members of the American Bankers' Association were protected by Pinkertons, as were the Jewelers Protective Union and Jewelers Security Alliance: they had signs in their windows announcing this. The Pinkertons even provided their services to the Barnum and Bailey Circus. In fact, the security of President-elect Cleveland was supplied by private detectives hired by a group of his friends. In many ways, then, law enforcement and public safety at the turn of the century depended on the services of private detectives.

Sherlock Holmes They Were Not

There is plenty of contemporary evidence to demonstrate that from the mid-19th century onward people turned to private detectives and not the police to take care of both criminal matters and to assist with personal and social issues. The latter was more curse than blessing, because becoming engaged with people's personal lives was one of several growing stains on private detectives as a profession. Becoming involved in personal problems has always been the bane of any and every law enforcement agency. That private detectives commonly became involved in helping to sort out personal and social challenges is reflected in the fact that newspapers of the day regularly carried stories about private detectives' roles in equivocal and difficult social and domestic situations that were issues more of civil than of criminal law. A lot of these news stories were accounts of actions attendant upon divorce, like the piece appearing in *The New York Times* on January 30, 1874:

> James McDermott, editor of the *Brooklyn Sunday Express*, yesterday evening attempted to shoot Patrick Byrnes, a private detective whom he encountered in a Bowery drinking saloon. The feud between the two men has been of long standing. It would appear that a divorce suit was instituted against McDermott

by his wife, on the ground of adultery. Byrnes was employed by the wife's relatives to "work up" the case against McDermott.

In addition to divorce cases, private detectives were also called upon to deal with public indecency like the arrest of the captain of one of the Staten Island ferries for "continually insulting respectable ladies in the neighborhood" (*New York Times*, December 8, 1880). Private investigators also routinely carried out what are now known as background checks on prospective and even incumbent employees. In fact this practice motivated a protest in the *New York Times* (May 19, 1869) that examined and condemned this kind of invasion of privacy ("OUR SPECIAL SPIES The Private Detective System and Its Abuses. How Employees are 'Tested' —Young Men Living Above Their Means 'Shadowed' Day and Night— Inefficient and Irresponsible Men Employed as 'Shadows'"). Another article ("The Spy in Social Life" September 30, 1880) decried the practice of fathers hiring private investigators to shadow and report on the character and activities of prospective sons in law. These were not nice things for anybody involved, and became less and less nice when one of the parties was paid to pry into someone else's private life.

This kind of thing led to bad enough press for private detectives at the turn of the century, but worse things about their common practices also hit the papers. Private detectives routinely used kidnapping as a method that simplified investigations and eliminated the need for the process and delays of legal extradition:

> The alleged kidnapping affair in Jersey City is a little mysterious. So far as the facts are known, it appears that three private detectives from PINKERTON'S agency went on Tuesday afternoon to Bowe's Hotel, in that place, and without showing any warrant seized upon the proprietor and attempted to carry him off to this City [*New York Times* November 14, 1873].

Allied with kidnapping, one finds regular accounts of private detectives breaking and entering and, of course, committing fraud in their pursuit of their quarry, whether that quarries was a criminal or simply a potential witness at a trial. These acts were commonly winked at by the police and the courts, but other acts couldn't so easily be ignored. Reports of arrests of men claiming to be private detectives for bribery, extortion, perjury, reward splitting (splitting the reward for return of stolen goods with the thieves), and witness tampering were common in the press of the day: But what got private detectives the most bad publicity at the turn of the century was strike breaking. Pinkerton agents' involvement with the bloodshed in the 1892 strike at Andrew Carnegie's Homestead steel plant ended up as the subject of hearings before the U.S. Senate in 1893; and throughout the period other private detective agencies got into periodic trouble (with the press and the unions at least) for brutal strike breaking and union busting activities.

Even the best of private detective agencies at the turn of the century occasionally did some illegal things. But there were a lot of private detectives around, and some who did more than occasional illegal things. For most of the 19th century all it took to be a private detective was getting cards printed up, running an ad in the newspaper and simply saying you were a private detective. Across the country, beginning in the 1890s, self-proclaimed private investigators caused enough problems to catch the attention of state and local governments. And that attention led to licensing laws. Thus, in 1898 assemblyman McLaughlin introduced a bill into the New York General Assembly

> ... forbidding the hiring of private detectives unless such detectives shall have been licensed by the Chief of Police of the city, town, or village in which such detectives are located and forbidding persons who have not been residents of the State for one year to act as such detectives. The bill provides that a license fee of $200 per year shall be charged, and that no private detective shall receive more than $4 a day for his services [*New York Times* March 16, 1898].

With California requiring licensing in 1915, by the time of World War I, bills like the New York bill had been introduced and passed by state legislatures across the nation. This, however, did not entirely solve the problem of dishonest or incompetent people passing themselves off as private detectives. Even after the passage of licensing legislation, New York had to carry out a protracted campaign against unlicensed detectives. In 1899 the legislature granted the Controller $3,000 per year to hire agents to track down unlicensed detectives. These agents answered newspaper ads for detectives, as they did in the case of William K. Spengler:

> ... who earns $70 a week in the office of a large corporation, decided that he might make a little more money by working at night as a private detective. So he bought a brand new nickel badge and a card from a private detective agency, certifying that he was employed as one of its detectives, and inserted an advertisement in an evening paper announcing that he would do private detective work.... Then he sat down in his parlor to wait for his first customer.
> The customer came. He was a man who wanted detective work in a divorce case. Spengler, according to this customer, said that divorce detection was his specialty, and that $3 a day was his charge. The customer introduced himself as State Detective Frank Whitfield of the State Controller's Office ... saying that the agency that issued the card was itself unlicensed to do business and arrested Spengler on a charge of posing as a private detective without a license [*New York Times* May 23, 1911].

Spengler wasn't alone. The Controller's men continued to run sting operations, like the one that resulted in the *Times'* headline "ARREST 8 SLEUTHS IN A BIG CRUSADE. State Officials Enforcing Law Requiring Private Detectives to be Licensed. 100 OF THEM ARE TRAPPED" (*New York Times*, September 5, 1915).

The scene with respect to private detectives when the American public first met Sherlock Holmes was, at best, a confused one. On one hand they were portrayed (and some portrayed themselves) as heroes. Given the limitations and inefficiency of turn of the century police forces, it was very often private detectives who got their man or woman or who solved the case. It was private detectives who understood and mastered the new developments in law enforcement technology. Thus it was private investigator Mary Holland, for example, who became the nation's first fingerprint instructor and presented expert testimony at the first trial (People v. Jennings) that turned on fingerprint evidence. The best of them were lionized, as was William Burns when he went to England and with his reminiscences inspired Arthur Conan Doyle to write *The Valley of Fear.* On the other hand they were fired ex-policemen, criminals, predators, bullies, informants, spies. They participated in and represented a business enterprise that capitalized upon the basest and sleaziest of personal and social relationships. And these two perspectives on the private detective received equal coverage in the daily press at the turn of the century.

FICTION IS STRANGER THAN TRUTH

Before they could sort out whether the private detective was going to be a hero or a villain, writers who took to the detective story at the turn of the century felt the obligation to distance themselves from some of the false or the romantic conceptions of the profession fostered by earlier literature, distance themselves so that they could substitute their own romantic concepts for those of the dime and sensation novels. These efforts aimed at several attributes fostered in older fiction about detectives. The first was that disguise was a usual and normal part of the detective business. Leroy Mitchell, one of Ottolengui's detectives in *Crime of the Century,* says, "I do not admire this masquerading. It is too theatrical. It savors too much of the dime-novel detective" (115). There's a more detailed discussion in *Policeman Flynn* (along with an illustration) when Elliott Flower introduces a character who

> ... could not be persuaded that the life of a detective was not one long romance filled with disguises, thrilling adventures and fabulous rewards. He would make himself up in the most wonderful and outlandish way, and then

drop in on Flynn to ask if that would not fool the cleverest 'crook.' Later he amused himself by shadowing people in the neighborhood, and writing out reports of his 'work,' which he submitted to Flynn for approval or criticism [260].

In addition to shattering the illusion about disguises and thereby asserting that detective work differed radically from childhood dress-up play, writers also sought to dispel the notion that the detective's work—or the detective story itself—had any connection with the satisfactions of the traditional mystery or romance. It's one of the first things that O'Higgins deflates when he introduces his boy detective, Barney, who goes on his job interview under

> … the influence of these Nick Carter stories that had brought him now … in his Sunday best, with his hair brushed and his shoes polished, as guiltily excited as a truant, having lied to his mother and absented himself from his work in the wild hope of getting employment—confidential and mysterious employment—in the office of the great Babbing [www.gaslight.mtroyal.ca/].

Nowhere is the opposition of romantic illusions with the mundane reality of the detective's work and of the detective's story itself made more graphic than in Arthur Stringer's *The Shadow*:

> Then began the real detective work about which, Blake knew, newspaper stories were seldom written. This work involved a laborious and monotonous examination of hotel registers, a canvassing of ticket agencies and cab stands and transfer companies. It was anything but story-book sleuthing. It was a dispiriting tread-mill round… [86].

And along with this point made about routine, undermining the point about the detective's omniscience would become another familiar theme. This begins with the generic statement that "You and I can hardly be a shrewd as the detectives of romance" (*Final Proof* 2). And it extends to many of the allusions about Sherlock Holmes that contemporary writers put into their stories.

GIVE THEM THE BUSINESS

One of the ways in which a number of turn of the century writers tinged their private detectives with reality was to introduce detection not simply as a personal necessity or a recreation but as a business—as well as a calling. To make this point, the private detective agency makes a prominent appearance in a number of period works. Thus there's the Babbing Bureau from O'Higgins' Barney stories, Keen and Company from Robert Chambers' *Tracer of Lost Persons*, Coleman's International Inquiry Bureau from Alfred Dorrington's *The Radium Terrors*, Watkins Detective Agency from Kauffman's *Miss Frances Baird Detective*, the Isburn Agency in *The Further Adventures of Quincy Adams Sawyer and Mason Corner Folks*; the Asche Kayton Agency in Hornblow's *The Argyle Case* (1913), and the Blaine Agency with its "girl spies" in *The Crevice*, by detective William J. Burns and Isabel Ostrander (1915). Ottolengui's Mr. Barnes has his own agency with offices and operatives, Anna Katharine Green's Violet Strange works for an unnamed private detective agency, and Madelyn Mack runs her own shop in Hugh C. Weir's stories.

Readers often get a glance inside the offices of these enterprises, and what they find is not the miscellaneous accoutrements of the cozy Baker Street apartment, but those of a commercial enterprise. *A Husband by Proxy* (1909), for example, begins with "criminologist" Jerold Garrison admiring his Spartan new office:

> He was almost penniless, with his office rent, his licenses, and other expenses paid, but he shook his fist at the city, in sheer good nature and confidence in his strength... [5].

Just as Garrison's office is strewn with technical books, like "A Treatise on Poisons," instead of a room filled with wigs, revolvers, manacles, costumes, chemical apparatus, and wanted posters, O'Higgins' Barney finds that

> The office was as commonplace and average.... There was nothing on the walls but some framed photographs of office groups. There was no furniture but the desk and chairs. There was nothing on the desk but telephone instruments, pens and ink, paper-weights, and some shallow wire baskets that were filled with letters, telegrams, and typewritten reports. There was, in fact, nothing interesting in the room... [www.gaslight.mtroyal.ca/].

In *The Tracer of Lost Persons*, Chambers adds a waiting room crammed with prospective clients, and the hurley burley of the busy corporate office:

> Through an open door he saw a dozen young women garbed in black, with white cuffs and collars, all rattling away steadily at typewriters. Every now and then from some hidden office, a bell rang decisively, and one of the girls would rise from her machine and pass out of sight to obey the summons [15].

In Arthur Hornblow's novelization of Harriet Gord and Harvey O'Higgins' play, *The Argyle Case* (1913), readers are told that

> Practical, up-to-date methods have shattered many old-time traditions and brought about astonishing modifications in the manner of doing business in all kinds of industrial enterprises; but nowhere has the change been more apparent than in the personality and working system of the modern detective. The days of Lecoq, Gaboriau, Gorin, and other world-famous thief-catchers

are past. No longer does the sleuth resort to the clumsy expedient of dying his hair, wearing fierce-looking whickers, and assuming other elaborate disguises in order to shadow an unsuspecting quarry. All the picturesqueness, all the romance of the detective business has gone forever. The successful detective of today is essentially a shrewd, hard-headed business man. His success is the result of sound judgment, hard work, and, above all, a special aptitude for his calling. In investigating criminal cases he uses the same systematic, practical, common-sense methods as are found in the management of any important commercial house [36].

Detective agencies, moreover, aren't just busy offices, at their best they are machines:

To Barney, watching, it became as bewildering as the smoothly intricate activity of a complicated machine. Babbing dictated letters in a leisurely undertone that was continually intermitted for telephone calls, the arrival of opened telegrams, corroboratory references to filed records, consultations with Archibald, directions to operatives, and above and around and under it all an interested reciprocation of talk with Snider. "Hello? Yes. Where are you? Have you got the goods on him? I see. Who's with you? Can you get in to see me? I'll relieve you with Corcoran. Three-thirty this afternoon."... "Take this. William P. Sarrow, and so forth. Dear Sir. Yours of the fifteenth. Regret that I'm unable to meet you and so forth. Previous engagements in Chicago on that date. Suggest the twenty-seventh."... "Wire that fellow to stop sending me telegrams or he'll queer the whole plant. Sign it Adam Hansen."... "Yes, Chal? Did he bite?" [O'Higgins, www.gaslight.mtroyal.ca/].

O'Higgins' detective agency—and a lot of others—depends on information and upon employees who are as faceless as they are numerous. While they share anonymity, fictional agencies have two kinds of putative employees, the office staff and the field staff. With regard to the latter, in *The Snare of Circumstance* the hero hops in a cab and rushes off to hire a brace of shadowers off the shelf on the spur of the moment:

"Come, let us be off to an agency and get men to work at once. I'm willing to risk the cost of the men for a few weeks on the chances of getting him ultimately..."
We entered the vehicle and drove to the Pingree Detective Agency, where we engaged men who were detailed for immediate duty [225].

And, of course, there's a boss. But the bosses are more than bosses. Most of the proprietors of fictional detective agencies are middle aged (at least), solid, responsible, wise businessmen. O'Higgins' Babbing, for example, is "a brisk-looking, clean-shaven, little fat man—rather a 'dude' to Barney—with a mild expression and vague eyes" (www.gaslight.mtroyal. ca/). And they tend to be avuncular or even paternal: Babbing, for instance, serves Barney as a substitute father; Old Man Isburn leaves his agency to Mary Dana and Quincy Adams Sawyer; and Violet Strange's employer is consistently sympathetic to her upper crust sensibilities. While the eccentric hero held some fascination for American turn of the century detective writers and produced characters like Futrelle's grumpy polymath Professor Van Dusen or Clinton Stagg's blind detective genius Thornley Colton, most of them emphasized the personal warmth, geniality, and sociability of not just minor characters but their heroes as well, characteristics, incidentally, that are often held to be a necessary adjunct to success in business. They were also qualities not prominent in turn of the century detective fiction in Britain where sophisticated reserve attended high, knightly ideals. In America, however, personal warmth, geniality, and sociability were qualities that even a genius hero could possess, Carolyn Wells, therefore, stressed her detective hero's sociability and geniality as well as his brilliance:

> Fleming Stone's personality was not at all of the taciturn, inscrutable variety. He was a large man of genial and charming manner, and possessed of a personal magnetism that seemed to invite confidence and confidences [*A Chain of Evidence* 273].

On the more normal level, Quincy Adams Sawyer's success, Pidgin lets readers know, began with his inclination to make friends: "Quincy, purely in pursuit of his own inclinations, had made friends with the police inspectors and had entered into an enthusiastic study of police matters" (*Quincy Adams Sawyer, Detective* 2). And in *The Argyle Case* Hornblow makes a point of showing his infallible detective, Asche Kayton, flattering witnesses versus threatening or browbeating them. This kind of affability ramifies in several other ways as well as displaying warmth of character. It connects with the knowledge of underworld personnel, obtained through trust, that some private detectives possess, and it also connects with the numerous period detective stories in which there are assistant or companion detectives—as opposed to friend narrators like Sherlock Holmes' Watson. One of the first writers of the period committed to the detective story, Rodriguez Ottolengui, based his books on the relationship between Mitchell and Barnes, two friends with different views on methodology. There are also a number of romantically linked couple detectives, as in Burgess' *The Master of Mysteries* with Astro and Valeska Wynne or Pidgin's *The Further Adventures of Quincy Adams Sawyer and Mason Corner Folks* with Quincy and Mary Dana. Romantic couples also figure in the plots of Carey's *The Van Suyden Sapphires,* and Leroy Scott's *Counsel for the Defense.* In 1897 in *That Affair Next Door*, Anna Katharine Green paired Inspector Gryce with her new character, spinster Amelia Butterworth and readers could find middle aged, single women helping out in Wells Hastings' *The Man in the Brown Derby* and Will Irwin's *The House of Mys-*

tery, both of which pair a young searcher with a canny and ingenious older woman.

The linkage of private detectives with details and metaphors from business accomplished a number of things. First of all, it gave the fictional hero a degree of legitimacy in that it separated him or her from the free-range, cowboy style hero of the dime novel detective story and associated him or her with an enterprise like those in the news that achieved success in the detective business, like the Pinkerton or the Burns Agencies. Just as importantly the hero's connection with an agency acknowledges 1) that detection is rarely accomplished by one person but is the work of many hands, 2) that detection relies as much or more on information and routine than it does on inspiration or derring-do, and 3) that detection is work — versus the metaphors of play attached to the dime novel detective or even on a more sophisticated level attached to the detective stories of Poe and Arthur Conan Doyle. And, reflected in Green's Violet Strange stories as well as rare references to divorce investigations, the detective's work is sometimes more disturbing and distasteful than it is dangerous. The ultimate extension of this can be found in Ostrander's *At One-Thirty* in which the conflict between law and justice cause her blind detective, Damon Gaunt to quit the profession. Reflected in other places, like the passage from Stringer's *The Shadow* cited above, the detective's work is frequently mind-numbing, routine, and boring: It is worth noting that many of the offices of fictional detective agencies of the period emphasize the presence of a clerical staff (one that is almost always female) along side the field operatives. This reflects the reality that at the turn of the century large agencies like the Pinkertons had better personnel, information, and communications than any of the country's police forces. Finally the fictional detective agency with its offices and employees presents a muted, but conscious contrast to the purposefully homey atmosphere of the cozy fire and careless comfort of Sherlock Holmes's Baker Street bachelor establishment. Money, fees, remuneration, and retainers serve to make private detectives American. This happens even with characters consciously and explicitly patterned on Sherlock Holmes. Therefore, one of the first things that Carolyn Wells tells her readers about her detective, Fleming Stone, is that he's pricey:

> I knew the man [Stone] slightly, having run across him a few times in a business way, and I knew that not only were his services exceedingly high-priced, but also that he never took any case unless of great difficulty and peculiar interest [*A Chain of Evidence* 273].

PRIVATE ENTERPRISE

Certainly not all turn of the century fictional private detectives worked for a corporate employer. There are those who work for themselves. Distinctions here are not exactly simple because there are several characters who pretty much function as full time detectives but who either have day jobs tangentially related to detection or, a la Sherlock Homes, would classify themselves as consultants rather than detectives—even though as far as readers are concerned they really are private investigators. Characters like Professors Kennedy and Van Dusen, or the perpetually on leave chemist Scientific Sprague, for instance, fall into this category. There are, nonetheless, pure examples of private detectives who are in today's usage independent contractors. Adams' Average Jones, Balmer's Luther Trant, Pidgin's Quincy Adams Sawyer, Freeman's Mr. Dix, Steele's Jerold Garrison, Eldridge's Isaac Trafford, Carolyn Wells' Fleming Stone, and Isabel Ostrander's Damon Grant among others, are, as it were, owner-operators who have their own offices, deal directly with clients, gather their own information, and do their own leg work. There is also Greene's Violet Strange who is quite literally an independent contractor, hired by a private detective whenever he has a high society case. The Violet Strange stories stand out because they center on a woman detective, and their open presentation of cash payments for detective work add to their meaning and impact. In doing this, Green, to be sure, had no intention of attaching a mercenary element to private detection. Instead she used money to emphasize her hero's motivation, to stress the fact that she had a higher calling than detective work. The same kind of thing can be seen with Hanshew's hero Cleek who acts as a detective consultant to atone for his career as a master criminal. And this stress placed upon the hero's motives for being a detective becomes one of the defining features of a number of turn of the century writers.

RAISON D'ÊTRE

Indeed motive became especially important in turn of the century detective stories. Back when crime fiction was just crime fiction and not the detective story, things were simple. Back then there was only one clearcut motive to explain why individuals were connected with solving crimes. That primordial motive lay in the hero's selfless desire to promote the will of providence and assist in the triumph of justice. Nineteenth century fiction, however, added other motives. Sensation novels substituted personal emotional fulfillment, the hero's need to save someone close to him or her or to exonerate him or herself became the central motive. With Poe, there was another significant change. He added the intellectual's or the puzzler's motive and satisfaction. Thus Dupin solves crimes because in doing so he has an opportunity to exercise his logical faculties just as, Poe says, the athlete glories in the opportunity to show his strength and agility. This same justification for the hero's actions became the rage among detective story writers when readers picked up on the fact that this was also Sherlock Holmes' reason for dealing with crime and criminals. Added to the puzzler's pride, at the end of the 19th century there was also professionalism: lawyers and eventually police officers like Thomas Byrnes solved crimes not simply because they were paid to do so but because doing so supplied an opportunity to exercise and demonstrate their professional expertise. And all of it, of course, also served as justification for telling an exciting story.

One of the defining characteristics of the infant detective story at the turn of the century, then, was its interest in why detectives detected. Indeed that same interest in motive both defines American detective fiction of the period and distinguishes it from contemporary British detective fiction. This is not to say that American writers spurned the Sherlock Holmes approach. To be sure, there was plenty of fiction on both sides of the Atlantic that leaned on Conan Doyle's dependence on logic and reasoning that he borrowed from Poe to justify Sherlock Holmes' special calling. It certainly stands behind stories like Futrelle's oft-anthologized Thinking Machine story "The Problem of Cell 13" and comes across clearly in Severy's Maitland novels. It's also what the hero is getting at in *Scientific Sprague*:

> Later he had drifted into the Washington bureau as an expert [chemist]. Taking the job, as he explained, because it gave him time and frequent leisurely intervals for the pursuit of his principal hobby, which was the lifting of detective work to the plane of pure theory, treating each case as a mathematical problem to be demonstrated by logical reasoning [*Scientific Sprague* 70].

While it's pretty difficult to deny that satisfaction derives from solving knotty problems or that this was the central motivation of a class of neo-Sherlockean heroes like Fleming Stone, a number of turn of the century writers made their heroes serve other gods. Luther Trant, for example, becomes a detective because he has become an apostle of psychology:

> Why, you and I and every psychologist in every psychological laboratory in this country and abroad have been playing with the answer for years! For years we have been measuring the effect of every thought, impulse and act in the human being. Daily I have been proving, as mere laboratory experiments

to astonish a row of staring sophomores, that which—applied in courts and jails—would conclusively prove a man innocent in five minutes, or condemn him as a criminal on the evidence of his own uncontrollable reactions. And more than that, Dr. Reiland! Teach any detective what you have taught to me, and ... he can clear up half the cases that fill the jails in three days [2–3].

While in a number of his works Ottolengui inserts a playful, running debate between an amateur detective and a private investigator about logic versus leg work, crime becomes more than part of a logic puzzle in *The Crime of the Century*; it becomes an entrenched societal problem that must also concern the hero:

... I can almost believe that it is of more utility to study the causes which have made a given crime possible, than to capture and kill the criminal. We think that we have thus gotten rid of him. We have put him away; out of the world. We have ended his career. Ah! But have we? Can we be sure that his crime will not breed another crime, as a direst sequence to the one for which he is punished? And do we know whether his punishment will advance or check the tendency toward crime which he has left as a heritage to his offspring? [20].

And then, too, there is the allied impact of muck raking on the detective hero's character where exposing and punishing the corrupt politician, plutocrat, or cartel becomes part of the hero's mission and supplies a large measure of his satisfaction. This, after all, was one of the things that private detectives like Parkhurst's Charles W. Gardner did in the real world.

THE OTHER SIDE

A general distaste for private detectives hovers in the background of a lot of turn of the century fiction. Some of it rested on fears about invasion of privacy. Brander Matthews in "The Twinkling of an Eye" makes the same point about employees' privacy as made by the piece from the *New York Times* ("OUR SPECIAL SPIES The Private Detective System and Its Abuses. How Employees are 'Tested'—Young Men Living Above Their Means 'Shadowed' Day and Night—Inefficient and Irresponsible Men Employed as 'Shadows'") cited above:

These clerks have all served us faithfully for years, and I don't want to submit them to the indignity of being shadowed—that's what they call it, isn't it?—of being shadowed by some cheap hireling, who may try to distort the most innocent acts into evidence of guilt... [212].

It turns out that not all private detectives in fiction at the turn of the century were unblemished, high-minded, dedicated, intellectually agile heroes.

A few of them were just plain boobs or conformed with the slinky, slimy stereotype generated by the dark side of real private detectives. Shortly after the Sherlock Holmes stories appeared in America, some of the Great Detective's accoutrements came to symbolize detectives, so anybody with a magnifying glass, deerstalker hat, Inverness cape, and meerschaum pipe (even if those things came more from Sidney Padget than Arthur Conan Doyle) was a detective. It's something cartoonists picked up on in a flash, and it was there in the fiction as well, blatantly and obtrusively in the parodies and burlesques and more subtly in the straight fiction where it was as much attitude as appearance that made the cliché detective. What happened, then, in some fiction was that anyone who looked like a detective wasn't going to be much of a real detective. In Leroy Scott's *Counsel for the Defense*, for instance, there are two private detectives, one of whom looks like a detective:

> He's Westervelle's best and only. He thinks he's something terrible as a detective—what you might call a hyper-super-utra detective. Detective sticks out all over him—like a sort of universal mumps. He never looks except when he looks cautiously out of the corner of his eye; he walks on his tiptoes; he talks in whispers; he simply oozes mystery, Fat head!—why Stone wears his hat on a can of lard! [199–200].

And the other is the real thing:

> One reason I went to New York was to try to get a particular person—Mr. Manning.... He has six children, and is very much in love with his wife. The last thing he looks like is a detective. He might pass for a superintendent of a store, or a broker. But he's very, very competent and clever, and is always a master of himself [200].

Interestingly enough Scott bases this ideal detective character on metaphors drawn from business and the family, bringing together two distinct varieties of moral rectitude.

As in England, reactions against Sherlock Holmes' infallibility gave rise to the bumbling (or human) detective hero. The principal example of introducing this kind of character in turn of the century American fiction was Kauffman's hero in *Miss Frances Baird Detective: A Passage from Her Memoirs* (1906). That novel begins with Francis Baird being read the riot act by her boss at the detective agency:

> "You started off so well," the Chief pursued, "that I began to have high hopes for you, but this last year you have more than undone all that you did at first. You let Donald Dugan get away with a three days' start on us, and it was no fault of yours that he was nabbed at all. You were all wrong in the Durham robbery. You botched the Van Hambrugh jewel case. You were really worse than useless in the matter of old Eben Stoner's divorce" [3].

While in the end, she does win the laurels, Kauffman follows this early dose of criticism with several episodes of bumbling detective work by both Frances and her male partner on the case. As a hero, however, her motives, her conscience, and behavior are all unquestionably upright. There were other detective characters about whom that could not be said.

Moral rectitude, however, was something that fictional detectives lacked in those stories that portray private detectives gone bad. Private detectives, of course, sometimes suffered for the sins of others Some writers, especially early ones, lumped all professional detectives together and thus all vices of the police—except, perhaps, buying their jobs—attached to the private as well as the public detective. Arthur Stringer's *The Shadow* offers a unique example of a character who shares the vices attached to all detectives, public and private. There Stringer follows Jim Blake from his origins as a Milwaukee newsboy through a career that moves from strike breaker to private detective to policeman to one of New York's top police officials. As a private eye he suborns perjury, is in league with petty thieves, acts as a scab, breaks and enters, and "… did bodyguard service, … handled strike-breakers, … rounded–up freight car thieves, … was given occasional 'spot' and 'tailing work to do" (35). He thrived as a private detective and then as a policeman because "… deep in his nature was that obliquity, that adeptness at trickery, that facility in deceit, which made him the success he was" (39). But as a central character, the detective gone truly bad is an anomaly in turn of the century fiction. While Eldridge's *The Millbank Case* (1905) has a private detective who attempts to blackmail his client, he's prevented by the book's hero private detective; most fictional private eyes of the period lacked the leprous corruption of the dark side of real private investigators of Eldridge's detective gone bad—so one rarely sees a detective guilty of intimidation, brutality, indiscriminate extortion, etc. Even divorce work doesn't get a lot of extended comment when it is mentioned—which is not often. In part the absence of the real dark side of real private detection at the turn of the century derived from the fact that period fiction did not display, could not display, any real brutality or violence, one of the signature vices of detectives gone bad in the real world. Instead, when turn of the century writers wished to characterize the gray side of private detectives, they trivialized the characters and the profession. How can a detective go bad if he or she is a negligible character with less than modest intellectual capacity to begin with? In *The Snare of Circumstance*, therefore, private detective Barney Rafferts crosses the hero's path a number of times: "He was a measly cur, a discredit to his profession, but he was too small to win more than a passing contempt…" (26). Added to this generalized distaste and dismissal, comments in the fiction sometimes concentrate on the issue of honesty as in Charles Carey's *The Van Suyden Sapphires* "Now, Bender is that rara avis among detectives, an absolutely incorruptible man." (153). Wells Hastings diminishes the profession both by showing an ineffectual detective and by associating him with a less than mundane assignment:

> Don't you go wasting your money on any of those silly detectives. I had a cousin once who hired one to detect who stole her silver tea pot. And he detected around for a couple of weeks, and after he'd accused the cook, who had been with her twenty years, he got mad and sent in a bill that would have paid for a whole tea-set, and said the thief had probably melted it up [*The Man in the Brown Derby* 182].

Occasionally one also finds objections made to private detectives based on what seems now to be a naively utopian view of humankind. Thus one of the things that discredits the city private detective in *The Four Pools Mystery* is his unacceptable, ungenteel conviction that "There is just one kind of evidence that doesn't count for much in my profession, and that's a man's word" (96).

While it is not a common recognition, at least Mary Roberts Rinehart and Harvey O'Higgins do mention the necessarily problematic morality associated with private detectives and their work, work that sometimes calls upon them to perform dubiously legal or even downright illegal actions. In Rinehart's *The Man in Lower Ten* this comes in with a virtual throw away line when one of her characters makes the observation that "Jolson's a blackguard, but he's a good detective" (133). The detective, here, is alternately made a pariah for what he does and then praised because he will do what others will not stoop to do. The case is presented in a more detailed fashion in *Barney the Boy Detective* where his boss and mentor gives the apprentice detective a lecture about morality and the detective's duty:

> "Well, then"—he came forward—"as a detective, you're allowed to do a great many things that would be punished in a private individual. You're expected to swindle, and steal from, and lie to, and betray the enemies of society in any way you can, in order to defeat them and defend society. It's your duty to do it, and do it diligently. If you don't, you're as bad as the criminal. And that's the only moral law that binds you professionally.
>
> "But in your private life,"—he wagged an emphatic forefinger—"you're bound by all the moralities that bind everyone else" [www.gaslight.mtroyal .ca/].

Here the detective's duty to society requires that he possess both a public and a private set of morals, and that maintaining them in separate spheres, maintaining two separate selves is the difficult but necessary sacrifice that the good detective makes.

A WOMAN'S WORK?

Detective Babbing bases his homily to Barney on the importance of the detective's service to society. Violet Strange, however, performs the role of the detective for more personal reasons—to support her wrongly disinherited sister. But there were fictional women private detectives who went before Anna Katharine Green's hero whose motives were quite different. And there was at least one other who came later. The motives of these women detectives, in fact, were closer to those of women detectives in real life. And there were, apparently, a goodly number of them.

The role of women in late 19th century law enforcement and detection is a largely unexplored field. Contrary to the notion that until the twentieth century women served on police forces exclusively as matrons and female searchers, even a cursory examination of contemporary newspapers yields an impressive, albeit a short, list of named women police officers and private detectives before World War I. Mary Holland, mentioned above, of course, received a good bit of press in the early 1900s. And there was also Miss Fleshauer, a store detective in New York City in the 1890s; Kitty Parker and Jennie Hughes were both Pinkerton agents; Mrs. Ellen Peck, a former confidence woman, was employed as a consultant by the New York City police; Catherine R. Gilkinson was "the only woman ever licensed by the courts in this county [i.e. Pittsburg's] to operate a detective agency" (*Washington Post*, June 8, 1896); Lola Baldwin was given police powers in Portland, Oregon in 1905; Lina Cameron was "New England's Famous Woman Detective" (*Washington Post,* March 7, 1910); Alice Stebbin Wells became a police officer in Los Angeles in 1910, Mrs. Mohan (nee Keelan) was associated with the Boston Police Department; Isabella Goodwin was a 1st grade lieutenant in the New York City Police Department (*Washington Post*, August 15, 1915); Luvena Mabry was "the only female detective in the South" (*Washington Post*, December 25, 1888); Mary Owens, widow of a policeman, was given the rank of policeman in the Chicago Police Department in 1893, and there was also Lulu Parks who "… CARRIES TWO GUNS: Chicago Policewoman 'Totes' Pistols, but Where?" (*Washington Post* March 25, 1914). This list, to be sure, hardly suggests that at the turn of the century public or private law enforcement was overrun with women agents. What does seem to be true is that women of the times were early and enthusiastic supporters of professions that served and protected and many expressed the desire to take part in them. In this context, an item run under the "Quaint and Curious" column in the *New York Times* on May 1, 1885 is now neither quaint nor curious:

A Fairfield lady of small size has applied to Gov. Robie to be appointed a private detective under the new law. The lady was formerly an editorial worker on a Fairfield paper. His Excellency is a very stalwart friend of women's rights. The female detective question is now being considered by the Executive Council—*Lewiston* [Maine] *Journal*

At the opening of the new century, women became more forceful. Thus a piece in the *Washington Post* (November 16, 1911) begins with the headline "WOMEN SEEK POLICE JOBS Office of Indianapolis Mayor is Stormed by Applicants" and the flowing story goes:

The idea of appointing women detectives grew out of the supposed murder of Dr. Helene Knabe and the inability of male members of the department to find the murderer. Suggestions from a number of women that female detectives would be better equipped in such cases than males led the mayor to suggest such appointment. But the rush to the office was so great that he slipped out by a back door and told his secretary to send all inquirers to the police superintendent.

In addition to having as much or more skill than male detectives, many believed that women possessed moral authority that men lacked, authority that could be applied to police work. In 1899, therefore, when a woman was elected mayor of Beattle, Kansas, the *Washington Post* ran a piece, "TOWN RUN BY WOMEN" stating that in Beattle

A large proportion of the city employees, including the police, will be women. It is believed that an attractive but dignified policewoman would enjoy a moral authority far greater than that of a mere policeman. No Kansas man will dare become drunk and disorderly under the eye of a policewoman [May 21, 1899].

In spite of the date, however, it appears that with respect to women in law enforcement the millennium did not arrive in Kansas ... or anywhere else in the United States for that matter.

More Heat than Light

For all of their efforts in Indianapolis, as police officers, at least, women made only miniscule progress at the turn of the century. In fact, Chief Sylvester, one of the important, reform-minded police officers of the early 20th century, had to deny an international rumor in 1907 that there were women in the Washington, D.C. police department:

According to current belief in Belgium, Washington has "police women," for in a recent communication to Superintendent Sylvester, the commissioner of police of Ghent requests information concerning that class of enforcers of the law, to the end of establishing a force of fair "coppers" in his city.

As a matter of fact, although private detective agencies find use for women "spotters," none has ever graced the roster of the Washington central office [*Washington Post*, April 2, 1907].

With only a few exceptions, the press of the day regularly continued to treat women in detection or law enforcement as curiosities, jokes, examples of mental illness, or all three. Hence these headlines:

THE FEMALE DETECTIVE
HER IDENTIFICATION BY NEWPORT POLICE—SHE IS BELIEVED TO BE INSANE [*New York Times*, July 18, 1878]
    SENT TO THE WORKHOUSE
    Mrs. Abbott, the Female Detective, Supposed to Be Deranged [*Washington Post*, October 1, 1891]
    HUNTING FOR A HUSBAND
    A Woman Detective Who Surprised the Police Officers [*Washington Post*, August 22, 1897].

In spite of introducing Miss Butterworth as co-detective in *That Affair Next Door*, Anna Katharine Green, the most popular woman writer of the period, demonstrates contemporary feelings about women police when Miss Butterworth gives a less than complimentary introduction to a woman operative in that novel:

... I will introduce the report of a person better situated than myself to observe the girl during the next few days. That the person alluded to was a woman in the service of the police is evident, and as such may not meet with your approval, but her words are of interest... [220].

Nonetheless, there is plenty of evidence to show that even if they were often banned from being members of official police forces, women played a significant role in real world detection at the turn of the century. One of their first roles, in this respect, was serving as store detectives in large dry-goods/department stores. Dashiell Hammett's *Black Mask* story "The Assistant Murderer," in fact, features one such woman store detective. As with male private detectives, women in the business regularly appear in news stories about divorce trials. It is clear, moreover, that in New York (and probably other cities) the all-male detective force pretty routinely contracted women (whom they could not hire) to assist them or to undertake independent investigations: "Inspector Byrnes owes some portion of his phenomenal success as a rogue catcher to the fact that he has not hesitated to employ women whenever he could do so to advantage, although all traditions of the central office were opposed to them" (*Washington Post*, December 7, 1890). Especially in the first decade of the 20th century, women detectives became increasingly identified with investigations related to progressive causes, chasing down quack physicians, spiritualist mediums, drug dealers, and white slavers. Take this 1912 headline as an example:

GAVE HER TREATMENT BY PULLING OF TOES
  Woman Sleuth Tells How a "Back to Nature" Healer Undertook to Cure
  Her [*New York Times*, March 8, 1912].

Perhaps more insight into women in law enforcement at the time occurred in the pre war *Washington Post*. Thus while the boys in the city room snickered at Lulu Parks, in their headline (SHE CARRIES 2 GUNS Chicago Policewoman 'Totes' Pistols, but Where?"), the story that follows notes that "… her experience as a social worker had led her to become one of Chicago's policewomen" (March 7, 1914). Women, it seems, made a real difference.

THE WORLD OF FICTION

Keeping in mind that there are not that many male heroes in turn of the century fiction who are depicted as realistic private detectives—professionals who conduct investigations as a business, for money and not friendship, self-protection or self-gratification—four women private investigators is a significant number. In order of appearance, they were Francis Baird from Reginald Kauffman's *Miss Frances Baird Detective: A Passage from Her Memoirs* (1906), Hugh C. Weir's Miss Madelyn Mack from *Madelyn Mack, Detective* (1914), Anna Katharine Green's Violet Strange from *The Golden Slipper and Other Problems for Violet Vane* (1915), and Arthur B. Reeve's Clare Kendall from *The Ear in the Wall* (1916). Additionally, there was New York police detective Katherine, "Lady Kate," Maxwell, a main character in Varick Vanardy's (Frederick M. Van Rensselaer Day) *Alias the Night Wind* (1913).

In any number of ways Green's presentation of women and detection was the most conservative one of the women detective books written before World War I. Green depicts her Violet Strange as the child of wealth and social prominence who reluctantly undertakes assignments from a private detective agency in order to earn money to support her sister, disinherited because of a marriage for love and not social position. Repeatedly she finds the work repugnant. Her employer chooses Violet because her family's wealth and prominence allows her entry into the homes of the rich and famous. The majority of the short stories that Green fits into the frame narrative (i.e. answering the question of why a woman would stoop to be a detective in the first place) essentially focus on sensation novel issues, matters concerning families, wills, estates, false heirs, and missing papers.

THE REAL WORLD

These are issues ignored by Kauffman and Weir in their portraits of their fictional women private investigators. While Kauffman adds a flash of sentiment to his hero's choice of vocation ("Here you are, Frances Baird, with good looks and wit and a finishing school behind you,—not to mention a year or two abroad,—and, just because you were once a little fool, nothing ahead but—detective work!" 27), both men try to ground their heroes in reality. The first step is in the dedications to their books. Kauffman's goes

MY DEAR FRANCES—
You tell me that, as a detective, your professional ethics forbid me to call you by your real name in any printed record which I may make of your achievements. I have tried to prove to you how, in the present instance, I have so altered scenes, dates—and even a fact or two—that the result should exculpate you.... But it was all no use. You are firm. The least, then, that I can do must be the most, and so I have coined a name as like your own as may be, have given it to the real you—and have told this story *as nearly as possible in the words in which you told it to me*... [v].

Weir's comes right out and names Mary Holland, one of the best known woman detectives in the nation:

TO
MARY HOLLAND
This is your book. It is you, woman detective of real life, who suggested Madelyn. It was the stories told me from your own note-book of men's knavery that suggested these exploits of Miss Mack. None should know better than you that the riddles of fiction ever fall short of the riddles of truth [iii].

Kauffman, at least, is not naïve about the reasons why agencies employ female detectives. Frances' boss reviews the qualifications for female detectives early in the book:

You have most of the requirements of a first-rate woman detective. You are not afraid of a mouse; you're quick-witted; you know how to behave among the best sort of people; you're young, and—ahem!—you're pretty [4].

It's the same thing that the narrator says about Kate Maxwell's qualifications as a detective: "she was competent, skillful, and apparently fearless ... she possessed remarkable eyes ... [and] she was undeniably attractive and beautiful" (*Alias the Night Wind* 53). Reeve makes his Clare

Kendall try to minimize all of the things standing behind Mr. Watkins' "ahem":

> It was not only her features and eyes that showed intelligence, but her gown showed that without sacrificing neatness she had deliberately toned down the existing fashions which so admirably fitted in with her figure in order that she might not appear noticeable [www.online-literature.com].

In addition to attaching their characters to real women detectives, and declaring that good looks were a vital component to women's success in the profession, both writers emphasize that their heroes have gained wide recognition for their achievements: thus Kauffman alludes to Frances' successful cases in New York, Philadelphia, Allentown, Buffalo and even England, and Weir throughout his book shows Madelyn coming from or going to another city for another important case. Throughout *Frances Baird* Kauffman inserts passages in which his hero makes comments and gives advice about being a real detective. If Frances Baird had a mysterious and sentimental past, however, Weir grounds Madelyn Mack's early career in the place that many actual women detectives began:

> The salient points of that portion of her life, I presume, are more or less generally known—the college girl confronted suddenly with the necessity of earning her own living; the epidemic of mysterious "shop-lifting" cases chronicled in the newspaper she was studying for employment advertisements; her application to the New York department stores, that had been victimized, for a place on their detective staffs, and their curt refusal; her sudden determination to take the case as a free lance, and her remarkable success, which resulted in the conviction of the notorious Madame Bousard, which secured for Miss Mack her first postion as assistant house-detective with the famous Niegel dry-goods firm [2–3].

In addition to being a successful detective and businesswoman, Reeve made Clare Kendall a feminist:

> I knew something of her history already. She had begun on a rather difficult case for one of the large agencies and after a few years of experience had decided that there was a field for an independent woman detective who would appeal particularly to women themselves. Unaided she had fought her way to a position of keen rivalry now with the best men in the profession [*The Ear in the Wall* (www.online-literature.com)].

While all of the writers equip their female private detective heroes with motifs of modern, real world detection by making them conversant with and adept at forensic science, Kauffman's novel presages the puzzle centered whodoneit of the 1920s with its collection of suspects in the big house whereas Weir's collection of short stories, like the muckrakers, possesses a more pronounced interest in social issues—thus "Cinderella's Slipper," as noted above, is about the misdeeds of big business, and "The Purple Thumb" turns on racial issues. And police detective Kate Maxwell's semi-final action is resigning from the New York Police Department because she believes it to be corrupt and corrupted by its own culture beyond redemption.

SO WHAT HAPPENED?

In turn of the century fiction private investigators play two distinctly different roles. On one side they are new model heroes. They are middle class or upper middle class individuals who are sociable and socially acceptable, sometimes even socially prominent. They're both smart and educated. It's a point to be made that a lot of writers who create detective heroes—Samuel Hopkins Adams, Balmer and McHarg, Pidgin, Edith Buckley ("criminal detection had been the profession to which he turned naturally after leaving college" [10]), Jack Steele, and Hugh C. Weir—mention that their heroes are college graduates. Brander Matthews, who taught English at Columbia and, therefore, had more than a passing interest in education, gives more detail than most about his hero's education in "The Twinkling of an Eye:"

> He had spent four years in college, carrying off honors in mathematics, was popular with his classmates, who made him class-poet, and in his senior year he was elected president of the college photography society. He had gone to a technological institute, where he had made himself master of the theory and practice of metallurgy. After a year of travel in Europe ... he had come home to take a desk in the office [201–202].

All of these heroes understood and used all of the advances in natural, physical, and social sciences that aid in the detection of crime. They operated both within the law and according to strict, self-imposed codes of professional ethics fused to their own personal integrity. And they are associated with both the private and the public good—tracking down those guilty of committing crimes that affect both individuals and those that affect everyone's health and well-being. And then there are the other private detectives who represent the exact opposite characteristics: they are ignorant, boorish, unprincipled, despised social pariahs who do jobs that range from being dirty to being illegal.

It's very tempting to say that after World War I the two sides of the character of the private detective merged. And maybe it's even true. But if it's true, it's because a lot of things changed. One thing that changed was police science. Shortly after the war private individuals simply could not do what the new police laboratories could. And with the beginnings of police reform in the 1920s, initiated by Vollmer on the West Coast and Sylvester on the East, the boys in blue could be depended upon to do much of the information gathering and routine work hitherto the province of the detective agency—until Prohibition changed the nature of police forces, once more, for the worse. The other thing that changed the private detective was the nature of crime—or the nature of crime that became the object of fiction. Other than a few notable exceptions, like Rex Beech's *The Net* about the New Orleans Mafia and books that mention gangs of New York like the Whyos, turn of the century fiction largely ignored organized crime in favor of fiction about a domestic crime that enabled the writer to highlight the hero's problem solving prowess. While that kind of story remained, the intrusion of organized crime into fiction called for a new kind of hero, one that embodied both sides of the private detective developed at the turn of the century.

8

Women

GUESS WHO'S COMING TO DINNER?

Those women who made the mayor of Indianapolis scurry out the back door in 1911 were not alone. The formative years of the detective story in America corresponded with the beginning of and first fruits of the women's suffrage movement. Shortly after Poe invented the detective story, in 1849, Elizabeth Blackwell became a physician. Three years after Metta Victor published *The Dead Letter*, in 1869, Arabella Mansfield was granted admission to practice law in Iowa and in 1870 Ada H. Kepley became the first woman to graduate from a law school. In 1878, the year Anna Katharine Green published *The Leavenworth Case,* the women's suffrage amendment was introduced in the United States Congress. Nine years later, the year of Julian Hawthorne's *The Great Bank Robbery*, the U.S. Senate rejected the suffrage amendment by a two to one margin. At the same time that Americans were reading the Sherlock Holmes stories in their newspapers, equal rights for women became one of the headline causes of the progressive movement, and in the nineteen teens state after state gave women the right to vote—Washington in 1910, California in 1911, Illinois in 1913—leading up to the post war passage of the Nineteenth Amendment to the United States Constitution. In the mean time, Ellen Swallow Richards became the first female professional chemist; Mary Baker Eddy founded the Church of Christ, Scientist; Susanna Medora Salter was elected mayor of Kansas City; Alice Guy Blaché became the first woman film director; and Jeannette Rankin became the first woman elected to congress. Then, too, Annie Edson Taylor was the first person to go over Niagara Falls in a barrel, Harriet Quimby was the first woman to fly across the English Channel, and Nellie Bly (Elizabeth Cochran) beat Jules Verne's Phineas Fogg by traveling around the world in seventy two days. And when he visited New York in 1894, the newly famous Arthur Conan Doyle stopped by to visit with Anna Katharine Green.

Fear of Commitment

Prominent and popular women writers stand at both ends of the detective fiction of the period, Anna Katharine Green at one end and Mary Roberts Rinehart at the other. Both were prolific writers. Between 1878 and 1923 Green turned out thirty four novels as well as short fiction, a play, and a book of verse. Her first novel, *The Leavenworth Case*, became an instant best seller and made her famous overnight. The end of the pre-war period saw the publication of Rinehart's *The Circular Staircase* (1908), the beginning of a celebrated career as a mystery writer that stretched into the 1950s. The accomplishments of each are known to many devotees of mystery fiction: indeed, Green is sometimes hailed as the "mother of detective fiction." Yet for the literary world Green and Rinehart remain largely unknown, their work eclipsed by other writers of the period like Edith Wharton and Willa Cather. Even among aficionados their work is sometimes disregarded because of its sentiment and sentiments. Part of this fate derived from the characteristic fickleness of taste and circumstance, but part of the reason for Green and Rinehart's partial obscurity lies in their attachment to old forms, and in part in their fear of commitment to what was rapidly becoming the modern detective story.

While Green 1) either invented or made popular some of the devices that would become standard in the detective novels of the 1920s and 1930s — crime scene diagrams, lists of questions asked and later systematically answered, some narrative legerdemain, etc. 2) created one of the first continuing detective characters (and a police officer at that) in Mr. Gryce, and 3) in Amelia Butterworth introduced a woman as a very early subsidiary detective, she publicly distanced herself from the detective story. Thus, in an interview with *The Washington Post* in 1902 Green told the reporter that

> I wish that people would not class my novels among the list of detective stories…. My stories are not detective stories, but come under the head of criminal romances [February 23, 1902].

Here Green doesn't link herself with Poe or bound on to the Sherlock Holmes bandwagon as did so many of her contemporaries, but identifies her work with the "criminal romance," the sentimental Victorian form perpetrated by the likes of Bulwer-Lytton (in novels such as *Paul Clifford* [1830]) that would transform into the sensation novel in the hands of Collins and even Dickens. What this means is that for Green depicting the exquisite, unmerited, heroic suffering of victims on one side of her work outweighed the dispassionate play of and with logic on the other, the detective side of her work. Then, too, even though she introduced two female detectives, Amelia Butterworth and Violet Strange, nonetheless she leaves readers with the impression that it was an unseemly occupation for women, one that should be undertaken only under the strongest provocation. This Green demonstrated in the frame tale of the Violet Strange stories that informs readers that Violet has turned detective only to support her cruelly disinherited sister. The same attitude shows in Miss Butterworth's low opinion of women as police agents—even if part of that attitude comes from Green's intent is to characterize Miss Butterworth as much as the subject of her speech.

Fifty four years after Green denied that she wrote detective stories, Mary Roberts Rinehart made the same admission. In 1956 she told Harvey Briet that

> I've never written a detective story in my life.... I'm not primarily interested in clues.... I'm interested in people and their motivations. When the crime story began to be interested in people it began to grow up. My contribution was *The Circular Staircase*, which came out in 1908 ... [quoted in *The Circular Staircase*, University of California Extension, San Diego vii].

Combined with a bit of amateur and fanciful literary history, Rinehart pointed to *The Circular Staircase* as her signal contribution to the formation of the detective story. And she also maintained that that novel, rather than being a detective story was a satire of detective stories. And, sure enough, it was and it wasn't. *The Circular Staircase* is a relatively long novel full of alarms and excursions about things that keep going bump in the night in a big, rented house in the country. There is a secret room and a character or two pops up in disguise; there are other characters who harbor secrets—romantic and sinister—that they won't divulge, even if it means (as it must) perpetuating the confusion and suspense; there are couples kept apart by perverse circumstance, and there's even a guy who is supposed to be dead but who isn't. There are also a couple of official detectives who investigate this and that, but do not solve the mystery. And the mystery is solved, not by the exertions of those investigating it but by the villain's greed coupled with the natural curiosity (or nosiness) of the narrator hero, Rachael Innes, who is, like Green's Amelia Butterworth, an unmarried woman of a certain age. Here there's purposely very little that's new, except, perhaps, Miss Innes. And that's the point: Rinehart has satirized the old, quasi-gothic sensation novel variety of the mystery and not the Poe-revival detective story that began with the introduction of Sherlock Holmes to American readers in the 1890s. Unlike Rinehart, Carolyn Wells—the fourth important woman detective writer of the turn of the century—became part of the new wave of detective story writers and, as such, showed in more than one place and in more than one way her admiration for the Sherlock Holmes stories. The trouble with Wells in this chapter is that she chose to make her genius detective a man and not a woman.

OLD FASHIONED VICTIMS

It goes without saying that women play significant roles in all turn of the century fiction. Most of those roles, but not all of them, require of their actors nothing more than varying degrees of naiveté, submissiveness, and passivity. Keeping in mind that murder had not yet become one of the inevitable requirements of the detective novel, in the murder victim department, women while not quite non-starters, come in a distant second to men. While there are women murdered in the fiction of the period–there's a woman victim, for example, in "The Denton Boudoir Mystery" in *The Master of Mysteries* as well as in Green's *That Affair Next Door*—female corpses affronted the sensibilities of the period in several ways, not the least of which was the notion that women, even by accident, could become involved in crime or violence or both. On top of that, there were better roles for women to play as victims. Tapping into the favorite plot of the sensation novel, as noted above, women appear in turn of the century fiction frequently in order to have their inheritances stolen from them. Rather than being a device to simply induce outpourings of readers' sentiment, in the detective fiction of the period the stolen inheritance also provided a showcase for the writers' cleverness and inventiveness. Stealing inheritances, after all, increasingly called upon the villain to know and use tricks from the repertoire of the confidence man. And consequently, just as it did with Conan Doyle's "The Speckled Band," this called upon the writer to invent clever or outré tricks for his or her villain to use on virtuous and helpless women and for the genius detective to solve. Futrelle, for one, plots different ways to rob someone of their birthright in "The Superfluous Finger," "The Problem of the Hidden Million," "The Problem of the Cross Mark," and "The Fatal Cypher." Ingenious variations on the theme of women as persecuted heirs also occur in Adams' "The Million-Dollar Dog," Burgess' "Miss Dalrymple's Locket," and Green's Violent Strange episode "Problem VI: The House of Clocks." And there's also a not so helpless woman heir in *Husband by Proxy* (1909). Every one of them based on a crafty ruse exposed by the detective hero.

If it's not their inheritance that the villains want, it's their jewelry. Women's conspicuous display of garlands of expensive, rare, and famous jewels serves as one of the hallmarks of the period in fact and it became the basis for a lot of detective fiction. Here, too, theme combines with new opportunities for writers to show off their inventions. Losing one's jewelry either by accident, design or theft became a way, albeit a superficial way, to say something about relationships—reflecting on wives' attitudes toward husbands' attitudes toward the loss of something worth a whopping amount of money. On top of that, finding the jewels also gave the writer an opportunity to exercise his or her ingenuity in plotting new ways to play the old game of Button Button. Indeed the finding things game goes all the way back to "The Purloined Letter." Thus, to cite only a handful, ingenious jewel thefts and smart solutions stand at the center of Futrelle's "The Rosewell Tiara," Burton Stevenson's *The Mystery of the Boule Cabinet*, Arthur Train's "The Baron De Ville" in *McAllister and his Double*, Geraldine Bonner's *The Castleton Diamonds Case*, and Burgess' "Mrs. Selwyn's Emerald" in *The Master of Mysteries*.

New Ways to Make Victims

If turn of the century writers put to use traditional ways of using women as victims, they also invented new ways to achieve the same end. Most prominent of these were female characters created by the ripple effect from George DuMaurier's 1894 novel *Trilby*. This obnoxiously anti-Semitic book about the pathetic fortunes of Trilby O'Farrell and her fate as the mesmerized puppet of the repulsive Svengali became wildly popular. One manifestation of *Trilby's* popularity was the use in period detective fiction of women victims made even more helpless by artificial means. In *Through the Wall* (1909), for example, Cleveland Moffet's villain uses the ingénue's amnesia instead of mesmerism as the basis of an elaborate, Trilbyesque plot to filch her inheritance. But other writers returned to hypnotism as a means of persecuting women victims. Thus "The Chalchihuitl Stone" in *The Achievements of Luther Trant* turns on hypnotism, and Will Irwin's *The House of Mystery* recounts the rescue of a young woman hypnotized by her aunt and made to serve as an unwitting accomplice in her spiritualism con game. There were, however, even more contemporary ways than hypnotism to show women as unwitting and unwilling victims of powers that overwhelmed their conscious wills.

That's where the new interest in psychiatry and all of the manias came in. As noted above, stories based on women who obey the promptings of irrational urges occur with some frequency in turn of the century detective fiction. Kleptomania, for example, looms pretty large. It comes in as early as Ottolengui's *The Final Proof* in 1898 and virtually every short story writer had a go at writing kleptomania into a story. And the unwitting criminals in these stories are invariably women. So important it was as a women's theme that Green used the mental illness in her first Violet Strange story, "The Golden Slipper." Period writers used kleptomania because it possessed numerous advantages. It was a topic of significant serious interest and equivalent to gossip about a juicy scandal among the patricians as well, just as importantly, as permitting writers to decriminalize the detective story: Kleptomania was invariably treated as an illness to be cured rather than a crime to be punished, and because of this freedom from the need to provide either implicit or explicit punishment or censure, plots turning on kleptomania allowed some of the writers of the period to invent fanciful, even playful plots—like Butler's plot in *The Exploits of a Physician Detective* in which a monkey eats a stolen jewel. Somnambulism was also a device used to show women as victims. Perhaps because it had such a long history and carried so much explicit meaning, however, somnambulism never inspired the kind of fanciful plotting permitted by kleptomania. Sleepwalking's principal function—along with its role as a plot device—was almost always to demonstrate the superior sensitivity of women: after all, it's not Macbeth but Lady Macbeth who sleepwalks, and turn of the century somnambulism stories tend to stress the inherent nurturing qualities of women. In short, women in the fiction generally walked in their sleep to do good things or to undo bad ones. In Green's Violet Strange story "The Dreaming Lady," for instance, a sleepwalking woman hides a copy of a will because of her misguided fear that it might represent an early draft that would bequeath the estate to the wrong heirs. In the case of afflictions like kleptomania and sleepwalking, however, writers present women characters who are more to be pitied than censured—even if they do misguided or even borderline bad things. They used women's imagined susceptibility to illness to excuse or at least to mitigate whatever guilt they might have.

But there was some aberrant behavior attached primarily to women that was much more difficult to blink away or to use and still maintain the playful mood gradually developing in the genre. One type of this is in the first story, "The Hautover Case," in Butler's *The Exploits of a Physician Detective*. There the detective discovers that the murder of a five year old boy was caused by "religious mania" suffered by the women murderers. The same motive comes up, again attached to women, in Harvey O'Higgins' "The Marshall Murder" published after the War in *Detective Duff Unravels It* (1929). In spite of explaining the women's actions by labeling them as the results of mental illness, calling the motives "religious mania" if anything makes matters worse for contemporary readers because it makes the women, expected by society to be both nurturing and spiritual, perverse, monstrous, and villainous. A less disturbing variant of this theme was in stories in which women are duped and victimized by spiritualists—Samuel Gardenhire's detective, for instance, needs to expose a spiritualist and free a woman victim in *The Long Arm* (1906). The other type of disturbing element that comes into the characterization of women as victims lies in the debilitating effects and after effects of dysfunctional relationships. A particularly modern awareness of this comes into Butler's "The Lodging House Mystery" in which a woman brutalized by her fiancé bears false witness and complicates the solution to a crime committed by her partner. Here the discovery of the motive for the woman's actions evokes an entirely natural response of pity. It's not so much pity, but perhaps fear that the other extreme of dysfunctional relationships calls up. That other extreme is when romantic fantasies and possessiveness drive a character to commit a crime. To be sure, this kind of dysfunction in the real world claims far more women than men as victims. In turn of the century fiction, however, in the few stories that have this variety of sexual underpinning, it is often the woman whose romantic fantasies and possessiveness drive her to criminal acts—women like the one in Mary Wilkins' story *The Long Arm*.

THE LAND OF OPPORTUNITY

One partial sign of progress in both American culture and literature was the increased opportunities afforded women to do bad things—and the growing recognition of this fact is reflected in turn of the century detective fiction. At first there's denial (in 1892, for example, Ottolengui's detective posits that "No woman would have been clever enough to plan it all, and then carry it out so thoroughly" *An Artist in Crime*, 67) and then there's skepticism: in 1909 "Criminologist" Jerold Garrison in Steele's *Husband by Proxy* "... doubted if any clever woman, perhaps excepting the famous and infamous Lucrezia Borgia, could have fashioned a plan so utterly fiendish and cunning" (104). The next year, however, John McIntyre's detective in *Ashton-Kirk Investigator* does concede that women can be criminals—but not really good ones:

> "Some of the world's most daring and accomplished criminals have been women," he went on. "But Nature never intended women to be the bearer of burdens; there is a weakness in her soul structure somewhere; she usually sinks under the consciousness of guilt" [222].

They're not really good criminals except if they're southern and honor is concerned—that's the take on women and crime in Isabel Ostrander's *At One-Thirty* (1915):

In Kentucky, where we came from, the women are honored and protected, even when they're not loved. And, when a woman is cruelly, vilely treated by a man; when, although innocent, she is dragged through scandal, and—worse, just to get her out of the way—why, then, Sir we kill. Not murder—kill! We don't knife in the dark, or strangle, or poison, or strike down with a blow, but we shoot, and shoot straight! If my father, or my brothers, or any man kin to us had been alive, Garrett Appleton would have been in his grave long ago. But there wasn't anyone left, just us two, little Natalie, and—me [295].

It took another woman, Mary Wilkins (Freeman), however, to demonstrate a more radical change in attitudes about women and crime illustrated in the following exchange between her female narrator and Mr. Dix, the private detective in *The Long Arm* (1895):

"It would have taken a man's strength to kill with the kind of weapon that was used," I said.

"No, it would not. No great strength is required for such a blow."

"But she is a woman!"

"Crime has no sex."

"But she is a good woman—a church member. I heard her pray yesterday afternoon. It is not in character."

"It is not for you, nor for me, nor for any mortal intelligence, to know what is or is not in character," said Mr. Dix [57].

While the vast majority of writers in period fiction exempt women from active roles on either side, good or bad, of the detective story, some portrayed classes of women born bad, some drew those who had bad things thrust upon them, and some created active female characters who just chose to live the life of criminals. The second class of these fictional women, the driven ones, have made their appearance above: they are the persecuted ones, the kleptomaniacs, the mesmerized, the sleepwalkers, the victims moved to commit crimes by forces outside of their control. But there are also a select few women characters from the first category—the ones who are just bad with no real explanation given, about whom motive hunting is either fruitless or irrelevant. And they are downright scary. The most extreme case is the woman murderer under discussion in the passage cited above from *The Long Arm*. At the end of that novella the narrator struggles to understand the murderer's character:

I cannot describe the dreadful calmness with which that woman told this— that woman with the good face, whom I had heard praying like a saint in meeting. I believe in demonical possession after this [65].

There are other, less extreme cases of bad women in period detective fiction. There's one in "The Affair of Lamson's Cook" from *Quincy Adams Sawyer, Detective*; a double jeopardy story in which a husband gets away with killing his vile, shrewish wife who had run away and faked her own death for which he had been sent to prison. As opposed to punishment for a truly vile act, Butler's story "The Wetchell Job" ends with a woman being rebuked not for any criminal act but for a purely domestic personal flaw, her lack of charity. Here a couple of just plain nasty women simply deserve what they get. On a less moral level, there are a number of stories in which female criminals function pretty much like male criminals do. Thus Futrelle has two stories about bad women, one "The Fatal Cypher" in which a woman creates a bogus code to steal an inheritance, and "The Superfluous Finger" in which a woman has a finger amputated in an attempt to impersonate an heiress. In Burgess' "Miss Dalrymple's Locket" a woman intends to blow up a rival with an "infernal device." Like their male counterparts, it goes without saying that these women are motivated by greed. And the writers who introduce this kind of women go without saying it. They are not accomplices but principal actors in these crimes. Their motives may be—in fact they seem to be—different, so frequently involving, as they do, inheritances, but in spite of that they still serve the same purpose—as antagonists, as opponents for the protagonist, the master of reason, the genius detective.

And then there are those who choose to be bad, the professionals, the female Raffles, the gentlewomen, as it were, burglars. As long as there have been policemen, it seems, there have been in fact or fiction women who have chosen to be criminals. One early example of this in fiction is in the exceptionally rare *Nick Bigelow: and the Female Burglar; and other Leaves from a Lawyer's Diary. By a Member of the New York Bar*, published in 1846. *The Fireside Companion*, a family story paper, published a "dime novel" in the Old Sleuth series called *The Lady Burglar*. Contemporaneous with Poe, neither of these works caused much of a stir. But Hornung's *Raffles, the Amateur Cracksman*, published five decades later in 1898 caused a stir and a half. And it wasn't long before a few prominent women crooks began to turn up in the pages of American crime fiction. There's Laura Bingham, known in England as Laura Brice, in the United States as Frances Latimer, and to the police of both countries as Laura the Lady in Geraldine Bonner's *The Castleton Diamond Case* (1906) as well as a young woman burglar in Louis Vance's *The Brass Bowl* (1907). A woman crook operating under the name Silver Mag plays a significant role in Frank Packard's *The Adventures of Jimmy Dale* (1914). And Arthur B. Reeve's female hero in *Constance Dunlap* (1913) is perhaps the best known lady criminal of the era. The problem (or situation), however, is that none of them is completely, totally, really a criminal. Thus, in *The Brass Bowl* the young woman has turned burglar to save her father from prosecution for his innocent involvement with crooked investors. Packard's Silver Mag is really one Marie LaSalle, an heiress whose father and uncle have been murdered and in the novel she acts more social worker than crook. Finally after the opening where she was involved in crime to save her doofus husband from being jailed for embezzlement, Constance Dunlap acts primarily like a private detective who is particularly effective because she is smart and knows how crooks carry on their trades. It's both her skill, dexterity, and inventiveness that Reeve admires about Constance Dunlap and if he had not invented Craig Kennedy first, perhaps he would have made Constance Dunlap a detective from the very beginning. Even more than the men who choose to be gentlemen criminals—but who, at heart, really aren't (about whom there will be more below)—turn of the century women crooks, as skilled at their trade as they certainly are, aren't really criminals at all, but are often women in the same predicament as the sensation novel woman—only they choose to and can do something about the people trying to steal their birthrights. Along the way they either wind up with a virtuous man as their reward or, as in Arthur Stringer's wire tapper stories and Packard's Jimmy Dale novel, they convert their companions from their lives of crime.

SUPPORTING ROLES

Just as turn of the century detective fiction occasionally allowed women to be more than victims of one kind or another in the crime department, it also provided the opportunity for them to be more than admiring bystanders in the area of detection. This occurred on a couple of different levels. First of all, there was the role of assistant detective. And several writers found it an appropriate job for a woman. Perhaps the most accurate reflection of women's place in real world detection can be found in Arthur B. Reeve's Clare Kendall from *The Ear in the Wall* (1916). There, as noted above, Reeve draws Kendall as an accomplished detective, owner of a detective agency specializing in helping women. But she's not the principal detective in Reeve's book; that role is reserved for Professor Craig Kennedy. This seems to pretty much mirror the place and use of women detectives as reflected in contemporary newspaper accounts. Entering the realm of literature, perhaps the most conventional way of employing a woman as an assistant detective can be seen in books like Burgess' *The Master of Mysteries*. There Astro, the genius detective, incrementally in each of the stories teaches his beautiful and intelligent assistant, Valeska Wynne, the art and science of detection. At the end Valeska becomes a real detective and she also falls into her teacher's arms. Going in the opposite but still archly conventional direction, in *Alias the Night Wind*, policewoman Katherine, "Lady Kate," Maxwell unlearns her job as a detective member of the police department when she discovers the lengths to which the police will go to frame an innocent man; she gives up her job as a detective to run off with the man she loves. But before this mixture of romance and the profession of detection, there was a small but significant cohort of older women characters, starting off with Green's Miss Butterworth, who filled a very different role. Green introduced Amelia Butterworth in *That Affair Next Door* in 1897 where she advises (and does not always agree with) *The Leavenworth Case's* Inspector Gryce. Almost a decade after Green, Mary Roberts Rinehart contributed to a revival of middle aged spinster assistant detectives with her Miss Rachael Innes in *The Circular Staircase* (1908) and even in some small way with her more openly satiric Letitia Carberry introduced in 1911 in *The Amazing Adventures of Letitia Carberry*. Shortly after Rinehart's debut, Will Irwin introduced Rosalie LaGrange the middle aged woman in *The House of Mystery* (1910) and the next year Wells Hastings created the spry Mrs. Lathrop in *The Man in the Brown Derby*. Even though a couple of them narrate the adventures they encounter, none of these women functions as the principal detective. There's always either someone else or circumstance that clears things up in the end. In spite of a few differences, some of which reflect the politics of their creators—Green and Rinehart, for example, stood on opposite sides of the women's suffrage issue—this group of women has some important similarities. Most obviously, these writers chose not young women, but women of a certain age to serve as assistant detectives. This removed the issues of romance, marriage, and child rearing and focused the characters' efforts on problem solving. That they are all unmarried—either spinsters or widows—and that most of them enjoy the benefits of some sort of unspecified independent income (which, of course, helps to make them independent) also frees them from the era's implicit and explicit expectations about women's roles in marriage. That independence and age also gave these women license to be direct, frank, or blunt as well as to possess low thresholds of tolerance for nonsense, foolishness, and other impediments to discovering the truth. In a number of cases (especially with those female characters created by women writers) the female assistant detective sees things differently than her male companion. This includes attention in the narratives to domestic items, like Rachael Innes' vexation with servant problems or broken china. And the difference and acuteness of these women's perceptions sometimes turns out to be better than that of the male detectives—confirming not only the view of the women who stormed the mayor's office in Indianapolis but also anticipating Susan Glaspell's "A Jury of Her Peers" (1917).

Before any of these female characters appeared, however, Mary Wilkins set a very high standard for women assistant detectives with her Sarah Fairbanks, in *The Long Arm* (1895), a standard that would not be equaled for decades. Sarah Fairbanks narrates Wilkins' novella and recounts the events surrounding the murder of her father, a miserly tyrant who had forbidden her from seeing her true love. During the course of the story the lover is imprisoned and released, Sarah comes under suspicion—the story takes the form of her report to the Grand Jury—and is released. And finally a detective is brought in from Boston. He solves the case—puts assembled evidence together—and the young lovers are free to marry. But Sarah is not a victim; indeed she is resolved not to be made a victim by incompetent police work. The significance of Sarah's character lies in her determination to solve the crime herself. But it's not just that. It's also in the way in which she undertakes her mission: she does it, on her own, like a scientist.

> My father's murderer I will find. Tomorrow I begin my search. I shall first make an exhaustive examination of the house, such as no officer in the case has yet made, in the hope of finding a clue. Every room I propose to divide into square yards, by line and measure, and every one of those square yards I will study as if it were a problem in algebra.
>
> I have a theory that it is impossible for any human being to enter any house, and commit in it a deed of this kind, and not leave behind traces which are the known quantities in an algebraic equation to those who can use them [32].

After she has completed her grid search and collected her evidence, she examines it under the microscope she used in her job as a school teacher. This approach to detection and evidence is almost three decades before the first appearance of what would become known as Locard's Exchange Principle found originally in Edmond Locard's *Manuel de Technique Policière* (1923): "Il est impossible au malfaiteur d'agir avec l'intensit que suppose l'action criminelle sans laisser des traces de son passage"; "It is impossible for a criminal to act, especially considering the intensity of a crime, without leaving traces of this presence" (www.modernmicroscopy.com/main.asp?article=11). Having collected most of the evidence, it remains only for Mr. Dix, the Boston detective, to put it together and collar the criminal—something that Sarah cannot do. She cannot put the evidence together not because she is incapable of doing so, but because it proves that a woman murdered her father and in her innocence this is something she cannot accept. But it is something that Mr. Dix, sadly, knows only too well.

ENTERING THE SPOTLIGHT

Although there were not many, there were a few women who served as the principal figures in turn of the century fiction. From the dime novel world there was Denver Doll, created by Edward L. Wheeler, who appeared in *Beadle's Half-Dime Library* in 1882 and 1883; Lady Kate, created by "Old Sleuth" who appeared in "Lady Kate, The Dashing Female Detective" in *Old Sleuth Library* in 1886 (www.geocities.com/jessnevins/vicl); and *Mrs. Donald Dyke, Detective* published by Smith and Street in 1900. From more mainline publishers, there was hero Gwendolyn Bramblestone in Charles Carey's *The Van Suyden Sapphires* (1905), Frances Baird in Kauffman's *Miss Frances Baird Detective: A Passage from Her Memoirs* (1906), Leroy Scott's Katherine West in *Counsel for the Defense* (1912), Hugh C. Weir's *Miss Madelyn Mack, Detective* (1914), and finally Anna Katharine Green's late entry *The Golden Slipper and other problems for Violet Strange* (1915). What readers got with all of these characters was women who were not canny, semi-comic spinsters but independent, enterprising, intelligent, knowledgeable, capable, and successful women, women who, in spite of romantic distractions, succeeded in doing things conventionally associated with men. Not only do these women succeed in a traditionally male profession but they also do so without significant outside help—particularly male help. In the most extreme case, Violet Strange becomes a detective explicitly behind her father's back and her employer stands pretty much in awe of her. In *Counsel for the Defense*, Katherine West assumes the parent's role in defending her father from calumny and trumped up charges. Gwendolyn Bramblestone, in *The Van Suyden Sapphires* fends off her wealthy and love struck male friend until she can straighten out what happened to the missing jewels. And other than Frances Baird's purposely enigmatic aside about her past (having been a "little fool"), neither of the female private investigators has a past or family to lend them support. In one way or another, all of these women are associated with work—Gwendolyn Bramblestone is enjoying one last outing before facing the necessity of finding employment, Madelyn Mack found her first job in the want ads, Frances Baird seems to have no alternative other than working as a detective, and Katherine West has a job as a lawyer for the Municipal League. Even Violet Strange, child of wealth, becomes a detective as a job—as something one does for money. Oddly enough, the most conservative of the books featuring a woman detective was the one written by a woman, the rest were written by men.

The Van Suyden Sapphires is mostly a divertissement in which it serves the writer's purpose to have a woman play the lead. In the manner of stage farce, the novel begins with a silly stunt gone wrong—a bubble-brained actress' publicity ploy of stealing her own jewels—an enterprise which Gwendolyn Bramblestone reluctantly joins. Then follows a series of mistakes, misadventures, and bizarre collisions characteristic of stage farce. The fact that the lead is a woman is part of the pattern of role reversal that is one of the conventions of farce and it adds, as well, to the comedy of incident—as when Gwen attempts to explain the smell of smoke in her rooms:

> "Because of the tobacco smoke? It is unkind of you to discover me. We lonely women, you know, are apt to pick up that rather solacing habit."
>   As I spoke, partly to bear out my words, and partly to conceal a confusion I could not overcome, I took up a cigarette from the table and pushed the box toward him. But, truth to tell, I really loathe tobacco, and for my efforts I could not repress a slight grimace of disgust as I drew in the smoke.
>   "I am afraid, like myself, you prefer a cigar" [he said]... [151–152].

Part of the context of the Carey's novel is that of the fad for Sherlock Holmes' burlesque—"Did not Conan Doyle's sagacious hero once deduce the entire structure of a complicated case from the half-smoked butt of a 'Trichinopoly'?" (150). And Carey also adds a bit of Raffles burlesque when Gwendolyn imagines the newsboys calling

> "Wextray! Wextray! Society lady relieves her friends of a fortune in jewels! Miss Gwendolyn Bramblestone, Feminine Raffles in the Great Onyx Court robbery!" [82].

As in stage farce, the ending needs to clear up all of the confusion that the characters have created for themselves; and so in the end of *The Van Suyden Sapphires* Gwen figures out how the burglary was effected, gets the sapphires from their hiding place, saves the gentleman crook from the cops, and everything gets wrapped up. And then she can sail off to England with her fabulously rich and compliant fiancé.

AN AGENCY DETECTIVE

Reginald Wright Kauffman's *Miss Frances Baird Detective: A Passage from Her Memoirs* moves the woman hero from amateur to professional status. As noted above, Kauffman gives a wash of realism to his novel. Thus in the preface/dedication he describes himself as a journalist whose published descriptions of the successes of the woman detective pseudonymously called Frances Baird have contributed to his success. And he cites some of those cases: the murdered librarian Wilson in Philadelphia in 1897, the Molineaux case in New York, the Burdick mystery in Buffalo, the Phares case in Mt. Holly, etc. He follows this up with a brief but semi-realistic description of the Watkins Detective Agency and with seemingly believable backgrounds for his private detectives. Kemp, Frances Baird's male rival at the agency,

> ... I understood, had something of an education, but had early got into some trouble at school and was forced to take a place as a clerk in a large department store. There, by means best known to himself, he had worked his way into the shop's detective force [10].

Frances, as noted above ("Here you are, Frances Baird, with good looks and wit and a finishing school behind you,—not to mention a year or two abroad,—and, just because you were once a little fool, nothing ahead but—detective work!" 27) became a detective out of necessity, a necessity that Kauffman repeatedly underlines by seeding in references to her straightened financial condition. There is also Watkins' frank admission that part of Frances' utility to his detective agency lies in the fact that she is an attractive woman, a fact that she is not altogether reluctant to use: "The jailer ... tried to stop me, but I flattered him first and impressed him with my position as a New York detective afterwards" (157). The novel displays some interest in scientific detection—Frances carries scientific apparatus around with her—and throughout its length Frances, the narrator, provides readers with several asides commenting on detective business:

> To the ideal detective, the scientific attitude is indispensable. He—or she— must work, not in defense of a theory, but for the determination of the truth. Indeed, the theory should come last in the detective's calculations. All the available facts should be first gathered, and from them only should a theory eventually be erected. No brief should be held, no cause espoused, save for the cause of justice [208].

One of the main complications in the novel is that Frances falls in love with the principal suspect:

> Here, indeed, was a pretty kettle of fish! Frances Baird, a detective, if you please, sentimental enough to fall in love at all, foolish enough to fall in love during business hours, and mad enough to fall in love with a man whose stolen love-letters, from another woman were in my possession,—a man whom I knew to have committed theft and murder for the sake of that other woman, and, finally, a man whose arrest I must cause by six o'clock the next evening if I didn't want to starve to death [97].

Throughout the novel Frances works at solving the crimes (theft and murder), competes with Kemp, her irritating male colleague from Watkins Detective Agency, and deals with her attraction to Lawrence Fredericks. All of which contribute to emotional exhaustion and her belief that perhaps some kinds of detective work are not suitable for her:

It seemed to show that I was not cut out for murder cases. They are the thing that every good detective delights in, they are for him what the mitre is for the priest and the bench for the lawyer, but for me they appeared to be too strenuous—altogether too strenuous. They packed too much emotion into too short a space. They were bad art [129].

In the end Frances does find the criminal (who is a woman) and exonerate Fredericks.

Kauffman pays significant attention in *Miss Frances Baird* to defining his view of the nature of a detective who happens to be a woman. Part of the reaction against Sherlock Holmes and the great detective, he made his character fallible, Frances makes mistakes. And Kauffman added details to the novel to give it at least a gloss of reality—indeed as much reality as one can put in a millionaire's house party book. Like the hero in *The Van Suyden Sapphires* Kauffman has his hero define herself not simply as a detective, a problem solver, a thinker as contemporary male heroes would define themselves, but in a most significant way he makes Frances Baird define herself by her relationships and by her emotions.

CROSSING THE BAR

Leroy Scott's *Counsel for the Defense* features a woman lawyer—one of if not the first woman attorney in American fiction. In the novel, attorney Katherine West, against the odds, makes justice happen and, at the same time, defines herself by her relationship with her father and with her prospective husband. The novel revolves around the efforts of corrupt politicians to sell the municipal water works to a private conglomerate that has been taking over utilities all over the Midwest. Part of those efforts involve framing Dr. West, Katherine's father and a retired physician, for taking bribes as a member of the town's water board. Katherine leaves her job with the Municipal League in New York in order to defend her father. At the trial, in spite of her skill and eloquence, Dr. West is found guilty, whereupon his daughter, the editor of the local paper, and two private detectives eventually find the means to free him. So on the detective side, *Counsel for the Defense* is a muckraker's tome, exposing corruption in high places—including the local clergyman. It's also a book in praise of the new woman.

The fact that Katherine West has made something of herself comes as something of a shock to the town elders:

"I guess you'll find she's grown right smart since then. She went to one of those colleges back East, Vassar I think it was. She got hold of some of those new-fangled ideas the women in the East are going crazy over now—about going out in the world for themselves and–"

"Idiots—all of them!" snapped Bruce.

"After she graduated she studied law. When she was back home two years ago she asked me what chance a woman would have to practice law in Westville. A woman lawyer in Westville—oh Lord!"

...

"Oh I know the kind!" Bruce's lips curled with contempt. "Loud-voiced—aggressive—bony—perfect frights" [28–29].

This, moreover, serves only as a reedy prologue to a chapter entitled "When Greek Meets Greek" (a shortened version of Nathaniel Lee's line about opposing sides of equal strength in *The Rival Queens*: "When Greek meets Greek, then comes the tug-of-war"). Scott devotes the entire chapter to a debate between Katherine and the aforesaid sneering Bruce who finds Katherine neither loud, aggressive nor bony, and who now aspires to be her husband. Its subject is women in the workplace: she's for it and he's against it. The discussion proceeds with points like this one:

"Do you know any man, any real man I mean ... who stops work in the vigor of his prime merely because he has enough money to live upon? Would you give up your work to-morrow if some one were willing to support you?"

"Now, don't be ridiculous, Katherine! That's quite a different question. I'm a man, you know."

"And work is a necessity for you?"

"Why of course."

"And you would not be happy without it?" she eagerly pursued.

"Certainly not."

"And you are right there! But what you don't seem to understand is, that I have the same need, the same love, for work, that you have.... I demand for myself the right that all men possess as a matter of course—the right to work!" [284–5].

And this one:

"You can't combine children and a profession."

"But I can!" she cried. "And I should give the children the very best possible care, too! Of course there are successive periods in which the mother would have to give her whole attention to the children. But if she lives till she is sixty-five the sum total of her forty or forty-five married years that she has to give up wholly to her children amounts to but a few years. There remains all the balance of her life that she could give to other work" [288–89].

She, of course, wins the argument—hands down. Indeed Katherine rejects the marriage proposal made on terms that would take from her the right to self-fulfillment. Ultimately, Bruce, in the way of happy endings, learns to appreciate Katherine's wisdom and professional expertise when she does something that he, as editor of the newspaper, has been unable to do: she cleans up the town, vindicates her wronged father and gets him out of jail.

MARY HOLLAND TRANSFORMED

Just as in his description of Katherine West Leroy Scott opposes the notion that a woman committed to progressive ideas—in a word, a suffragette—must necessarily be an angular, grim-visaged virago, so does Hugh C. Weir in his description of his woman detective in *Madelyn Mack, Detective:*

> I had vaguely imagined a masculine-appearing woman, curt of voice, sharp of feature, perhaps dressed in a severe, tailor-made gown. I saw a young woman of maybe twenty-five, with red and white cheeks, crowned with a softly waved mass of dull gold hair, and a pair of vivacious, grey-blue eyes that made one forget every other detail of her appearance [4].

Indeed, as with his description of Madelyn Mack being both smart and beautiful, in other aspects of his presentation of his hero Weir also tries to cover all of the bases and, in some respects, to have it both ways—to be normal and routine and at the same time sensational and exotic. This shows up particularly in the way in which he treats his hero as a detective. On one hand he portrays Madelyn Mack as an organized, energetic, successful businesswoman. Thus, when Nora Noraker, the Watson-narrator, first meets Madelyn she makes her out to be a busy, successful business person:

> She had just returned from Omaha that morning, and was planning to leave for Boston on the midnight express. A suitcase and a fat portfolio of papers lay on a chair in a corner. A young woman stenographer was taking a number of letters at an almost incredible rate of dictation [4].

Additionally Weir makes Madelyn protest that there is nothing uncommon about being a detective or about what detectives do:

> "Oh, there isn't anything wonderful about it! You can do almost anything, you know, if you make yourself think you really can! I'm not at all unusual or abnormal" [5].
>
> "Are you a detective?"
> "Why?" I parried.
> ...
> "I—I always thought detectives different from other people."
> ...
> "You will find them human enough" I laughed, "outside detective stories" [26].

Part of the reason for all of the protestation about normalcy derived from the fact that Weir based his character on Mary Holland. Mary Holland was very much a real business woman whose successes as a detective derived, as most do, from determination and hard work. The other reason Weir's narrator insists on Madelyn as a normal person was in his attempt to distance his hero from Sherlock Holmes:

> There are only two real rules for a successful detective, hard work and common sense—not uncommon sense such as we associate with our old friend, Sherlock Holmes, but common, *business* sense [Weir's italics 5].

But perhaps in doing all of this he makes the ladies protest too much? Madelyn Mack is not really the kind of person one meets every day nor is her expertise as a detective a pedestrian accomplishment. Weir knows it—and so do his readers.

Take the text of dedication to Mary Holland: it seems to suggest that Weir is really interested in the exotic, even outré aspects of Ms. Holland's experience as a detective. Thus the dedication says

> None should know better than you that the riddles of fiction fall ever short of the riddles of truth. What plot of the novelist could equal the grotesqueness of your affair of the Mystic Circle, or the subtleness of your Chicago University exploit or the Egyptian Bar? [iii].

Grotesqueness? Mystic Circle? Subtleness? Exploit? Egyptian Bar? These all sound pretty much outside the realm of business sense. On top of this, at the same time that Madelyn tells Nora that it all depends on hard work and common sense, she acts like Sherlock Holmes, tantalizing her companion (and readers) with enigmatic clues that she unriddles at the end of the stories. And in the stories themselves, Weir inclines toward the novel and bizarre—the pistol hidden in the piano and rigged to shoot when a specific note is played, the hashish loaded in a secret part of the victim's pipe. And, perhaps, more difficult of solution, several of the Madelyn Mack short stories turn on complex marital relationships, a field usually impervious to either common or business sense. All of this, in the end, amounts to solving the same conundrums faced by all post-Holmes detective story writers—how to make the hero like Holmes but different? And how to concoct a plot with the right mixture of spine tingling sensation and brain stretching exercise in reasoning? In the Madelyn Mack stories readers can see Weir doing this before their eyes.

They can also see Weir face up to some of the central issues involved with creating a woman detective in the nineteen teens. One of the most obvious is prejudice, a fact that Weir confronts in the first story in the book. There Madelyn receives a letter from a prospective client putting it on the line: "While I will say at the onset that I have little faith in the analytical powers of the feminine brain, I'm prepared to accept Hamilton's judgment [that Madelyn is an exception to that rule]" (12). And, of course, the narrative disposes of that prejudice pretty handily. In addition to being able to analyze as well as men, Madelyn, like the women who stormed the mayor's office in Indianapolis, holds that women possess abilities that men do not:. Thus Madelyn continues her description of the criteria for being a successful detective cited above:

> There are only two real rules for a successful detective, hard work and common sense—not uncommon sense such as we associate with our old friend, Sherlock Holmes, but common, *business* sense.

And she adds

> And, of course, imagination! That may be one reason why I have made what you call a success. A woman, I think, always has a more acute imagination than a man [5]!

WHY ASK?

It is hardly likely that anyone is going to ask why women didn't take over or even get equal attention as heroes of detective stories at the turn of the last century. After all, they couldn't even vote.

But women in detective fiction were hardly in the same category into which Samuel Johnson put women preaching: "It is not done well; but you are surprised to find it done at all." At the turn of the century American women were closely identified with the kind of progressive causes that came to characterize one type of period fiction, that influenced by the muckrakers. At the turn of the century, too, women, although unrecognized and unheralded, were engaged in private and even public detective work, often detective work connected, in a large sense, with public welfare—something that could rarely be said of male detectives. In fiction, however, the progress was slower even than it was in life. Most writers had a hard time figuring out whether women could be more than victims or models of heroic ... suffering. Women writers, in general, shied away from the evolving form of the detective story, with its focus shifting from sensation to reason and entertainment; instead they essentially continued to write sensation novels. There is more than a bit of irony attached to the fact that the most active, realistic, and progressive female characters in turn of the century fiction were those created by men—Kauffman, Scott, and Reeve.

9

Lawyers and the Law

FOUNDED BY LAWYERS?

It seems altogether fitting to associate lawyers and the law with the formation of the detective story at the turn of the century. Lawyers, after all, were there at the beginning, or almost at the beginning. Gaboriau may have been only a notary, but Wilkie Collins was a full-fledged lawyer and so was Anna Katharine Green's father—she made the subtitle of *The Leavenworth Case* "A Lawyer's Story" and her book is reputed to have been once used at the Yale law school to demonstrate the fallibility of circumstantial evidence. And at the turn of the century the law in America was, more than ever before, in the process of accommodating seismic changes in the culture—from women's suffrage to the testimony of expert witnesses. It seems altogether fitting, then, that a profession and an institution so intimately connected with crime and with vested interests in statute law and legal documents (especially wills) be closely associated with the birth and growth of the modern detective story.

But there were problems with the incorporation of lawyers in the detective story. One problem was that crime and the testamentary transmission of a family's name and fortune from one generation to the next formed the core not of the new detective story but of the crime fiction of the last generation; it was the central issue, first, of Bulwer-Lytton's criminal romances and then of the sensation novel. Not only that, as it developed, the central business of the detective story was finding facts, not necessarily defending anyone, even those who are innocent or falsely accused—as seen in the growth and popularity of the "least likely suspect" plot formula and the writer's admonition to "suspect everyone." Therefore the more the plot in a detective story leaned toward defending a suffering innocent—one of the principal things that can turn a lawyer into a hero—the more connected it was with the sensation novel whose central purpose was emotional versus the more intellectual intent of the kind of detective story that was developing at the turn of the century. Therefore, those connections with old-style crime fiction, insofar as the creation of the modern detective story is concerned, became strike one.

And then, in the hero department, there are problems with lawyers because they are lawyers. As sympathetic, honest, and estimable as many lawyers surely are, nobody really wants to go to see one. First of all, to many it seems fundamentally unfair to have to pay in order to achieve justice or security. Then, too, the stereotype of the lawyer as a dishonest and conniving scoundrel existed long before the turn of the 20th century; and it was highlighted by a number of period writers, including Arthur Train in his *The Confessions of Artemas Quibble: Being the ingenious and unvarnished history of Artemus Quibble, Esquire, One-Time Practitioner in the New York Criminal Courts, Together With An Account of the Diverse Wiles, Tricks, Sophistries, Technicalities, and Sundry Artifices of Himself and Others of the Fraternity, Commonly Yclept "Shysters: OR "Shyster Lawyers"* (1921). Turn of the century readers, in fact, could find lawyer villains in crime fiction with relative ease. Arthur Stringer's *The Phantom Wire* (1906), like Train's later work, also discourses briefly on the method of making of a shyster lawyer, and that species of attorney turns up, too, in Roman Doubleday's *The Hemlock Avenue Mystery* (1908), and in Meredith Nicholson's *The House of a Thousand Candles* (1908). Setting aside shysters and ambulance chasers, even with those lawyers who are pillars of virtue, there's something about the profession that makes a lot of people nervous, reticent, and even makes them withhold the truth. That's why, in addition to all of the other tangible things that Arthur Conan Doyle added that changed the detective story permanently, it was important that he also brought the point of view not of a lawyer but of a physician—a profession in which bedside manner is important, a profession people willingly, anxiously seek out, confide in and trust, and one for which visitors are patients and not clients. And thus, for no real fault of their own, for lawyer heroes that was strike two. There were also a couple of near misses in the lawyer-hero department: one of them was the notion (or the reality) that lawyers just don't do detective work, that they are professionals who hire detectives versus doing the "dirty work" or "leg work" themselves—the sort of thing lawyer writer Erle Stanley Gardner would later enshrine in the formulaic relationship between Perry Mason and his private detective Paul Drake. If there were to be a strike three with respect to lawyers as heroes of the new detective story, however, it wasn't going to matter all that much. After World War I lawyers were going to have their own literary niche—in the legal thriller, a form customarily seen as beginning with Richard Noyes Hart's *The Bellamy Trial* of 1927. But for a while at the turn of the century lawyers had a chance, albeit a small one, of becoming the heroes of the new detective story.

STRANGE SCHEMES

One of the things that perhaps confused the issue of lawyers as potential heroes of the new detective story was the success of lawyer writer Melville Davisson Post's stories about attorney Randolph Mason, collected as *The Strange Schemes of Randolph Mason* (1896), *The Man of Last Resort or, the Clients of Randolph Mason* (1897), and *The Corrector of Destinies* (1908). In his introduction to *The Strange Schemes of Randolph Mason* Post sees himself as a detective story writer, working in the tradition of Poe and Conan Doyle:

> Exacting is this taskmaster. It demands that the problem builder cunningly join together the Fancy and the Fact, and thereby enchant and bewilder, but not deceive. It demands all the mighty motives of life in the problem. Thus it happens that the toiler has tramped and retramped the field of crime. Poe and the French writers constructed masterpieces in the early day. Later came the flood of "Detective Stories" until the stomach of the reader failed. Yesterday, Mr. Conan Doyle created Sherlock Holmes, and the public pricked up its ears and listened with interest [3].

But he also sees himself as an innovator:

> *It is significant that the general plan of this kind of tale has never once been changed to any degree.* The writers, one and all, have labored, often with great genius, to construct problems in crime, where by acute deduction the criminal and his methods were determined; or, reversing it, they have sought to plan the crime so cunningly as to effectually conceal the criminal and his methods. The intent has always been to baffle the trailer, and when the identity of the criminal was finally revealed, the story ended.
> *The high ground of the field of crime has not been explored; it has not even been entered.* The book-stalls have been filled to weariness with tales based upon plans whereby the *detective*, or *ferreting* power *of the State might be baffled. But, prodigious marvel! no writer has attempted to construct tales based upon plans whereby the* punishing *power of the State might be baffled.*
> *The distinction, if one pauses for a moment to consider it, is striking. It is possible, even easy, deliberately to plan crimes so that the criminal agent and the criminal agency cannot be detected. Is it possible to plan and execute wrongs in such a manner that they will have all the effect and all the resulting profit of desperate crimes and yet not be crimes before the law?* [3–4, my italics].

In the main, Post's stories fall into the same category as those of other progressive or muckraking writers: while some purposely aim to outrage readers with respect to the perversity of the law, others are about the lawyer finding the means for the protagonist to outwit the perverse purposes of either titanic corporate, ubiquitous political evil, or just plain bad luck. Thus both "The Governor's Machine" and "The Grazier" in *The Man of Last*

Resort, for instance, show individuals besting grasping corporations because they simply deserve to win and because they have a lawyer who knows the back alleys and disused rights of way of the law. To do this Post builds each of the Randolph Mason stories around a specific point of law: one of the stories in *The Strange Schemes*, for example, is entitled "corpus delecti" and revolves around that Latin term and its particular legal meaning and precedent. Because he can, Post also often cites case law in order to both bolster and drive home the technical point of his stories—the non-technical point usually being the triumph of virtue or at least of the lesser of available evils. His story from *The Strange Schemes*, "The Animus Furandi," for example, begins with this head note:

> See the case of State vs. Brown at al, 104 Mo, 365; the strange case of Reuben Deal, 64 N.C., 270; also on all fours with the facts here involved, see Thompson vs. Commonwealth, 18 S.W. Rept., 1022; and the very recent case of The People vs. Hughes, 39 Pacific Rept., 492; also Rex vs. Hall, Bodens case, and others there cited, 2 Russell on Crimes [249].

And because the stories pivot on points of law, some of them culminate in trial scenes or other forms of review that test the validity of the legal loophole Randolph Mason has invoked for his client. In those scenes, unlike the usual detective story, the facts are obvious and undisputed—they do not need to be identified or uncovered. Post doesn't want the surprise to come from the discovery of facts, but from the obscure, arcane, and often unjust points of law Randolph Mason introduces which turn not the facts but the direct implications of justice upside down.

Post cast his hero Randolph Mason as a reclusive, brooding, arrogant, angry, intemperate, demanding, cynical misanthrope who is also a genius capable of using the law for both good and evil purposes. Clients have to seek Mason out and his counsel is given both reluctantly and guardedly. In some ways Post made his hero this way because he had to. The implication of all of the Randolph Mason stories is that the dilemma that gave rise to the cynical and misanthropic characteristics is that the hero's profession, his membership on the bar, brings with it an implicit belief in the majesty of the law as well as a commitment to uphold the law. Mason can't accept either easily. Seeing its impact on the weak and the helpless he neither believes in the law's majesty nor can he uphold the law as doing so is conventionally understood. Instead he turns the law on itself sometimes in order to protest the perversion it has suffered in the hands of the rich and powerful and preserve virtue and sometimes apparently out of a kind of demonic satisfaction in demonstrating the law's inadequacy. This tension between what ought to be and what is progressively erodes his character. In the first series of stories Post makes him out to be a kind of reclusive,

Dupinesque genius, only a lot grumpier. At the end of the second book, *The Man of Last Resort,* readers hear a report of Mason being sedated (a process that requires two hypodermics of morphine), being diagnosed as suffering from "acute mania," and being taken off to an asylum.

A LAWYER'S LIFE

To suggest that Post's success gave rise to a stampede of lawyers writing detective stories about lawyers or even detective stories featuring lawyers written by lay writers would be gross hyperbole. But there were some in each category. Setting aside detective fiction for a moment, there seems to have been some small stirrings of interest at the turn of the century in publishing fiction portraying lawyers' lives as being interesting and even exciting. Although all of the contents are British, Estes and Lauriat of Boston emphasized the lawyer as action hero in their *Legal Adventure Library* (1880) consisting of *The Experiences of a Barrister and Confessions of an Attorney* by Samuel Warren, *Recollections of a Policeman* by Thomas Waters of the London Detective Corps, and *The Adventures of an Attorney in Search of a Practice* by Sir James Stephen. Frederick Hill presented an American attorney as hero in his *The Case and Exceptions Stories of Counsel and Clients* (1900). There were, however, a couple of lawyers (in addition to Post) who wrote detective stories during the period. There was Nathan Winslow Williams, a State's Attorney in Baltimore (and eventually Maryland's Secretary of State) who wrote one detective novel, *A Master Hand* (1906) under the pseudonym Richard Dallas. And there was the prolific Arthur Train who sometimes included "Formerly Assistant District Attorney New York County, N.Y." on his title pages. While most of his fiction dates from after the War (including his series of stories about lawyer Ephraim Tutt), at the turn of the century Train contributed a number of true crime pieces for *The Saturday Evening Post* as well as some stories that qualify as detective fiction. Perhaps as important as lawyers entering the field was the fact that a number of titles of turn of the century detective fiction show a close association between the detective story and the law: every title that uses the word "case," for example, adds legal overtones to what follows. It is ubiquitous in period magazine titles for both non fiction (e.g. Frank Norris' "A Case for Lombroso," *The Wave* September 11, 1897) and fiction (e.g. William Shryer's "A Case in Equity," *The Popular Magazine* June 7, 1917). And titles of novels like Ottolengui's *The Final Proof, or The Value of Evidence* (1898), Richard Marsh's *A Case of Identity* (1908), and Carolyn Wells' *A Chain of Evidence* (1907) point pretty directly to these writers' linkage between detective fiction and the law—or at least one facet of the law. In addition to legal terms that sometimes crop up in period titles, turn of the century fiction had a virtual obsession with circumstantial evidence. But back to lawyers for the time being.

More so than any other profession, in early detective fiction lawyers performed yeoman duty as narrators. After all, who else was a family to call upon in times of trouble? Surely not the police, and the persistence of lawyers in detective fiction would continue to reflect this fundamental distrust of all public authority, particularly that of the police. And so lawyers acting as both advisors and friends of the families serve as narrators for *The Dead Letter* and *The Leavenworth Case*. And, protecting the families' interests as they do, it's altogether appropriate that they tag along with the detectives as they investigate the crimes in the novels—protecting their clients from the power of the State. The same thing holds true of the lawyer narrators at the turn of the century—Otis Landon in Carolyn Wells' *A Chain of Evidence*, Mr. Lester in Burton Stevenson's novels, Mr. Drew (a fictional lawyer who has written a fictional book on evidence) in Henry Kitchell Webster's *The Whispering Man*, and Mr. Crosby in Jean Webster's *The Four Pools Mystery*. As opposed to the narrators in Green and Victor, however, these turn of the century lawyer narrators had been influenced not just by Poe's unnamed narrator but also by Conan Doyle's Watson. So they all try (and fail) on their own to solve the cases in which they become entangled and end up requiring the assistance of a friendly expert in these matters. Even when, as is sometimes the case, the attorney is the principal detective, there is a tendency in turn of the century detective fiction to bring in at least a pair of lawyers, because of the assumption then as now that a lawyer without partners, like Pudd'nhead Wilson, wasn't much of a lawyer. Thus in Scribner's *My Mysterious Clients* there are stories featuring lawyer partners—one young and busy and the other old and eloquent. There is the same pattern in *Counsel for the Defense* where attorney Katherine West seeks the advice and counsel of a wise, old lawyer. The denouement of Burton Stevenson's *The Holladay Case,* in fact, shows readers lawyer Lester and one of his senior partners setting off to France to uncover the facts that lie under the book's central mystery. And in *A Master Hand*, Dallas, the Assistant District Attorney narrator, convinces an old friend to leave retirement and take on the defense of a man he believes to be innocent.

As heroes, lawyers play a variety of roles in addition to that of the Watson in turn of the century detective fiction. The most conventional of these is the lawyer as detective, as the one who uncovers and interprets clues. The hero of Twain's *Pudd'nhead Wilson* (1894), with his collection of fingerprints, defines this category as does Stevenson's Lester with his discovery and revelation that a key witness is colorblind in the beginning of *The Holladay Case*. Then there is the lawyer as strategist—the Randolph Mason model—who sets traps and waits off stage for ignorance, greed, and evil to spring them. Dallas' *A Master Hand* also follows this pattern with a lawyer maneuvering so that there will be a hung (deadlocked) jury. From muckraking writers comes the lawyer as crusader. Thus there is lawyer David Kent in Francis Lynde's *The Grafters* (1904) who takes on corrupt politicians and evil businessmen and the genius blind corporate lawyer in Balmer and McHarg's *The Blind Man's Eyes* (1916) who has been misled by agents of the cartels. There are also some novels in which lawyers represent order. A fair number of lawyer books during the period take place outside major cities. Thus some of Post's stories happen in West Virginia, Twain's David "Pudd'nhead" Wilson hangs his shingle in the miniscule burg of Dawson's Landing. Scott's *Counsel for the Defense* takes place in a small Midwestern city, Jean Webster's *The Four Pools Mystery* in the rural South, Scribner's *My Mysterious Clients* in small town Lyons (probably) Ohio, and Eldridge's *The Millbank Case* (which is about the murder of lawyers) is "A Maine Mystery of Today." Whatever other roles the lawyers play in these novels, one of their functions (like that of summoning the expert, big city, private detective) is to bring order, particularly the order of law, to locales unused to crime, controlled by custom, and uncomfortable with asking the right questions.

CHANGE OF VENUE

Just as the geographic locale of the novel plays a role in a number of lawyer-detective books at the turn of the century, the significance of other venues looms large. Indeed, courts and trials of various sorts become a defining feature of this particular variety of fiction. That some of them end in trials, in fact, is one of the things that serves to mark off turn of the century detective fiction from its sensation novel progenitor. In sensation novels, after all, solving the family's problems and meting out punishment in a public, state run judicial proceeding would have been unthinkable: haven't these people suffered enough without exposing them to public humiliation? On top of that, from the sensation novel's point of view, trials place justice in the hands of the state instead of providence, and in the sensation novel, sooner or later, providence will take care of crime and criminals pretty much by itself. But in turn of the century detective stories this is definitely not the case. And so the intent to secularize justice that lies at the heart of the modern detective story sometimes is made manifest by thrusting the reader into the midst of court proceedings. And the American judicial system (unlike the British system) at the turn of the century, as now, provided plenty of different kinds of those proceedings to use: coroner's juries, grand juries, petit juries, administrative courts, district courts, appellate courts, state courts, federal courts. It may be confusing, but the American judicial system provided and provides plenty of settings for drama in the courtroom. Perhaps the single most important virtue of our graduated judicial process for the triumph of justice and for the development of detective fiction lies in the fact that it is possible for mistakes to be made and then corrected. All of this has myriad applications, particularly in detective fiction. Trials, for instance, can be put to a variety of uses from milking the sentiment from a wrongly accused or wrongly convicted hero as in George Allan England's *The Greater Crime* (1917) or Cleveland Moffit's *Through the Wall* (1919) to demonstrating the virtue of logic and science—the latter seen in the courtroom use of the lie detector in Melvin Severy's *The Mystery of June 13th* (1905). At the turn of the century, moreover, things in the world of the judicial system were, if anything, made more complicated because parts of the judicial system were visibly and essentially changing to accommodate the accelerating capacity of science to explain the material world. And those changes had a significant impact on the content and construction of detective stories. These changes can be seen pretty clearly in the prominent roles played by coroners and the coroner's juries in turn of the century detective fiction.

The office of the coroner and the institutions of the coroner's jury and the role they play in the coroner's inquest have been mentioned in passing above. Because of their function in period fiction, they merit a bit more than passing mention. Like a lot of other parts of the American system of jurisprudence, the office of coroner originated in England around the time of the Norman Conquest. The coroner was a crown official whose job it was to seize the property of persons who died: if the death were due to violence, then the property went to the crown; if the death were accidental then it went as alms to the poor. Eventually this process led to the establishment of the formal inquest:

> Once the Coroner had viewed the body, he then held the inquest, just as he does today in certain classes of death. In medieval times, this may have been done on the spot, with the body present before him, or it may have been adjourned for a few days. Originally the inquest was a massive affair, as the jury had to consist of all the males over twelve years from the four nearest townships, together with additional men from the Hundred [www.britannia.com/history/articles/coroner3].

By the 18th century in Britain it became increasingly apparent that determining causes of death was the province of a medical professional and not of lay persons and this duty began to be shifted to appointed professionals with medical expertise. But even as that reform was taking place, the old system of lay coroners and juries was being established in the colonies—William Penn, in fact, served as an appointed coroner. As had happened earlier in England, by the middle of the 19th century there began significant outcry in a number of jurisdictions against lay people making medical and legal decisions about causes of death. As a response to this movement, Boston, in 1877, replaced its coroner with a professional medical examiner. But because of its linkage to political patronage, coroners became the subject of protracted debate in other parts of the country. The debate, as one would expect, was particularly pointed in New York City and Albany; thus the following from *The New York Times*:

> The abolition of the Coroner and the establishment of a rational system of medical examination will put an end to the abuses and scandals which have sprung from a clumsy and incongruous method of dealing with the solemn incident of sudden death in the community [February 12, 1896].

Indeed the debate was so protracted that some parts of the country did not abandon the elected office of coroner for decades—Oklahoma jurisdictions, for example, did not give up elected coroners until 1962. Small wonder, then, that the coroner controversy spread to detective fiction.

Coroners come into American detective fiction almost from the beginning. The *medias res* beginning of *The Leavenworth Case* in fact takes readers into the coroner's inquest held at the Leavenworth home as soon as the novel begins. There Green gives a snapshot of the coroner's jury:

> As for his jurymen, they were, as I have indicated, very much like all other bodies of a similar character. Picked up at random from the streets, but from such streets as the Fifth and Sixth Avenues, they presented much the same appearance of average intelligence and refinement as might be seen in the chance occupants of one of our city's stages [11].

Unlike the jury, Green presents the coroner as an intelligent and perceptive individual. Insofar as turn of the century detective fiction was concerned, Green's coroner was, perhaps, the last of his breed: his descendants in fictions are almost universally boobs. Charles Walk presents the typical coroner in *The Silver Blade* (1909):

> Mr. Merkel was fussy, important, and wholly incompetent; and the [police] Captain was so accustomed to his repetition of phrases that were not, to say the least, pregnant with meaning that he ignored them... [31].

The imposition of the typical fictional coroner's fussy, pompous incompetence on the inquest makes possible using that public hearing as a significant element in the detective story's plot. Thus in turn of the century detective stories the inquest commonly 1) presents incomplete facts, 2) misinterprets the facts brought out in evidence, and 3) accuses an innocent person. Each one of these, in turn, serves as an occasion for the detective to demonstrate his or her acumen in finding facts, interpreting them correctly, and freeing the falsely accused by identifying the real criminal. In this respect, the dumber, more ignorant, and more hostile the coroner, the better, because each of these traits serves to magnify the hero's positive ones. Additionally, while the public exposure of an individual's or a family's problems at a coroner's inquest or even a trial takes away the emotional substance of the sensation novel, it replaces or redefines private suffering by presenting opportunities for public displays of fortitude (on the part of the wrongfully accused), pathos (on the part of his or her family and friends), and determination (on the part of the lawyer, detective, or lawyer-detective) who can only play a passive, watching role at the inquest.

Victims of Circumstance?

In turn of the century detective fiction, when coroners' inquests go bad (which is almost always), inevitably "circumstantial evidence" gets the blame. The nature of evidence, it turns out, was a hot topic at the time and most of the controversy focused on the relative validity of direct versus circumstantial evidence. Both sides of the argument had their points. While direct evidence (the testimony of witnesses, documents, etc.) establishes facts without the need for inference, it does have its problems. In fact and in fiction the possibility exists that people cannot and do not always tell the truth, both on their own and because of outside pressure exerted by others. There's not only that, but people are not always able to accurately report or correctly interpret what they have witnessed. On the other hand, circumstantial evidence (evidence that does not come from an eye witness and therefore requires some inference or reasoning to establish its meaning) may rest on reasoning that is spurious and calls on others, whether judge or jury, to accept that one particular set of inferences or line of reasoning is superior to another.

In one way or another, the argument about direct versus circumstantial evidence rears its head in almost every detective story of the period. It comes into the titles of books like James Barnes' *The Clutch of Circumstance* (1908) and Edith E. Buckley's *The Snare of Circumstance* (1910). It pops up in the titles of chapters like the one in Carolyn Wells' *The Maxwell*

Mystery entitled "Circumstantial Evidence," or in Charles Carey's *The Van Suyden Sapphires* where the chapter is "The Web of Circumstance," or in Burton Stevenson's *The Holladay Case* where the chapter is "In the Grip of Circumstance." Mary Roberts Rinehart, who was pretty acute in gauging the mood of the mystery marketplace, begins the opening paragraph of her second novel by pointing to circumstantial evidence — in part as inducement for readers to read on and in part out of mischief:

> McKnight is gradually taking over the criminal end of the business. I never liked it, and since the strange case of the man in lower ten, I have been a bit squeamish. Given a case like that, when you can build up a network of clues that absolutely incriminate three entirely different people, only one of whom can be guilty, and your faith in circumstantial evidence dies of overcrowding [*The Man in Lower Ten* 1].

In response to these kinds of allusions and references to circumstantial evidence, *The Washington Post* singled out fiction, no doubt detective fiction, for distorting the public's perception of the nature of evidence in real world legal proceedings:

> The discrediting of circumstantial evidence arises, no doubt, from a misapprehension as to the degree of certainty required by the law in the application of evidence, both direct and circumstantial, in order to sustain a conviction. Inferences to be drawn are not mere guesses or probabilities, such as form the plots of some very interesting romances, whose authors have done more perhaps than others to discredit legal circumstantial evidence [July 2, 1896].

But did the writers of those romances categorically dismiss circumstantial evidence? or was the very nature of indirect, circumstantial evidence changing? or were writers using circumstantial evidence as the basis for their detective stories because it gave them some ready-made plot devices?

First of all, it is past argument that circumstantial evidence receives near universal condemnation in turn of the century detective fiction. Attorney-writer Nathan Winslow Williams, writing as Richard Dallas, for example, began his novel *A Master Hand* with a preface that included an opening salvo against circumstantial evidence: "To me the history of this tragedy has always seemed convincing proof of the insufficiency of circumstantial evidence, except where such evidence is conclusive" (iii). Futrelle's Thinking Machine, as is his wont, is even more outspoken on the subject:

> "One of the most astonishing things to me," Hatch added, "is the complete case of circumstantial evidence against Mrs. Dudley, beginning with the quarrel and leading to the application of the poison with her own hands. I believe she would have been convicted on the actual circumstantial evidence had you not shown conclusively that Osaka did it."
> "Circumstantial fiddlesticks!" snapped the Thinking Machine. "I wouldn't

convict a dog of stealing jam on circumstantial evidence alone, even if he had jam all over his nose" [*The Great Cases of the Thinking Machine* 40].

In trials at the time, real and imaginary, however, some things that had never before been evidence or at best were considered circumstantial evidence were being transformed by science into forensic evidence—evidence that, it could be and was argued, was more reliable than the testimony of human witnesses. For example, although it took almost a century, blood stains progressively worked their way from meaningless red blotches to being human versus animal blood, to being blood of a specific type to being the seemingly irrefutable blood-based DNA evidence that convicted Colin Pitchfork in 1988. Part of the detective story's obsession with circumstantial evidence, then, came from the faith in or longing for scientific certainty in the detection of crime, the kind of thing that Luther Trant goes on and on about in 1910:

> Juries have convicted thousands of other innocent people on evidence less trustworthy. The numerous convictions of innocent persons are as black a shame today as burnings and torturings were in the Middle Ages; as tests by fire and water, or as examinations for witchcraft. Courts take evidence to-day exactly as it was taken when Joseph was a prisoner in Egypt. They hang and imprison on grounds of 'precedent' or 'common sense." They accept the word of a witness where its truth seems likely, and refuse it where it seems otherwise.... There is no room for mistakes ... in scientific psychology. Instead of analyzing evidence by the haphazard methods of the courts, we can analyze it scientifically, exactly, incontrovertibly—we can select infallibly the true from the false [*The Achievements of Luther Trant*, 94–95].

But it was more than faith in science that so pointedly put circumstantial evidence on the turn of the century detective story map. It was also there because it had to be. Without circumstantial evidence, there is no such thing as the detective story. If it's all uncontested direct evidence, there is no need for detection. The same thing goes if there's no evidence. It has to be circumstantial. And so what readers find is writers of the period, in effect, playing with circumstantial evidence because of its nature, because it depends on inference and reason and not demonstrated facts. Thus we find writers setting up a first set of straw man circumstantial evidence in order to replace it with another set, one that the writer will build the rest of the plot upon, thereby convincing the readers it is more credible than the first set because they have watched or learned that the hero has discovered the new set of evidence. Thus at the end of the story the writer seeks to convince readers there are not really hundreds of reasons for the presence of that tobacco ash, as its status as circumstantial evidence would have it, but only one. And that reason is true and not just circumstantial because the detective says so. When one set of facts supplants another, it is also credible to readers because the conventions of the detective story had so thoroughly discredited the police and coroners as interpreters of both people and facts. In addition to this kind of play with circumstantial evidence, period writers developed a second method of using it to make their plots. This one depended on the growing acceptance of scientifically-based forensic evidence, and features writers taking forensic evidence that had been accepted as incontrovertible and turning it into misleading circumstantial evidence. One can see this especially in the appearance of stories about faked fingerprints that appeared shortly after fingerprints were universally accepted as valid, dependable forensic evidence.

THE JURY WAS STILL OUT

Lawyers doing what lawyers do—as opposed to doing what police or private or amateur investigators do—occupied a precarious position in turn of the century detective fiction. They stood between the kind of justice implicit in the sensation novel and the novel as play that was to soon take over mainstream detective fiction. Neither one of them had anything to do with law as lawyers and judges know it. The principal function of lawyers in sensation novels was to keep problems in the family, out of the eye of the public, the police, and the courts. The underlying purpose of the sensation novel, however, lay in the demonstration of the workings and ultimate justice of providence, and there wasn't a lot of use for lawyers in that particular arena. Increasingly this kind of resolution to problems and to plots of crime novel became less tenable. Criminals, and crime were a public concern and so was the determination of guilt or innocence, and the administration of punishment manifestly became the province of the state. That being the case, lawyers were admirably suited for roles as heroes, as the wise, ingenious and eloquent defense attorney or the prosecutor crusading against evil. The problem was that beginning at the turn of the century the literary detective story was slowly transforming into a game, a light-hearted contest between the writer and the reader with the idea of intellectual exercise thrown in as an excuse for having fun. In this kind of fiction, the business of the state, the machinery of the criminal justice system necessarily ending in the death house and the electric chair, is so discordant as to defeat the purpose of the endeavor. And so writers evolved ways of wrapping up criminal matters without the police, without the criminal justice system, without lawyers.

10

Everybody Else

Pro Am Match

The detective story began by focusing on the amateur detective, or at least on the non-professional detective—it being hard to call Dupin an amateur at anything he chose to set his hand or part of his mind to. In addition to demonstrating Dupin's genius, Poe's tales illustrate the virtues of individualism and the incompetence and impotence of established authority. As an amateur, it's Dupin who chooses to solve problems which he does either for his own amusement (as in "Murders in the Rue Morgue") or to show up the police (as in "Marie Roget" and "Purloined Letter") and it's Dupin to whom the authorities turn with hat in hand when they meet a problem they cannot solve. All of that, one should recall, went on before the creation of the institution of the police or detective police in America. Once they were in place, after the mid-19th century, solving crime—what there was of it in fiction—became the job of the police—and providence. Thus Victor, Green, and Hawthorne all put the crime solving (as opposed to the expression of sentiment) into the hands of hero police officers. Wracked by scandal as the police were at the turn of the century, however, writers had to look elsewhere for the heroes of the detective stories they began to write in response to the popularity of the Sherlock Holmes tales published at the beginning of the 1890s.

There was a lot to copy from among the many characteristics of Sherlock Holmes besides his role of reasoner and problem solver. There was Holmes as the scientist, Holmes as the actor, Holmes as the logician, Holmes as the knightly protector of the weak, Holmes as the athlete, Holmes as the eccentric, Holmes as the romantic enigma, Holmes as the polymath, and so much more. But, unlike Poe or Dupin, Conan Doyle, who was himself a professional, created Holmes as one too: he repeatedly makes it clear that being a detective is something Holmes has devoted all of his energies toward learning and mastering (hence his first meeting with Watson at St. Bart's) and that he is a renowned specialist—a consulting detective to whom the police and others appeal when they encounter problems they cannot solve. The workman deserves his hire, and as a professional Sherlock Holmes even sometimes accepts fees from clients—when they can conspicuously afford it. Conan Doyle, however rarely mentions this. Indeed Sherlock Holmes in the main doesn't seem like a professional. In part this happens because of the emphasis Conan Doyle places on his cozy home in Baker Street. In part it happens because Holmes has far more skills and attributes than one can expect in a narrowly accomplished specialist. And in part it happens because the stories are adventures with a friend and not just cases with clients on the clock. On top of that, Holmes wasn't the only developed character in Conan Doyle's detective stories, there was also Watson. Indeed, one of Conan Doyle's principal changes to Poe's formulas was in giving the narrator not just a name but also memorable characteristics, and often significant roles in the action of the stories. In other words, Conan Doyle increased the importance of the role of the amateur in the detective story. Watson is more than narrator and friend, he is the assistant detective.

Indeed, that Conan Doyle made Sherlock Holmes a professional in the first place stands as something of an anomaly. The Sherlock Holmes stories in addition to being detective stories derived from Poe owe much to the Victorian schoolboy story and the books written for the first generation to benefit from universal education on both sides of the Atlantic, books like *Treasure Island* and *The Prisoner of Zenda* and even (on a much lower level) the Horatio Alger tales. This kind of fiction placed emphasis not on professionals but on heroes who acquire skills, who learn responsibility, who become—sometimes in spite of their ages—adults. They are about amateurs, and by extension, they are about the amateurs who were going to run the Empire; in America the same kind of stories were about youths whose pluck and gumption were going to create industrial empires.

Boys Will Be

There were boy detectives in America almost as soon as detectives began appearing in family story paper yarns and then in dime novel stories in the mid-19th century. While there certainly was opposition to stories that featured crime and criminals voiced by Anthony Comstock and other Victorian moralists, from the predominant point of view the detective story in general and the Sherlock Holmes stories in particular could be used as part of a boy's education. Detective stories could help boys to develop their powers of reasoning and deduction. It is no coincidence, then, that Arthur Baden-Powell in the Boy Scout manual, *Scouting for Boys* (1909), urged Boy Scout leaders to read the Sherlock Holmes stories to their troops as examples of deductive reasoning. Detective stories could teach them about precision and the powers of observation—hence the popularity of fictional deduction demonstrations based on minutiae like Watson's watch. Detective stories could also teach boys about responsibility and about chivalry. It is no coincidence that Conan Doyle also wrote books about knights whose attributes toward the weak and humble as well as toward women carried over pretty clearly and emphatically to Sherlock Holmes. It's also no real coincidence that Horatio Alger used the character of the detective as a frame upon which to hang a fable about virtue being more than its own reward. His *Dan the Detective* (1884) spins a yarn about Dan Mordaunt, newsboy, who recovers his family's stolen assets, catches counterfeiters, and is noticed and taken under the wing of Mr. Rogers who makes him a real detective in the Barton and Rogers Detective Agency. Unlike Poe's stories, then, the rebirth of the detective story in the 1890s had a lot to do with character-building tied in with justice. Given that pedigree, then, it is not altogether surprising, when reviewing the status of amateurs in turn of the century detective fiction to find, from early on, a number of heroes who are literally (and some who are figuratively) boys.

Boy detectives climbed out of the slough of the dime novel in 1896 when Mark Twain made Tom Sawyer one in *Tom Sawyer, Detective*. Richard Harding Davis introduced cub reporter Gallagher in 1906, and Harvey O'Higgins wrote a series of short stories about the exploits of the messenger boy who becomes detective Barney in 1915. Twain's work is another one of his jabs at the popularity of the detective story, or at the kind of detective story based on arthritic plot devices like mistaken identity and missing relatives. Significantly, though, in addition to the spoof, Twain links Tom and Huck's absorption with being detectives with youthful hi jinx and, more importantly, with the impulse toward playing, the same impulse found in Poe's allusions to games in "Murders in the Rue Morgue" and Dupin's dressing up found at the end of "The Purloined Letter." Just as Twain's burlesque focuses on affronting authority—both the authority of literary form of the last generation's sensation novel detective story and the world of adults overturned by smart boys—so does Richard Harding Davis' boy hero Gallagher who catches a crook and gets the story that the adults are unable to accomplish. It is not until O'Higgins' Barney that professionalism takes over and Barney, while bright and capable, instead of being able to live out his youthful fantasies needs to abandon them and learn the mundane intricacies of being a detective. With the advent of the 20th century, however, the thread of boy detective heroes would separate off and become a significant part of adolescent literature with the Hardy Boys books that began in 1927 and then with the Nancy Drew series for girls that began three years later.

Husband Material

But boys were not the only amateurs to enter turn of the century detective fiction. There was also the male lead in the sensation novel who may have qualified as a hero in the sense that he was sensitive, patient, honest, helpful, and understanding—in a word, he was ideal husband material—but, because the focus is upon women's suffering, and because providence is going to do the heavy lifting in the crime solving department, he's not the hero. But this character-type would eventually become more of an amateur detective than empathetic bystander with the approach of the 20th century. What one finds in the male leads in both *The Dead Letter* and *The Leavenworth Case,* moreover, is a response to events that is both lawyerly and one that carries with it a heavy dose of patience, of what can be construed (in light of later influences) as unmuscular Christianity. In both novels the male leads rely on constituted authority, the police, to do the majority of the investigating, the responsible citizen's fundamental duty in any orderly community—and one hammered away in British law from the time of the Tudors. Faith is the principal virtue of these two men, faith in the providential nature of the universe and faithfulness to women who will not be available until said providence clears up the crime that has disrupted the community. Virtues though they surely are, the kinds of qualities demonstrated by the men in these books and in sensation novels in general are passive, and from the perspective of later generations, wimpy. They are scarcely the makings of an amateur detective hero.

Part of what the sensation novel does is to make its central problem not only socially disruptive but also one that is both decidedly gothic and that has assumed proportions that seem larger than life. Things aren't just confused or puzzling or enigmatic, they're mysterious, eerie, threatening. Bad guys aren't just bad guys, they're larger than life evil geniuses. In this sense the master criminal detective story—a la John Buchan or Sax Rohmer—would become one of the offshoots of the sensation novel. With respect to this kind of villain, at the turn of the century one of the most immediate modification taking place in the sensation novel in America was in changing the male lead from passive observer into a detective (or into more of a detective than the sensation novel hero used to be) and into an action hero. One can see this happening in novels like Burton Stevenson's. *The Holladay Case* (1903), Meredith Nicholson's *The House of a Thousand Candles* (1905), Charles E. Walk's *The Yellow Circle* (1909), Will Irwin's *The House of Mystery* (1910), and Wells Hastings' *The Professor's Mystery* (1911) and *The Man in the Brown Derby* (1911). These novels center on a closely guarded, sinister secret that disrupts the world of the book, largely by denying the hero access to the woman he loves and, underlying everything, denying her access to her birthright—i.e. her family's money. That's all classic sensation novel stuff. Unlike traditional sensation novels, however, for one thing, turn of the century writers acknowledge that the police do exist, but now they have the added advantage of being able to portray them as corrupt or incompetent, aloof from the problems or impotent to assist the hero. This adds to the underlying sense of persecution of the hero who must either solve the book's problem by himself or find assistants or companions to help. These companions or assistants differ significantly from the Watson narrator-assistant invented by Poe and employed in *The Dead Letter* and *The Leavenworth Case*. These new assistant detectives actually do materially assist the hero and do things he cannot do. Thus in Hastings' books the heroes find an alienist, a "sociologist," and a middle aged spinster; in McIntyre's Ashton-Kirk books the companion, significantly, is a former amateur boxer and owner of a gym who provides brawn to the hero's brain. What happens here is that when the male lead is faced with mysterious, seemingly obdurate evil associated with the central problem, he first does some detection to find out what is going on and then he actively intervenes to save the suffering, persecuted, often kidnapped woman—in Wells Hastings' *The Man in the Brown Derby*, for example, the woman in the case is being held against her will (a la *The Woman in White*) in an insane asylum. Unlike the traditional sensation novel, in books like these the women's suffering, although certainly implied, happens largely off stage and the focus has shifted from empathy for women's sufferings to the man's determination to discover what happened as well as the whereabouts of the woman whose wealth and social position are imperiled by powerful enemies. Consciously a group of turn of the century writers had in mind modifying the sensation novel to make it more male centered. They would keep the gothic, titanic, inaccessible evil but would make the hero more knight than patient bystander. Thus when the hero sets off to find the lost formula (and subsequently to meet a frightening French count and to save a kidnapped woman) in William D. Pitman's *The Quincunx Case* (1904) he says

> Will you wish me good luck? I don't know how it will all end—I feel like one of those old chaps in Mallory going off on a quest... [89].

And like those old chaps in Mallory, accomplishing the quest means more than saving the lady. In a number of turn of the century detective stories the detection and the action has as much to do with the hero changing from being useless to being useful, as much to do with the hero acquiring and demonstrating virtue as it has to do with solving a crime problem. This had a connection with the influence of "muscular Christianity," the movement inspired in Britain by Charles Kingsley and manifested in Thomas Hughes' *Tom Brown's School Days* (1856) and then propagated first by Arthur Conan Doyle and seconded by the imperial romances of John Buchan. In the U.S.

> The heyday of muscular Christianity ... lasted roughly from 1880 to 1920. During that time, the YMCA invented basketball and volleyball, the Men and Religion Forward Movement sought to fill Protestant churches with men, and the churches took the lead in the organized camping and public playground movements. These efforts to make muscular Christianity an integral part of the churches lasted throughout World War I [www.infed.org/christianeducation/muscular_christianity].

As part of this movement the male sensation novel—and other kinds of turn of the century detective novels, too—shows the hero abandoning a frivolous, aimless, and self-indulgent life and becoming engaged in a purposeful one. Thus Philip Adrian in *The Quincunx Case* takes on the job of discovering the whereabouts of the secret formula to prove himself not only to himself but also to 1) his mother, 2) his uncle, and 3) his female cousin. And in so proving himself, Adrian's success, and that of all of the other heroes of male sensation novels, depends not just upon finding clues and solving a puzzle which is the detective part of the story but also upon traveling to unfamiliar places, encountering strangers who may help or hinder, saving innocents from harm, and facing down and defeating powerfully evil people. This is the kind of thing one can trace back to *Mort D'Arthur* and then watch the explicit application of morality to the adventure story in *Pilgrim's Progress*. In some turn of the century detective fiction, therefore, it is not simply the suffering of courageous women that lies at the emotional core of the story but the sensations that come from obstacles and adversaries that test and demonstrate the hero's personal worth. The thrills and chills are significantly different. But the turn of the century had another way for readers to experience these kinds of sensations. They could read about heroes who operated on the other side of the law.

OH BROTHER-IN-LAW, WHERE ART THOU?

In 1899 Ernest W. Hornung dedicated his collection of short stories, *The Amateur Cracksman*, to his brother-in-law Arthur Conan Doyle. This volume, along with *Raffles: Further Adventures of the Amateur Cracksman* (1901) and *A Thief in the Night* (1905), recounts the escapades of one A.J. Raffles, a toff with exquisite manners, the right clothes, the right schools and clubs, and impeccable social connections who is also a burglar. In the first story in the first collection, "The Ides of March," Raffles explains his peculiar criminal proclivities to his friend Bunny who narrates the stories:

> "How came you to begin?" I asked, as curiosity overcame mere wonder, and a fascination for his career gradually wove itself into my fascination for the man.
>
> "Ah! that's a long story," said Raffles. "It was in the Colonies, when I was out there playing cricket. It's too long a story to tell you now, but I was in much the same fix that you were in to-night, and it was my only way out. I never meant it for anything more; but I'd tasted blood, and it was all over with me. Why should I work when I could steal? Why settle down to some humdrum uncongenial billet, when excitement, romance, danger and a decent living were all going begging together? Of course it's very wrong, but we can't all be moralists, and the distribution of wealth is very wrong to begin with. Besides, you're not at it all the time. I'm sick of quoting Gilbert's lines to myself, but they're profoundly true. I only wonder if you'll like the life as much as I do!" [http://hornung.thefreelibrary.com/The-Amateur-Cracksman/1–1].

As the century turned there came to be something of a Raffles boom, especially in the United States. Raffles became a cinema hero when portrayed first by John Barrymore in 1917 and later by Ronald Coleman in 1930. Barrymore's Raffles, however, differed from Hornung's Raffles. The original Raffles had more than a bit of the blackguard about him and possessed no socially redeeming qualities other than good taste in clothes and sophisticated manners. Barrymore made his Raffles into a Robin Hood figure, a move that was conditioned by a number of developments. The popularity of Baroness Orczy's portrayal of Sir Percy Blakeney's double life as a mincing sophisticate and a swashbuckling savior of those threatened by the Reign of Terror in *The Scarlet Pimpernel* (1905) had something to do with that change. But more specifically the character of the gentleman crook was shaped when Maurice Leblanc introduced his knock off of Raffles in *Arsène Lupin, Gentleman Cambrioleur* in 1907 (*The Confessions of Arsene Lupin*, 1913). Arsene Lupin possessed a flair for the dramatic, a Gallic élan, and a sense of humor largely absent in Raffles:

> Arsene Lupin, the fastidious gentleman who confines his operations to country-houses and fashionable drawing-rooms, and who one night, after breaking in at Baron Schormann's, had gone away empty-handed, leaving his visiting card:
>
> Arsene Lupin

Gentleman Burglar

with these words added in pencil:

"Will return when your things are genuine."

Arsene Lupin, the man with a thousand disguises, by turns chauffeur, opera-singer, book-maker, gilded youth, young man, old man, Marseillese bagman, Russian doctor, Spanish bull-fighter! [www.gaslight.mtroyal.ab.ca/gaslight/lupin].

Arsene Lupin became the Robin Hood that Raffles wasn't. Not only that, Leblanc's light tone dissipated the moral implication of having a criminal hero and allowed readers to savor the hero's style as well as his ingenious criminal technique.

So popular was the gentleman crook that for decades the character type echoed in American popular culture. In the 1920s Dashiell Hammett commented on the fad for gentleman crooks by making them the object of satire in his early pieces in *The Smart Set* and *Brief Stories*. At the turn of the century the gentleman burglar even became the subject of urban myth, embodied in a style of walking stick called the "Gentleman Burglar's Cane":

This gentleman burglar's cane is a square forged iron rod with a 4–1/2 inch wide, L-shaped handle and integral fluted ferrule. The handle and collar are nickel plated and the shaft is ebonized. Overall length is 34 inches. The walking stick belonged to an older New Yorker who terrorized jewelry stores, smashing showcases while his wife scooped up the jewels. He stayed at the scene of the crimes, leaning on his cane, with his elegantly dressed wife, the jewelry in her pockets. He never got caught. It is said he financed an orphan's home with the proceeds of the jewelry he fenced. In business he was known as Iron Rod. This modern-day Robin Hood left his belongings and this relic to charity [http://showcase.goantiques.com/detail,early-20th-gentleman, 403031.html].

These echoes existed partly because of Raffles and Arsene Lupin but also because a number of turn of the century writers in America turned their attention to grafting the character of the gentleman burglar onto the body of the detective story.

Don't Make Me Laugh

Gaston Leroux wrote the Arsene Lupin stories with his tongue pretty firmly in his cheek: his hero's second outing, after all, was *Arsène Lupin contre Herlock Sholmes* (*Arsene Lupin vs. Herlock Sholmes* [1908]). Just as the introduction of Sherlock Holmes inspired both emulation and parodies, so did the idea of the gentleman criminal. And that's the way in which the gentleman crook was introduced to turn of the century American fiction. Arthur Train surely had his tongue in his cheek when he introduced the gentleman crook to America in his *McAllister and his Double* (1905). The first three stories in Train's collection ("McAllister's Christmas," "The Baron De Ville," and "The Escape of Wilkins") involve McAllister, a tubby, bonhomous clubman, and his valet, McAllister's aforesaid double, who has left his employer and, dressed in his clothes, embarked on a career as a gentleman burglar, known to the police as "Fatty Welch." What follows has a great deal in common with stage farce based on social inversion, mistaken identity, and assorted hi jinx. The following year Nelson Lloyd moved the gentleman burglar from burlesque up the scale to comedy combined with social comment in *The Robberies Company, Ltd.* (1906). In it Captain Herberton Wade's home is invaded by a gang that takes the places of his servants and holds him "prisoner" for a month. They, however, are not garden variety criminals, but a collective of educated, sophisticated gentlemen who believe that materialism is the root of society's ills and intend to use Wade to bilk wealthy New Yorkers out of some of their cash. In the end Wade accepts their premise and becomes one of their number. In 1906 Geraldine Bonner also used the gentle, but this time gentlewoman burglar in her comic redaction of *The Moonstone*, *The Castlecourt Diamond Case*. The last of the initial prewar run of American gentleman crook stories was Arthur Stringer's *The Night Hawk* (1908). In that collection Edward Elton Gahan, the Night Hawk, narrates a series of eight stories, all of which involve the hero from the "under groove" (i.e. underworld) in adventures with criminal activity but which also have chivalric leanings. In "The Adventure of the Emerald Pendant," for example, the hero protects an innocent woman's reputation by blowing open a safe and then returning her emerald necklace. Chivalry aside, like Raffles Gahan was addicted to excitement:

> I waited at the corner of Broadway and Fourteenth Street, lazily debating with myself whether it should be the Criterion or the Casino. I didn't care which, for those play-acting places seemed mostly a waste of time. When I wanted amusement, I always hankered for the real thing: I never cared to sit in a plush chair and watch a two-dollar picture of it. That make of mental cocktail was good enough for tired workers and hall roomers. It was good enough for souls of flat-dwellers who longed to obliterate their twelve hours of by a two-hour daub of melodrama. But when I wanted thrills, I preferred getting them from the jolts and bumps of the crazy, happy-go-lucky Under Groove itself [78].

Gahan even provides a philosophic underpinning for his style of life:

> It was the same old and shallow self-deceit, the same old salve for the sore

conscience, the weak will; the same old whine of the man who'd never learned to make offense against law a philosophy of conduct. As for myself, I used to read Neitzsche in my younger days; but now I acted him [134].

All of this heady stuff, however, turns out to be fantasy. Edward Elton Gahan is not really a suave, internationally famous gentleman crook, but a telegraph operator from Michigan who developed an alternate, fabricated personality after receiving a knock on the head during a robbery of his office. And it's to that identity as a telegraph operator he returns, a la *A Connecticut Yankee*, at the end of the book. In spite of the sententae in *The Night Hawk* about excitement and ubermensches, Stringer, like Train, Lloyd, and Bonner doesn't take the figure of the blue blooded criminal very seriously. Neither does Frederick Anderson with his entry into the gentleman criminal sweepstakes just before the war with *The Adventures of the Infallible Godahl* (1914). Sure enough, it's about a suave, sophisticated gentleman about town who, like Arsene Lupin, mostly robs from the pretentious nouveau riche. Part of Godahl's panache comes from the fact that he possesses the same kind of technique and chutzpah as Erich Weiss, the magician who changed his name to Harry Houdini in 1913. The interest in Anderson's stories resides both with the Robin Hoodish character of the gentleman criminal and in piquing readers' interest in showing how his schemes work—an attraction parallel to magicians explaining how magic tricks work. Their interest also comes from Anderson's light-hearted double perspective: the stories in Anderson's book are really about Oliver Armiston, a writer who has created stories about exquisitely brilliant schemes executed by a gentleman crook, the Infallible Godahl. So these pieces by Anderson, like those by Train, Bonner, and Stringer, focus on excitement—particularly the excitement provided by the prospect of being caught doing something illegal—as well as on the freedom to go and do whatever one pleases to do. But they don't take themselves too seriously—or don't take literature too seriously. Others would take the gentleman crook more seriously. Sort of.

WHO WAS THAT MASKED PERSON?

It's not that other writers in the teens took the gentleman criminal more seriously than Stringer, Train, Lloyd, Bonner or Anderson who used them for a variety of ultimately comic purposes; if anything the new writers in the teens took the character type less seriously, avoiding any meaningful thought about the moral, social, or economic implications of a gifted individual turning to crime while enjoying the fruits of social prominence.

The second wave of gentleman burglar writers avoided any of those implications by copying the conventions established by the Robin Hood stories as well as Robin's reincarnation in the form of the Scarlet Pimpernel. Those models yielded the stereotype of the outlaw hero and the excitement of secret identities and both of these had a discernable impact on the character of the gentleman burglar—as did motifs from the sensation novel.

Apropos to American notions about the gentleman's natural habitat, T.W. Hanshew set most of his stories about Hamilton Cleek (beginning with *The Man of Forty Faces*, 1910) in London. The Cleek stories are mostly scientific detective stories: they turn on things like x-rays, arrow poison and fingerprints. While Cleek, like The Thinking Machine and most other up to date private sleuths, has a lab, his signal advantage is possessing a malleable face that allows him to change his appearance almost at will. Except for the face part, all of this is pretty contemporary; indeed Hanshew's plots are detective story plots. But the hero is and isn't a detective and is and isn't a gentleman burglar. Hamilton Cleek was the celebrated and feared "Vanishing Cracksman." But he's gone straight. What takes the Cleek stories backwards to the sensation novel is his past as a criminal who has reformed and become a private detective—not because he's good at it or because he knows how criminals work, a la Vidoq—both of which, of course, are true—but to redeem himself with the woman he loves both by defeating others' villainy and by sending the fees he earns as a detective to those whom he had burgled during his old life of crime. Almost the same thing shows up in Arthur B. Reeve's hero in *Constance Dunlap* (1916). The stories begin with Constance Dunlap using her brains and dexterity to commit a crime that will cover up her inept husband's embezzling. She becomes practiced in the upper-level criminal arts and crafts, but she turns these skills to use helping others as an amateur detective. In both cases the writers' perspective shifts from the admiring description of the dexterity and élan of the criminal's technique to that of the detective. While Hanshew has his criminal turned detective work with the officials of Scotland Yard in the fictionally familiar role of "consulting detective," in the manner of the sensation novel Reeve's hero continues to he hounded by a thuggish and threatening member of the New York Police Department.

While both the new detective story based on science as well as motifs from the sensation novel stand behind Hamilton Cleek and Constance Dunlap, the influence of the sensation novel became more prominent in a set of ragingly popular novels. These began with Louis Joseph Vance's series of eight Lone Wolf books that started with *The Lone Wolf* in 1914 and ended after the War with *The Lone Wolf's Last Prowl* in 1934. The Lone Wolf is the name that the newspapers have attached to Michael Lanyard, an orphan who grows up as apprentice to a cracksman and becomes a master of his craft and a world-renowned felon. A gang of criminals attempts to make him a member of their syndicate and, when he refuses the offer tendered by International Underworld Limited, they become his implacable enemy. In response to their threats, the Lone Wolf goes straight, rescues a young woman who was in the gang's thrall, returns the booty from his most recent heist to its owners, and escapes to England—after a shoot-out between airplanes over the English Channel. Two years after this heady yarn, Frank Packard's novels about Jimmy Dale began with *The Adventures of Jimmy Dale* (1917) and extended to *Jimmy Dale and the Phantom Clue* in 1935. Jimmy Dale, like Michael Lanyard, is known to the police and the newspapers under another name—he's the Gray Seal because he leaves a diamond shaped gray paper seal glued to the safes he cracks. In reality Jimmy Dale is a millionaire clubman, heir of a family fortune made in the safe manufacturing business. He, of course, steals from the rich and gives to the poor, and does so especially after a mystery woman discovers his alternate identity and sends him instructions about whom to burgle and to whom to give the swag. She, it turns out, is one Marie LaSalle, an heiress who has been cheated out of her fortune by a Master Criminal (who is not a gentleman by any means), and who, in the character of Silver Mag, acts as an amateur social worker. By the end of the book, Jimmy Dale has rescued her fortune, defeated her nemesis, and clasped her to his bosom.

What Vance and Packard both do is to combine bits of Raffles and Arsene Lupin with added schoolboy fantasies and motifs from the sensation novel. Michael Lanyard, Jimmy Dale and Marie LaSalle all come under the influence of unseen threatening powers. Marie has the traditional maiden's curse of having her inheritance stolen and Michael and Jimmy both fear the exposure of their alter egos and, more immediately, both are subject to the double malevolent workings of the corrupt police and the vengeful underworld, both home-grown motifs in fiction. In these stories the emphasis in the characterization of the outlaw hero is moral rather than social. Even outlaw heroes of the period like the Scarlet Pimpernel and Zorro (introduced in 1919 in Johnston McCulley in *The Curse of Capistrano*) didn't mean a lot in the social justice department: even though their *raison d'être* was social justice, their causes were long ago and far away and the focus of their adventures was solely on the excitement of capture and escape. Vance and Packard don't deal with social implications—or, rather, they do deal with social implications but only of the most conservative sort. At least in their initial appearances, the significance of their outlaw heroes is that because of the influence of good women they quit being criminals, they become ideal husband material with a dangerous and romantic past and a domestic present. These narratives describing that domestication, however, were written in a dumbed-down style appropriate for adolescent readers, not the same class of readers who picked up the gentleman crook fiction of Anderson or Train or Lloyd.

FOR SALE: THE BROOKLYN BRIDGE

Forgetting, for a moment, about detective stories, that same class of readers who avoided Vance and Packard's oeuvre as jejune but who appreciated Anderson and company might have been inclined to dip into Gelette Burgess and Will Irwin. Burgess, to be sure, wrote detective stories. But with Irwin he also wrote about picaros. In *The Picaroons* (1904) they included a head note to explain their reintroduction of this antique character type:

> *Picaroon*—a petty rascal; one who lives by his wits; an adventurer. The Picaresque Tales, in Spanish literature of the beginning of the Seventeenth Century, dealt with the fortunes of beggars, impostors, thieves, etc., and chronicled the Romance of Roguery. Such stories were precursors to the modern novel.

Except that the picaro and the picaresque novel weren't that old any more. What Burgess and Irwin were doing here was following Mark Twain's lead. In 1884 Twain had dusted off the old literary form of the picaresque novel and used it as the backbone of *Huckleberry Finn*. And it wasn't just Burgess and Irwin who followed Twain's lead, Arthur Stringer, George Randolph Chester, Hugh Pendexter, O. Henry, George Allan England all made the rogue hero their own, the rogue hero whose acts danced on and sometimes over the edge of the law. Most of these writers' picaresque pieces started out as magazine fiction: Burgess and Irwin's yarns about four down-and-outers in San Francisco appeared in *Pearson's Magazine* in 1904; *The Saturday Evening Post* carried Hugh Pendexter's pieces on bogus impresario Tiberius Smith in 1905; and the same magazine ran Arthur Stringer's stories in 1907 and began George Randolph Chester's chronicling of the exploits of Get Rich Quick Wallingford in 1908. That same year also saw the publication of O. Henry's collection *The Gentle Grafter*.

Picaresque pieces like these play a problematic role in the history of the detective story. Even though they usually include crime of one sort or another, they are hardly detective stories. Even though their rogue heroes sometimes help to solve or to prevent serious crimes, they're not detectives, they're con men and the focus of the fiction is on the construction and articulation of their less than upright schemes. Although sometimes the victims of those schemes deserve to be victimized, Pod and Bender, Wallingford, and the rest are no Robin Hoods or gentleman burglars. They lack the physical dexterity, stamina, and even the ambition for that profession. They work in spurts—usually when they run out of money. And, appropriate to American fiction, they are peripatetic, moving from one place to another to find fresh sets of suckers. The knot of rogue stories that appeared in the first decade of the new century, however, added several things to the development of crime fiction in America. First of all, this kind of fiction emphasized technique: rogue stories focus on the way that con games are set up and sprung on the victim—not on their moral or criminal quality. In this sense, they contribute to the gradual movement of the detective story away from didactic, moral fiction and toward light entertainment. Thus in early 20th century detective stories the discovery of how a crime was committed gradually became equally important, even more important than who committed the crime. Along the same lines, like the ubiquitous parodies of Sherlock Holmes, this class of fiction added a much needed light touch to turn of the century crime fiction. In style, in incident, in character, most turn of the century rogue fiction intends to be comic—and some of it still is. And that was a significant contribution to the development of the detective story that was hi-jacked by moralists soon after it was invented by Poe.

THE NEW AMATEUR DETECTIVE

The creation of a new kind of hero serves as another indicator of turn of the century efforts to shift the focus of the detective story from sensation novel morality and Boy's Own Paper didacticism on to semi-intellectual entertainment—i.e. playing with logic seasoned with a chase or a pistol shot or two in the dark. Leaving out heroes who are victims of injustice (those who become detectives because they have to in order to save themselves or a loved one from prosecution or persecution), all of the heroes we have encountered—police officers, private detectives, lawyers, journalists, scientists—regardless of how committed they are or how well suited they are to what they do, solve crimes because it is their job to do so. They get paid. By definition, then, no matter how smart, knowledgeable, charming, or attractive they are, no matter how much fun they have doing what they do, what they do can't be a game, because it is not something they choose to do. This was a standard that Poe set for the detective and the detective story—Dupin is as far from a professional thief taker as one can get and the fact that he is not a professional both liberates his character and magnifies his success. There were a number of forces that moved Conan Doyle to make Sherlock Holmes a professional detective, not the least of which was the creation and evolution of professional detectives. Nonetheless, at the turn of the century the cult of the amateur was alive and thriving in Britain and America. It was there in athletics with the modern Olympics beginning in 1896 and in science and technology with unschooled inventors like the Wright brothers changing the world. It was there in Britain's sending off amateurs to govern the Empire and in Teddy Roosevelt's rounding up cowboys to serve as his "Rough Riders." And it was emphatically there in the world of business and commerce with Andrew Carnegie and Rockefeller illustrating the truth that anybody could become a millionaire. It was there, too, in the emergence of a new kind of hero of the turn of the century detective story.

Almost as soon as the Sherlock Holmes stories made their appearance in American newspapers, that new kind of hero began to emerge. In 1892 Roderiguez Ottolengui introduced his pair of sleuths, Barnes and Mitchell, in *Artist in Crime*; the pair would appear again in *The Crime of the Century* (1896), and *The Final Proof* (1896). Barnes is a private detective, and by most accounts (including his own) a pretty good one. Robert Leroy Mitchell isn't a private detective. He's a rich guy fascinated by crime and by criminals. Throughout the three books Barnes, the professional, and Mitchell, the amateur, engage in a usually friendly competition. This competition ranges from the joke Mitchell plays on Barnes in "The Missing Link" (one that revolves around planted clues and the body of an ape that is mistaken for that of a human) to the more wide ranging problems in *The Crime of the Century*. Seasoned with allusions to Sherlock Holmes, throughout Ottolengui's books intellect beats humdrum, old fashioned detective routines like dressing up in disguises and shadowing people. Hence this piece of intellectual flaunting from Mitchell:

> "Which only proves," said Mr. Mitchell, "that as usual you detectives have worked in routine fashion, and, consequently, by beginning at the wrong end, you have not reached the goal. Now I have not done half of the work that either of you have been compelled to bestow on your investigation" [*Final Proof,* 120].

Just as Ottolengui's Mitchell drops in allusions to Sherlock Holmes, Samuel Gardenhire lards his pieces about amateur detective LeDroit Conners, originally published in the *Saturday Evening Post* and collected in *The Long Arm* (1906), with references to Poe. Thus when the narrator first drops by the hero's rooms he sees

> Three pictures of a single man were grouped about the bust, all of a common likeness but expressive of different moods or impressions, as the artist had

painted some character that had laid hold of his fancy. I recognized the bust as that of Edgar Allan Poe, and upon the three pictures was the word "Dupin," painted in strong charcters in the lower corner of the canvas. This particular circumstance did not impress me at the time, but I remembered that the Chevalier Dupin was an astute character of several fascinating romances of the great author in which he displayed a singular and deductive skill in the discovery of crime [8].

LeDroit Conners, however, is not a detective, private or otherwise: he's an artist whose talents (with a bit of pseudo psychology bibble babble thrown in) make him an infallible detective:

> You cannot understand how strongly such matters appeal to me. It is a faculty with me almost to know the solution of a crime when the leading circumstances connected with it are revealed. I form my conclusion first, and, confident of its correctness, hunt for evidence to sustain it. I do this because I am never wrong. It is not magic, telepathy, nor any form of mental science; it is a moral consciousness of the meaning of related facts, impressed on my mind with unerring certainty [63].

Three years later Henry K. Webster would also play off of the artist as amateur detective in *The Whispering Man*, but Webster gave his artist the background of having been a police detective and a courtroom artist as explanation for his knowledge of the accoutrements of crime. Gardenhire does little to explain why Conners knows all about chemistry and counterfeiting beyond making him an avid newspaper reader—and a genius. That readers would accept that an accomplished amateur possessed such knowledge is yet another repercussion of the popularity of the original detective polymath, Sherlock Holmes. Unlike Webster's book about an artist-amateur detective where the solution has something to do with the artist's special talent, however, Gardenhire gives Conner's occupation as an artist no special connection with his talent for solving crimes. It's more something that marks him off as an amateur more than anything else. The problem with amateurs who become popular is maintaining their amateur status. Thus as the stories proceed, Gardenhire has something of a problem explaining the shift from an amateur solving problems that accidentally come his way to a celebrated expert who is sought out and rewarded for his expertise and acumen. Being an expert, however, does not make one a professional.

Being a polymath was a good thing for an amateur detective to be at the turn of the century, but being a rich polymath was a lot better if one was going to take up detection as a hobby. John T. McIntyre's Ashton-Kirk was one of them—the scion of a wealthy family who took up detecting as an all consuming hobby. Before the War, McIntyre wrote three Ashton-Kirk books—*Ashton-Kirk Investigator* (1910), *Ashton-Kirk Secret Agent*

(1912), and *Ashton-Kirk Special Detective* (1912). And with a somewhat different emphasis, three Ashton-Kirk films were made in 1915: *An Affair of Three Nations*, *The Menace of the Mute*, and *The House of Fear.* Here is the hero's first appearance in print:

> Ashton-Kirk, who had solved so many mysteries, is himself something of a problem even to those who know him best. Although young, wealthy, and of high social position, he is nevertheless an indefatigable worker in his chosen field. He smiles when men call him a detective. "No; only an investigator," he says.
>
> He has never courted notoriety; indeed his life has been more or less secluded. However, let a man do remarkable work in any line and, as Emerson has observed, "the world will make a beaten path to his door." Those who have found their way to Ashton-Kirk's door have been of many races and interests. Men of science have often been surprised to find him in touch with the latest discoveries, scholars searching among strange tongues and dialects and others deep in tattered scrolls, ancient tablets and forgotten books have been his frequent visitors. But among them come many who seek his help in solving problems in crime [*Ashton-Kirk Investigator* 5].

As with Gardenhire, McIntyre starts his amateur detective off with Poe, an allusion to whom is tucked into the catalog of books about crime in which the reader finds Ashton-Kirk engrossed in the first novel. Indeed, he sometimes goes into Dupinesque reveries: "Rather he sank deeper into the arms of the chair; the cigarette end became gray and dead between his fingers; the strangely brilliant eyes closed as though he had fallen asleep" (*Investigator* 118). In addition to his own literary and scientific arsenal, Ashton-Kirk has servants and paid private investigators to scour the globe, if need be, for the information he needs to close the case. Ashton-Kirk, however, retains, for McIntyre, the common touch. He goes to the gymnasium of his old friend Scanlon, a retired collegiate boxing coach, and he refuses to move from the family mansion in spite of the precipitous decline of the neighborhood.

Average Jones, the name that Samuel Hopkins Adams concocted for his amateur detective featured in *Average Jones* (1911), likewise summons up the common touch—even though Adrian Van Reypen Egerton Jones can scarcely be described as common. He has inherited millions from a grafter relative with proviso that he live in New York for five years so that he will "squander his unearned and undeserved fortune, thus completing the vicious circle, and returning the millions acquired by my political activities, in a poisoned shower to the city..." (3). Echoing the traditional conversion story, however, the money does not corrupt Adams' hero because he acquires a hobby, which begins with just collecting strange and bizarre newspaper advertisements and items from the personals columns. Along with the style of living of a carefree, affluent man about town—one that involves a lot of going to one's club—and savoring the slang and purposely carefree diction that was going to come to characterize the speech of the fast set after the War, Adams gives his hobby a higher purpose than simply passing time by centering on graft and corruption, the chosen venue of the muckraker. And so the amateur hero finds entertainment from the zaniness of the advertisements he finds in the newspapers, exercises his reason the way that he was taught at college, and completes the circle by using his skills and inherited wealth to uncover the kind of graft and corruption that earned it in the first place.

THE ECCENTRICS

While a number of period writers embodied reasoning and science in the art and discipline of detection undertaken as a hobby of the otherwise idle rich, others focused on characters who were superficially not the least bit like Sherlock Holmes. That, to be sure, would include women detectives both professional and amateur. On the amateur side it would include Gwendolen Bramblestone of Carey's *The Van Suyden Sapphires*, who functions in the novel pretty much as a male amateur would—except that she's a woman. Mary Wilkins Freeman in *The Long Arm* and Susan Glaspell in "A Jury of Her Peers" both include characters who are not like the conventional detective and, additionally focus on perceptions and the differences between the ways in which men and woman view the same evidence. This same impulse to create a unique detective character and to use the detective story to explore the nature and use of the senses was the motive that inspired Harrison Holt to create a blind detective, Stephen Garth, in 1912, two years before Bramah's *Max Carrados*. In 1915 Isabel Ostrander followed both by introducing Damon Grant, a blind private detective for his only appearance in *At One Thirty*. One year later Clinton Stagg created Thornley Colton, another blind detective, in *Silver Sandals* (1916) and continued his adventures after the War. Colton calls himself a "Problemist." In compensation for his blindness, Colton, like Grant, has developed his other senses, developed them extraordinarily—he can read regular print with his fingers, hear things inaudible to others, and even drive an automobile. He has a house full of assistants all of whom were foundlings adopted by the hero and who assist him when he needs help or, more often, need his help when they get into trouble doing what the hero has asked them to do. Thus the Thornley Colton books combine elements of the detective story with elements of the thriller—another British import from the likes of Edgar Wallace.

Play and Games

One of the most interesting uses of the amateur hero of the period was by John Prentis in *The Case of Doctor Horace A Study of the Importance of Conscience in the detection of Crime* (1907). It begins with an argument between Dr. Horace and his friend Wallace about why criminals are caught. Wallace maintains that criminals are caught because they're guilty—"the confession his conscience makes discloses his crime to the law" (16). Horace, however, contends that "A man's conscience has little to do with whether he is punished or not. There are plenty of criminals in the jails today who haven't conscience enough to trouble them any, and yet they have been caught. The law is simply wiser and better organized than the criminal and so it catches the majority of them" (16). To settle their dispute, Horace wagers $1,000 that if they fake a murder and Wallace acts the part of the murderer, that he will not be able to escape capture for a month. They do this and Wallace eludes capture for the stipulated period—although Hunter, the bright police detective, is hot on his trail. *Doctor Horace* crystallizes a number of turn of the century detective story themes. First of all it represents crime and the justice system as a hot topic for conversation among lay people—neither Horace nor Wallace has any connection with the law, the police, or any sort of professional detecting. Significantly the book presents the contrast and conflict between different points of view about justice: Wallace upholds the old view of providential justice and that "murder will out" and Horace advocates the view that ultimately goes back to Blackstone—that detecting and punishing crimes is the state's business not that of the deity. Finally, Prentis' novel explicitly makes the detective story into a game, not just a symbolic portrayal of tag or hide and seek, but one in which the participants consciously engage in playing a game.

In *Doctor Horace* Prentis put into practice something that had been happening with amateur detectives in American fiction almost as soon as the Sherlock Homes stories appeared on newsstands. The idea of play and the amateur detective started with Ottolengui's stories in the early 1890s. While Ottolengui's books certainly reflected his concern with some serious social problems—*The Crime of the Century*, for instance, focuses on the condition and fate of children of poverty—both the characters of the detectives and the fundamental justification of the narrative leave behind the sentimentality of the sensation novel and the didacticism of the boy's story and replace them with the concept that the principal purpose of the detective story is to play a game, to entertain. Ottolengui is quite open about this in preface to *The Crime of the Century*:

After all, the main object of fiction is to entertain, and even though a little instructive lesson may be deftly interwoven with the plot, I fear that the modern novel is sometimes too highly spiced with philosophic dissertations. And in seeking to entertain is it not best to offer something out of the common? Something a little different from the dull routine of daily existence? [iv].

And if the detective story could entertain readers by consciously presenting them with a game to watch, it was not a very long step to move the form from a spectator sport to one in which the readers could also be involved. And this was something that writers and their publishers wanted. Thus in the ads in the back of Webster's *The Whispering Man* (1909), someone at Appleton added that the novel was

A detective story you ought to read. Something altogether different in that the clues to the mystery lie open to the reader throughout the whole story, and are yet so concealed that the unsuspecting reader will be amazed at the outcome.

It's what Ellery Queen twenty years later would call the challenge to the reader.

11

Last Thoughts

As it stood on July 10, 1891, things didn't look all that good for the future of the detective story that Poe invented. In fact, as things stood, the detective story in America was in significant trouble. Poe's tales of ratiocination had loitered about for fifty years, more appreciated in Europe than in his own country. The home-grown detective yarns that had appeared in family story papers and then in dime novels from the late 1860s were under attack from Anthony Comstock and societies for the suppression of vice almost as soon as they began to appear on newsstands and in the mail: prompted, no doubt, by Comstock or the paranoia he engendered, contemporary newspapers occasionally ran stories about youths who had committed crimes under the influence of sensational fiction and a number of state legislatures considered and some even passed Comstock-inspired laws banning the production or sale of material (fiction or non-fiction) that contained criminal news, police reports, or accounts of criminal deeds. In the literary world—or the world that was more literary than that of the dime novel—crime and detection had become the exclusive property of sensation writers who focused on the emotional reverberations of crime, reverberations centered mostly on women, their suitors, and their families. Even Julian Hawthorne with his insider's connections with the New York Police Department focused on sentiment rather than on crime or its detection in his Thomas Byrnes novels. On top of that, the profession that had recently been invented to prevent and detect crime was in serious trouble. News of epidemics of debilitating police corruption was about to break out in New York and then across the country via Lincoln Steffens' reporting for *McClure's* that was eventually published as *The Shame of the Cities* (1904). On top of that, in spite of Allan Pinkerton's successes and efforts at marketing and publicity, private detectives, linked with divorce cases, violence, and a miscellany of other unsavory and illegal acts, attracted little public confidence or esteem. That lack of confidence and esteem was one of the things that ex-Pinkerton operative Dashiell Hammett commented on in his early ventures into print in H.L. Mencken's *Smart Set*. That lack of confidence and esteem led state after state at the turn of the century to require private detectives to be regulated and licensed.

And then, the next day, July 11, 1891, "A Scandal in Bohemia" started to appear in newspapers in cities across the nation and in the following months the rest of the short stories that would comprise *The Adventures of Sherlock Holmes* came out in papers from coast to coast. Arthur Conan Doyle's Sherlock Holmes stories not only made what was originally Poe's invention popular in the United States they also made the detective story legitimate. After Holmes appeared in the United States, pretty quickly writers recognized that detective stories were hot stuff. One of the first to appreciate this was Mark Twain, arguably the most famous writer in the country at the time—he had been given one honorary degree from Yale in 1888 and would receive another from Yale, as well as one from Oxford during the ensuing decades. Shortly after the American publication of the Holmes stories, Twain dashed off *Tom Sawyer, Detective* (1896) and six years later he overtly spoofed Conan Doyle's detective in "The Double Barreled Detective Story." He was hardly alone in his double barreled response to Conan Doyle, both serious imitations of Conan Doyle's detective and narrative technique as well as parodies of Holmes and Watson became popular items in American newspapers and magazines. That was the popularity part. The legitimacy that Conan Doyle's detective brought to American detective fiction occurred in two separate arenas. The first was from state legislatures. As noted above, from the early 1870s onward, Anthony Comstock and assorted societies for the suppression of vice had targeted, along with literature on birth control, literature about crime. Comstock, in fact, had tried to shut down *The Fireside Companion*, one of the most popular story papers and one of the original sources of what would become known as "dime novel" detective fiction. One of the most telling arguments against anti-dime novel legislation was the appearance of the Sherlock Holmes stories, a "higher class of detective fiction." And this made the New York legislature and others shy away from trying to keep the detective off of the newsstands and out of bookstores. The other side of legitimacy had to do with the recognition that the detective story was a separate and distinct literary genre. The publication of the Sherlock Holmes stories moved readers, writers, and miscellaneous intellectuals to look at what Conan Doyle had done and this, in turn, led to the rediscovery of Poe, to the creation of a prehistory for the genre going all the way back to the Egyptians and an examination of the intervening links between Poe and the publication of *A Study in Scarlet* and "A Scandal in Bohemia." And the rapid acceptance of the detective story as a legitimate form of literary expression and even literary diversion manifested itself in popularity—as the new century dawned detective stories became commonplace in American newspapers, magazines, and began to gain a significant and separate niche in the book trade.

That much about the turn of the century detective story is reasonably clear. Not a lot else is so easily traceable. Something, for instance, was happening to the sensation novel. Dominating crime fiction from the days of Bulwer-Lytton and reaching to the turn of the century and beyond, sensation novels used crime and detection as a means of stimulating the readers' sentiments. They accomplished this mostly by exhibiting female characters rendered isolated, threatened, and helpless by both crimes and the by intrusiveness of civil authority: often the women in these works are made thrall both by crime and the demands of propriety. Representing traditional views of criminals and crime, sensation novels presented criminals as bearing the marks of their warped natures and evil deeds on their countenances and their demeanors. They slouched, and sneered, and shivered. They recoiled when confronted with evidence of their perfidy. And that confrontation of the wicked with explicit proof of their guilt and their subsequent exposure and punishment, although in the later 19th century often aided by official detectives, was fundamentally the work of providence. In other words, sensation fiction rested on the same murder-will-out formula found in Chaucer's "Prioress' Tale" and Shakespeare's *Macbeth*. At the turn of the century, however, the sensation novel underwent a variety of changes, some of which affected detective fiction and some of which did not. One that did not was the gradual morphing of the sensation novel into part of the background of the modern love romance at the beginning of the 20th century. Concerning detective fiction, the most significant phenomenon was the increased role of detection and the decreased role of the unseen hand of providence in effecting a "happy" ending in fiction. In this respect, focus began to shift from the suffering of the woman hero to the reasoning and the stratagems of the male hero who increasingly displaced the police officer as the detective figure. Corresponding with this shift came writers' creation of devices to mask the identity of the criminal or to render the criminal inaccessible.

Out of necessity writers had to transform the sensation novel: they had to keep it up to date, and to do so they had to dispense with a variety of stock effects. One thing that changed the sensation novel was the invention of the police, the gradual emergence of new attitudes toward crime, and the growing prominence of urban settings. The traditional sensation novel feeds on isolation and helplessness. In spite of their desire for closure, the last thing the characters in *The Dead Letter* and *The Leavenworth Case* want to do is to expose their problems or their family's problems to strangers and to hold them up to public scrutiny. In *The Moonstone* as well as in American sensation fiction the police characters, representing a recently founded institution, largely serve as agents of upper middle class families whose job it is to both solve the crime and to keep everything hushed up. As the end of the century approached, this character pattern became increasingly difficult to maintain. As the police and police detectives became more established entities, as newspapers became more and more interested in reporting on crime and civic corruption, as private detectives and private detective agencies proliferated, and, especially in America, as society became in theory at least somewhat more egalitarian, it became less and less credible and less and less acceptable to have police detectives act as agents of the elite and to exempt the wealthy from the established processes of the rule of law.

Just as crime fiction came to accept new attitudes toward crime and justice as a public opposed to a private affair, at the turn of the century it also began to reflect changes in the nature of evidence and police work. Up until the end of the 19th century crime detection and the demonstration of guilt in fact and in fiction were not very complicated affairs. Putting aside torture, divination, and other extrasensory methodologies, guilt could only be incontrovertibly established either by an eyewitness or through the confession of the accused. There was no other kind of reliable evidence—no ballistics, no fingerprints, no blood analysis; in a word, justice had no access to scientific or what today is called forensic evidence. What that meant was that the principal job of the police officer or of the private detective until the end of the 19th century was identifying people and shadowing them. In the trickle of crime fiction that existed at mid-century, then, the detective's principal occupation became finding and following suspected persons. Corresponding with Arthur Conan Doyle's introduction of deductions based on minutiae in the Sherlock Holmes stories, the turn of the century witnessed a burst of scientific discoveries that aided in the detection of crime—fingerprints, blood types, modern ballistics, etc. This phenomenon ramified in several directions. First, it changed Anglo-American jurisprudence by bringing the expert witness into the courtroom to testify to the presence of things often unseeable by the naked eye. Correspondingly, it made the job of the detective far more complex and, therefore, a potentially more interesting subject for fiction than a narrative based on old police methods that boiled down to following suspects or, if they were lower class or minority individuals, physically intimidating them with Thomas Byrnes' third degree. Additionally, it changed the nature of one area of police work, and this, in turn, had its impact on the hero of the detective story. While from the beginning of police forces, the main qualifications for being a police officer were stamina, average intelligence, and discipline, the advent of scientific evidence required a new sort of detective — one with specialized, technical knowledge often associated with university education. And, realistically, that disqualified the police — even if the contemporary corruption scandals did not. This state of affairs, however, offered a variety of options to the fledgling detective story — in developing characters and in articulating plots.

One of those options was looking into the character of the criminal. In the way of cause and effect, the 19th century's exploding wealth and galloping urbanization led to a variety of attempts to explain and deal with the crime that attended the brave new world of modern capitalism. One of these, of course, was the creation of both preventive and detective police forces in Britain and in the U.S. There was also the growth of societies for the prevention of vice, the YMCA, evangelism, and a variety of off-shoots of muscular Christianity. Then, too, a good deal of thought was being given from a number of perspectives devoted to fathoming why people do bad things. First off, from the founding of the republic criminals had been defined by the country's ideas about prisons which began with the concept of reforming criminals versus just punishing them advocated by Benjamin Rush's Society for Alleviating the Miseries of Public Prisons created in 1787. Then followed the penitent concept embodied in the mandated solitary confinement and isolation of Pennsylvania's Eastern State Penitentiary opened in 1829. And after mid-century the reformatory concept returned in the 1870s. In another venue, American newspapers from the Civil War onward didn't try to explain crime but counted it and complained about it in periodic editorial campaigns mounted against perceived "crime waves." This broadened out from local to national concern when *The Chicago Tribune* compiled statistics on the number of homicides in the U.S. from 1881 to 1902 and commented on the increase of crime in the entire country. Journalists also made several period crimes part of the country's heritage — among others, Lizzie Borden's murder of her parents, the American Ripper case of Carrie Brown, and (Theodore Dreiser's favorite) Chester Gillette's murder of Grace Brown continue to resonate in popular imagination. On a more elevated plain, while American readers were exposed to European thinkers' notions of biological determinism to account for criminal behavior, first with Gall's phrenology and then with Lombroso's concept of atavism, American writers at the turn of the century like Jacob Riis began to examine how poverty lay at the root of criminal behavior. Imaginative literature had something to say about the subject, too. Separate from the sensation novel, the principal way in which fiction in the 19th century confronted the issues of crime and criminals was to divvy them up: some books centered on crime and its debilitating effect on the human soul and other books examined criminals as a social phenomenon. The former, in some respects, go back to Poe's gothic tales like "The Tell-Tale Heart" which center on abnormal psychology. The culmination of fiction examining the effects of crime on the individual's psyche at the turn of the century (and for all times) was Dostoevsky's *Crime and Punishment* published in the U.S. in 1886. Stephen Crane's *Maggie: A Girl of the Streets* (1893) and Frank Norris' *McTeague* (1899) represent the latter class—that which looks at criminals and criminal behavior as phenomena caused, aided, and abetted by social conditions. Josiah Flynt became the most persistent practitioner of this school with his *The Powers that Prey* (1900) and *The Rise of Roderick Clowd* (1903). Both kinds of books, quite obviously, concentrate on serious issues; most significantly, however, because they take criminals as their protagonists, both kinds of fiction treat police and detective characters as negligible, as villains, or as antagonists. They're not detective stories.

As they developed in the 1890s, detective stories shifted attention away from the criminal and exhibiting and exploring the perverse neural or social or metaphysical pathways that led him or her to commit an atrocities. And they focused attention on the detective. As such, the new detective story shifted readers' attention from interest in personality to fascination with technique, from the agonies of those whose lives had been wrecked and wracked by crime to the processes of discovery of the facts of the crime itself as well as the identity (but not necessarily the character) of the criminal. At the turn of the century several things happened that made this a possible and suitable scenario upon which to base fictions. For one thing, as noted above, science and technology changed police work and it became, in potential at least, more complex, demanding, and interesting than ever before in the history of humankind. Attendant on the addition of science to detection came the attention given at the turn of the century to the nature and function of circumstantial evidence. In other words, if in American (and English) courts an individual could be convicted solely on evidence that required inference and reasoning, why couldn't it happen in fiction? And indeed, it did happen in fiction, over and over again.

A lot of the reason all of this happened in fiction at the turn of the century was because of the publication of the Sherlock Holmes stories. In turn, a lot of the reason for the Sherlock Holmes stories was Conan Doyle's reintroduction of things that Poe had invented half a century earlier— Conan Doyle was always forthright about this. And a lot of the reason that Conan Doyle knew Poe in the first place was balled up with the history of Poe's biography which began with Rufus Wilmot Griswold's efforts to cast him as a drunken lunatic in the early 1850s which resulted in John Henry Ingram's efforts to reconstruct his life and works and establish Poe's reputation as an artist published in Edinburgh in the 1870s and early 1880s, precisely when Arthur Conan Doyle was studying medicine there at the University. As he freely admitted, Conan Doyle learned a lot about how to write detective stories from Poe. Indeed, without Conan Doyle, Poe's brand of detective character might not have survived. Dupin lacked most of the prerequisites of a popular, memorable, successful literary character. Sherlock Holmes, however, while exhibiting the same intellectual equipment possessed all of the human qualities that Dupin lacked. Nonetheless, in spite of Conan Doyle's successful transformation of Poe's Dupin into an appealing literary hero, Conan Doyle never quite fully understood the principal purpose of Poe's hero or of Poe's tales—he never understood that they were essentially designed to develop and satisfy a new relationship between writer and reader that shifted the purpose of the crime novel from evoking sentiment to playing a game. And, at the turn of the century, Conan Doyle was not alone in this. It was the same mistake made by Gaboriau and by almost everybody else writing detective stories in the 19th century who saw the core of the detective story as an exhibition of reasoning to be admired as opposed to a game to be played between the writer and reader. That recognition took another generation and became the motive force behind the golden age of detective fiction in Britain and America.

Very, very few turn of the century writers understood the underlying purpose of Poe's detective narratives, so the detective story as game would not fully emerge in this country until the late 1920s. Likewise, during the period there evolved no consensus about the character and characteristics of the detective hero. For a variety of reasons, turn of the century writers never settled on who the hero of the detective story should be. As seen above, there was no dearth of applicants for the job—reporters, police officers, lawyers, psychologists, physicians, private eyes, and scientists—all had their proponents, but none of them emerged as a clear winner in the hero department except perhaps the amateur. Thus while American writers would create a uniquely American hero in the 1920s and 1930s with the hard-boiled detective, turn of the century detective fiction offered no clearly defined John the Baptist or advance man preparing the ground for Race Williams or the Continental Op or Marlowe or even Dan Turner. Granted, the strain of muck raking evident in turn of the century fiction contributed something to their genealogy. Perhaps the period's connecting private detection and business played a microscopic role as well. But in a fuller sense, while some of the main ingredients of modern American detective fiction were latent in turn of the century stories, it took the

Great War, and then a society made cruel by economic want, and then new kinds of crime and new kinds of criminals to create both the escapist playfulness of Golden Age fiction and the poetic naturalism of the hard boiled story.

Works Cited

Adams, Samuel Hopkins. *Average Jones*. Indianapolis: Bobbs Merrill, 1911.
_____. *The Flying Death*. New York: McClure, 1908.
_____. *Great American Fraud: Articles on the Nostrum Evil and Quacks*. New York: P.F. Collier and Son, 1907.
Alger, Horatio. *Dan the Detective*. New York: G.W. Carleton, 1884.
Anderson, Frederick I. *Adventures of the Infallible Godahl*. New York: Crowell, 1914.
_____. *Book of Murder*. New York: Dutton, 1930.
Baden-Powell, Arthur. *Scouting for Boys*. London: Pearson, 1908.
Balmer, Edwin, and William MacHarg. *The Achievements of Luther Trant*. Boston: Small, 1910.
_____, and William McHarg. *The Blind Man's Eyes*. Boston: Little, Brown, 1916.
Bangs, John Kendrick. *Paste Jewels: Being Tales of Domestic Woe*. New York: Harper, 1897.
_____. *The Pursuit of the Houseboat*. New York: Harper Brothers, 1897.
Barnes, James. *The Clutch of Circumstance*. New York: Appleton, 1908.
Barton, George. *The Strange Adventures of Bromley Barnes*. New York: Page, 1918.
Beach, Rex. *The Net*. New York: Harper Brothers, 1912.
Bonner, Geraldine. *The Castleton Diamonds Case*. New York: Funk and Wagnalls, 1906.
Bradon, Mary Elizabeth. *Lady Audley's Secret*. New York: Dick, 1863.
Bramah, Ernest. *Max Carrados*. London: Methuen, 1914.
Brooks, Hildegard. *Without a Warrant*. New York: Scribners, 1901.
Buckley, Edith E. *The Snare of Circumstance*. Boston: Little, Brown, 1910.
Burgess, Gelett. *The Master of Mysteries*. Indianapolis: Bobbs Merrill, 1912.
_____, and Will Irwin. *The Picaroons*. New York: McClure, Phillips, 1904.
Burns, William J., and Isabel Ostrander. *The Crevice*. New York: W. J. Watt, 1915.
Butler, George F., M.D. *The Exploits of a Physician Detective*. Chicago: Clinic Publishing, 1908.
Byrnes, Thomas. *Professional Criminals of America*. New York: Chelsea House, 1969.
Carey, Charles. *The Van Suyden Sapphires*. New York: Dodd, Mead, 1905.
Carr, William Wilkins. *The Suggestion of Insanity in Criminal Cases and the Collateral Issue*. Philadelphia: T. and J. W. Johnson, 1890.
Chambers, Robert W. *The Mystery of Choice*. New York: Appleton, 1897.
_____. *The Tracer of Lost Persons*. New York: Appleton, 1907.
Chester, George Randolph. *Get-Rich-Quick Wallingford*. New York: A.L. Burt, 1908.
Cohen, Octavus Roy. *Jim Hanvey Detective*. New York: Dodd, 1923.
Collins, Wilkie. *The Moonstone*. New York: Harper, 1868.
_____. *The Woman in White*. New York: Harper, 1860.
Comstock, Anthony. *Traps for the Young*. New York: Funk & Wagnalls, 1883.

Crane, Stephen. *Maggie: A Girl of the Streets (A Story of New York)*. New York: Printed for the Author, 1893.

Crawford, Nelson. *The Ethics of Journalism*. New York: Knopf, 1924.

Curtis, Wardon Allan. *The Strange Adventures of Mr. Middleton*. Stone: Chicago, 1903.

Dallas, Richard. *A Master Hand*. New York: Putnam, 1904.

Davis, Richard Harding. *Gallagher*. New York: Scribners, 1906.

Dickens, Charles. *Bleak House*. New York: Harper, 1853.

Dorrington, Albert. *The Radium Terrors: A Mystery Story*. New York: W.R. Caldwell, 1912.

Dostoyevsky, Feódor. *Crime and Punishment: A Russian Realistic Novel*. New York: Thomas Y. Crowell, 1886.

Doubleday, Roman. *The Hemlock Avenue Mystery*. Boston: Little, Brown, 1908.

DuMaurier, George. *Trilby*. New York: Harper, 1894.

Eldridge, George Dyre. *The Millbank Case: A Maine Mystery of To-Day*. New York: Henry Holt, 1905.

Ellis, Havelock. *The Criminal*. New York: Scribner and Welford, 1890.

England, George Allan. *The Air Trust*. www.gutenberg.org.

_____. *The Greater Crime*. New York: Cassell, 1917.

_____. *Pod, Bender & Co*. New York: McBride, 1916.

Flower, Elliott. *Policeman Flynn*. New York: Century, 1902.

_____. *The Spoilsmen*. New York: L. C. Page, 1903.

Flynt, Josiah, and Francis Walton. *The Powers That Prey*. New York, McClure, 1900.

_____. *The Rise of Roderick Clowd*. New York: Dodd, Mead, 1903.

Futrelle, Jacques. *Best "Thinking Machine" Stories*. Ed. E.F. Bleiler. New York: Dover, 1973.

_____. *Great Cases of the Thinking Machine*. Ed. E. F. Bleiler. New York: Dover, 1976.

Gallomb, Joseph. *Master Man Hunters*. New York: Macaulay, 1926.

Galton, Francis. *Finger Prints*. London: Macmillan, 1892.

Gardenhire, Samuel M. *The Long Arm*. New York: Harper Brothers, 1906.

Gilbert, Nelson Rust. *The Affair at Pine Court*. Philadelphia: Lippincott, 1907.

Green, Anna Katharine. *That Affair Next Door* and *Lost Man's Lane*. Durham, N.C.: Duke University Press, 2003.

_____. *A Difficult Problem: The Staircase at the Heart's Delight and Other Stories*. New York: Luptom, 1900.

_____. *Doctor Izard*. New York: Putnam, 1895.

_____. *The Golden Slipper and Other Problems for Violet Strange*. New York: Putnam, 1915.

_____. *The Leavenworth Case*. New York: Dover, 1981.

Green, Sanford. *Crime: Its Nature, Causes, Treatment, and Prevention*. Philadelphia: Lippincott, 1889

Greene, Hugh. *The American Rivals of Sherlock Holmes*. New York: Penguin, 1976.

Griswold, Rufus Wilmot. "Memoir of the Author," *The Works of the Late Edgar Allan Poe*. 3 vols. New York: J. S. Redfield, 1850.

Gross, Hans. *Criminal Psychology: A Manual for Judges, Practitioners, and Students*. www.gutenberg.org.

Hand, Learned. *Historical and Practical Considerations Regarding Expert Testimony*. Albany, New York: Albany Medical Annals, 1900.

Hanshew, T.W. *Cleek, the Man of Forty Faces*. New York: Cassell, 1913.

Hardy, Arthur Sherburne. *Diane and Her Friends*. Cambridge, MA: Houghton Mifflin, 1914.

Hart, Alfred Noyes. *The Bellamy Trial*. New York: Doubleday, Page, 1927.

Hastings, Wells. *The Man in the Brown Derby*. Indianapolis: Bobbs-Merrill, 1911.

____, and Brian Hooker. *The Professor's Mystery*. New York: Grosset and Dunlap, 1911.

Hawthorne, Julian. *An American Penman*. New York: Cassell, 1887.

____. *Another's Crime*. New York Cassell, 1888.

____. *The Great Bank Robbery*. New York: Cassell, 1887.

____. *Section 558 or the Fatal Letter*. New York: Cassell, 1888.

____. *A Tragic Mystery*. New York: Cassell, 1887.

Hay, James, Jr. *The Melwood Mystery*. New York: Dodd, Mead, 1920.

____. *No Clue*. New York: Dodd, Mead, 1920.

____. *The Winning Clue*. New York: Jacobson, 1930.

Haycraft, Howard. *Murder for Pleasure*. New York: Appleton, 1941.

Henry, O. *The Gentle Grafter*. Garden City NY: Doubleday, Doran, 1908.

Holt, Harrison J. *Midnight at Mears House*. New York: Dodd, Mead, 1912.

Hornblow, Arthur. *The Argyle Case*. New York: Harper, 1913.

Hornung, E.W. *The Amateur Cracksman*. New York: Scribners, 1899.

Hughes, Thomas. *Tom Brown's School Days*. London: Macmillan, 1856.

Ingram, John H. *Edgar Allan Poe: His Life, Letters and Opinions*. 2 vols. London: John Hogg, 1880.

____, ed. *The Works of Edgar Allan Poe*. 4 vols. Edinburgh: Black, 1874–1875.

Irwin, Will. *The House of Mystery*. New York: A.L. Burt, 1910.

Kauffman, Reginald Wright. *The House of Bondage*. New York: Grosset and Dunlap, 1912.

____. *Miss Frances Baird Detective: A Passage from Her Memoirs*. Boston: L.C. Page, 1906.

Klinger, Leslie S., ed. *The New Annotated Sherlock Holmes 150th Anniversary: The Short Stories*. New York: Norton, 2004.

____, ed. *The New Annotated Sherlock Holmes: The Novels*. New York: Norton, 2005.

Leblanc, Maurice. *The Confessions of Arsene Lupin*. New York: Doubleday Page, 1913.

LeRoux, Gaston. *The Mystery of the Yellow Room*. www.online-literature.com.

Lewis, Alfred Henry. *The Apaches of New York*. New York: Donohue, 1912.

____. *Confessions of a Detective*. New York: A.S. Barnes, 1906.

Lindsey, Ben, and Harvey O'Higgins. *The Beast*. New York: Doubleday, Page, 1910.

Lloyd, Nelson. *The Robberies Company, Ltd*. New York: Scribner's Sons, 1906.

Lombroso, Cæsar, and William Ferrero. *The Female Offender*. London: Unwin, 1895.

Lombroso-Ferrero, Gina. *Criminal Man*. New York: Putnam, 1911.

The Long Arm and Other Detective Stories. London: Chapman and Hall 1895.

Lynch, Lawrence. *Against Odds: A Detective Story*. Chicago: Rand McNally, 1894.

____. *Shadowed by Three*. Chicago: Donnelley, Gassette and Loyd, 1879.

Lynde, Francis. *The Grafters*. Ridgewood, N.J.: The Gregg Press, 1969.

____. *Scientific Sprague*. New York: Scribners. 1912.

McFarlane, Arthur E. *Behind the Bolted Door*. New York: Dodd, Mead, 1916.

McGibeny, Donald. *32 Caliber*. Indianapolis: Bobbs-Merril, 1920.

McIntyre, John T. *Ashton-Kirk Criminologist*. Philadelphia: Penn Publishing. 1918.

____. *Aston-Kirk Investigator*. New York: Burt, 1910.

____. *Ashton-Kirk Secret Agent*. Philadelphia: Penn Publishing, 1912.

____. *Ashton-Kirk Special Detective*. A.L. Burt: New York, 1914.

Moffett, Cleveland. *Through the Wall*. New York: D. Appleton and Company, 1928.

Munsterberg, Hugo. *On the Witness Stand*. New York: The McClure Company, 1908.

Nicholson, Meredith. *The House of a Thousand Candles*. Indianapolis: Bobbs-Merrill, 1905.

Norris, Frank. *McTeague: A Story of San Francisco*. New York: Doubleday and McClure, 1899.

O'Higgins, Harvey. *Detective Barney.* www.gaslight.mtroyal.ca.

_____. *Detective Duff Unravels It.* New York: Liveright, 1929.

Orczy, Emmuska. *The Scarlet Pimpernel.* New York: Putnam's Sons, 1906.

Ostrander, Isabel. *At One Thirty a Mystery.* New York: W.J. Watt, 1915.

Ottolengui, Rodriguez. *An Artist in Crime.* New York: Putnam, 1892.

_____. *A Conflict of Evidence.* New York: Putnam, 1893.

_____. *The Crime of the Century.* Putnam, 1903.

_____. *The Final Proof, or The Value of Evidence.* New York: Putnam, 1898.

_____. *A Modern Wizard.* New York: Putnam, 1894.

Packard, Frank L. *The Adventures of Jimmy Dale.* New York: A.L. Burt, 1917.

Pendexter, Hugh. *Tiberius Smith: As Chronicled by His Right Hand Man Billy Campbell.* New York: Harper, 1907.

Pidgin, Charles F. *The Further Adventures of Quincy Adams Sawyer and Mason Corner Folks.* Boston: L.C. Page, 1909.

_____, and J.M. Taylor. *The Chronicles of Quincy Adams Sawyer, Detective.* Boston: L.C. Page, 1912.

Pinkerton, Allan. *A Double Life and the Detectives.* New York: G.W. Dillingham, Publishers, 1884.

_____. *The Expressman and the Detective.* Chicago: W.B. Keen, Cooke, 1874.

Pitman, William Dent. *The Quincunx Case.* Boston: Herbert Turner, 1904.

Poate, Ernest M. *Behind Locked Doors.* New York: Chelsea House, 1923.

Post, Melville Davisson. *The Man of Last Resort.* New York: Putnam, 1897.

_____. *The Strange Schemes of Randolph Mason.* New York: Putnam, 1896.

Prentis, John H. *The Case of Doctor Horace: A Study of the Importance of Conscience in the Detection of Crime.* New York: Baker and Taylor, 1907.

Reece, John James. *Text-Book of Medical Jurisprudence and Toxicology.* Philadelphia: P. Blakiston, 1884.

Reeve, Arthur B. *Constance Dunlap.* New York: Harper, 1913.

_____. *The Dream Doctor.* www.classicreader.com

_____. *The Ear in the Wall.* www.classicreader.com. 1916.

_____. *The Poisoned Pen.* www.classicreader.com

_____. *The Silent Bullet.* www.classicreader.com

Riis, Jacob. *The Making of an American.* www.bartelby.com.

Rinehart, Mary Roberts. *The Amazing Adventures of Letitia Carberry.* New York: Grosset and Dunlap. 1911.

_____. *The Circular Staircase.* San Diego: University of California Extension. 1977.

_____. *The Man in Lower Ten.* New York: Grossett and Dunlap, 1909.

Scott, Leroy. *Counsel for the Defense.* New York: Doubleday, Page, 1912.

Scribner, Harvey. *My Mysterious Clients.* Cincinnati: Robert Clarke Company, 1900.

Severy, Melvin L. *The Darrow Enigma.* www.projectgutenberg.org.

_____. *The Mystery of June 13th.* New York: Dodd, Mead, 1905.

Slee, Richard, and Cornelia Atwood Pratt. *Dr. Berkeley's Discovery.* New York: Putnam, 1899.

Stagg, Clinton H. *Silver Sandals.* New York: Watt, 1916.

_____. *Thornley Colton.* New York: Watt, 1923.

Steel, Jack. *Husband by Proxy.* New York: Desmond FitzGerald, 1909.

Steffens, Lincoln. *The Shame of the Cities.* New York: McClure, 1904.

Steinbrunner, Chris, and Otto Penzler. *Encyclopedia of Mystery and Detection.* New York: McGraw Hill, 1976.

Stevenson, Burton E. *The Holladay Case: A Tale.* New York: Holt, 1903.

_____. *The Mystery of the Boule Cabinet.* New York: Arno, 1976.

Stringer, Arthur. *Night Hawk*. New York: A.L. Burt, 1926.

____. *Phantom Wire*. Boston: Little, Brown, 1906.

____. *The Shadow*. New York: Century: 1913.

____. *The Wire Tappers*. Boston: Little, Brown, 1906.

Strong, Harrington. *The Brand of Silence: A Detective Story*. New York: Chelsea House, 1924.

____. *Who Killed William Drew? A Detective Story*. New York: Chelsea House, 1925.

Taylor, Alfred Swaine. *Medical Jurisprudence*. Philadelphia: Lea and Blanchard, 1845.

Thornwald, Jurgen. *The Century of the Detective*. New York: Harcourt, Brace and World, 1965.

Thwing, Eugene, ed. *The World's Best One Hundred Detective Stories*. 10 vols. New York: Funk and Wagnalls, 1929.

Train, Arthur. *The Butler's Story; The Camorra in Italy; and, an American Lawyer at Viterbo*. New York: C. Scribner's Sons, 1912.

____. *"C.Q." or, in the Wireless House*. New York: Century, 1912.

____. *The Confessions of Artemas Quibble: Being the ingenious and unvarnished history of Artemus Quibble, Esquire, One-Tome Practitioner in the New York Criminal Courts, Together With An Account of the Diverse Wiles, Tricks, Sophistries, Technicalities, and Sundry Artifices of Himself and Others of the Fraternity, Commonly Yclept "Shysters: OR "Shyster Lawyers," as Edited By Arthur Train Formerly Assistant District Attorney New York County*. New York: Scribners, 1921.

____. *McAllister and his Double*. New York: Scribner's, 1905.

Twain, Mark. *A Double Barreled Detective Story*. New York: Harper, 1902.

____. *Pudd'nhead Wilson*. Hartford: American Publishing Company, 1894.

____. *The Stolen White Elephant*. Boston: Osgood, 1882.

____. *Tom Sawyer, Detective*. New York: Harper, 1896.

Vanardy, Varick. *Alias "The Night Wind."* New York: Dillingham, 1913.

Vance, Louis Joseph. *The Brass Bowl*. www.gutenberg.org.

____. *The Lone Wolf*. New York: Triangle, 1938.

Victor, Metta Fuller. *The Dead Letter*. Boston: Gregg Press, 1979.

Walk, Charles Edmonds. *The Yellow Circle*. Chicago: McClurg, 1909.

____. *The Silver Blade: The True Chronicle of a Double Mystery*. Chicago: McClurg, 1909.

Webster, Henry Kitchell. *The Whispering Man*. New York: Appleton, 1909.

Webster, Jean. *The Four Pools Mystery*. New York: The Century Company, 1908.

Weir, Hugh C. *Miss Madelyn Mack, Detective*. Boston: Page, 1914.

Wells, Carolyn. *A Chain of Evidence*. Philadelphia: Lippincott, 1912.

____. *The Maxwell Mystery*. Philadelphia: Lippincott, 1913.

____. *The Technique of the Mystery Story*. Springfield, MA: The Home Correspondence School, 1913.

Wood, Mrs. Henry. *East Lynne*. New York: Dick, 1861.

Index